Girls in Trouble with the Law

D0962805

The Rutgers Series in Childhood Studies

Edited by Myra Bluebond-Langner

Advisory Board
   Joan Jacobs Brumberg
   Perri Klass
   Jill Korbin
   Bambi Schiefflin
   Enid Schildkraut

Girls in Trouble with the Law

Laurie Schaffner

Rutgers University Press

New Brunswick, New Jersey, and London

Library of Congress Cataloging-in-Publication Data

Schaffner, Laurie.
    Girls in trouble with the law / Laurie Schaffner.
        p. cm. — (The Rutgers series in childhood studies)
    Includes bibliographical references and index.
    ISBN-13: 978-0-8135-3833-4 (hardcover : alk. paper)
    ISBN-13: 978-0-8135-3834-1 (pbk. : alk. paper)
        1. Female juvenile delinquents—United States. 2. Juvenile delinquency—
United States. 3. Teenagers with social disabilities—United States. 4. Juvenile
corrections—United States. I. Title. II. Series.

HV9104.S3224 2006
364.36082′0973—dc22

2005028096

British Cataloging-in-Publication data for this book is available from the British
Library.

Copyright © 2006 by Laurie Schaffner
All rights reserved.
No part of this book may be reproduced or utilized in any form or by any means,
electronic or mechanical, or by any information storage and retrieval system, without written permission from the publisher. Please contact Rutgers University Press,
100 Joyce Kilmer Avenue, Piscataway, NJ 08854-8099. The only exception to this
prohibition is "fair use" as defined by U.S. copyright law.

Manufactured in the United States of America

In loving memory

Robert Schaffner
1949–1987

Paul David Shipley Schaffner
1921–2001

Eric Ellery Fiedler
1943–2003

Margaret Ann Shipley Fiedler
1919–2005

Contents

Illustrations

Tables

Preface

The first time I got arrested I was sixteen years old. To be exact, it was my sixteenth birthday. In those days, you couldn't go outdoors before 3:00 p.m. without getting arrested for truancy—until you were sixteen years old, the age when mandatory public education legally ended. So, to celebrate, my boyfriend and I hitchhiked from Berkeley to Ocean Beach in San Francisco. In front of what is now the Beach Chalet, a police car rolled up. I told my (twenty-one-year-old) boyfriend to keep walking. We knew about statutory rape laws, which could get him into trouble. When the police called my mother (in Los Angeles) to come get me out of detention in YGC (San Francisco's Youth Guidance Center), she refused. I guess I could say that my mother piqued my interest in this topic—girls who come to the attention of authorities.

It is difficult to acknowledge all the people who helped me work on this project because it is, essentially, a life work, and thus I feel the need to thank everyone. Because thanking everyone who ever saved my life is a life work of its own, I begin here by telling stories about writing this book and sharing gratitude with everyone along the way. I began this work under the brilliant auspices of my mentor, dissertation chair, and wise and soulful woman Arlie Hochschild. What a leap it was into the sociology department at Berkeley from where I had come and what a loving and astute spotter I had in Arlie. I was given the gift of true mentoring, spiritual support, and the rare gentle intellectual coach. Professor Hochschild lovingly altered my life in deep, meaningful ways, and I would like to acknowledge and express my gratitude to her. My entire committee, Troy Duster, Kristin Luker, and Pedro Noguera, were supportive and generous with their time and advice, for which I am indeed grateful as well.

During the course of the fieldwork for this book, a wide range of feelings came up, to put it mildly. Feelings in the field—mine and the participants'—mattered to the work. Any reliable methodology text no longer expects research to be "value free" and does not teach some kind of sterile objectivity. But being the emotional and theoretical receptacle for all the unhappiness of the study participants made my job very rich and very difficult. Although authentic, intimate, or emotional exchanges with my "subjects" did not violate my role as a researcher, feelings certainly complicated my relationship to this work.

The girls I met related the stories of their lives, including hours of accounts of violence and rape and abuse and misery. It was difficult to sit like a stone and listen to horrific, graphic details of gang rapes, beat-downs, and forced sex. I made comments such as "That shouldn't have happened to you." I cried sometimes during interviews. I explained to them that I believed it was possible that by telling their stories they could help other young women. One young woman said to me, "Cry for me 'cause I can't cry no more."

When some of the girls talked about beating each other with golf clubs and baseball bats and stabbing others, I felt strongly about their actions. I saw their anger, and I feared their rage. I became afraid as well when I glimpsed into the chasm of brutality that people can perpetrate against each other. I felt anger toward some girls for the awful things they had done, and I worried about their victims. Their narratives also sparked my outrage at a world that had allowed the conditions under which these children lived to materialize.

I also experienced large amounts of guilt—for studying unhappy girls, for leaving them in detention facilities while I hopped into a comfortable car and went home to a nice meal. These emotions led to the often-inevitable questions of a reflexive researcher: How objective should I have been? How objective could I have been? Did I get too close to my informants because their suffering moved me so? How dare I "study down"? Also, (how) can I speak for young women of color, as I am not one? Furthermore, (how much) does activism/advocacy impede socio-logical theorizing? I especially worried about simply titillating an academic pedophilia among middle-class, middle-aged (mostly male?) scholarly readers by writing about the secrets, sexualities, and violence of young girls.

A few thoughts about these questions carried me through the grueling fieldwork phase. The fact that I experienced considerable difficulty in my own adolescence gave me a sense of standing to share these stories. After all, it wasn't so long ago that I endured hardships, possibly for similar reasons as my informants. I often still feel more comfortable on the donated couches of community agencies than in the fancy hotels where I present my work to colleagues. That I had spent a few miserable weeks myself, thirty-five years before, in the exact same cell where I interviewed some of the girls for this study not only allowed me an insider's view but also inspired me to take action to change the system.

In writing this book, I had a number of important insights not only about girls in detention but also about myself and about the feminist sociology that I claim as my own. My work is deeply informed by my experiences as a girl in trouble. At the same time, I appreciate my years of training in research methodology and the history of theory in, arguably, the nation's top institutions. Ultimately, I am a citizen invested in social justice. Do these identities conflict with one another? Sometimes, but they also enrich all my work in important ways.

The demand to locate oneself in the work—that is, the autobiographical call from feminists and critical scholars—is now ubiquitous and requisite in my area of inquiry. The confessional imperative of the postmodern ethnographer seeks to interrupt the discourse of the researchers who located themselves above and outside the human action they studied. But even if I were to disclose a deep, dark past, my training as a researcher obligates me to turn information into data, not provide personal, traceable, individual facts. My intellectual task is to obscure, scramble, and disguise life histories in reporting back so that they become stories of people, not persons. We qualitative sociologists and critical researchers focus on uncovering patterns and meanings, spotlighting power inequities and social injustice, not exposing and intruding on individual privacy.

In the academy, at best, experience with the so-called lowlife may spark minor prurient interest. More often, having a past translates into the distinctly not respectful notion that one is less than a serious scholar. Locating oneself in the project becomes a treacherous balancing act for the less privileged and nondominant precisely because stigma adheres to the stigmatized. Sometimes I feel lucky to be able to draw on many types of social capital; other times I feel cursed with knowing too much about painful incongruities in these worlds.

I now know that caring about people and their social problems is not divorced from the work of analysis and interpretation. Being neutral isn't the same as being inhuman. I can live with the experience of having entered one hundred "cases" into the Statistical Program for Social Science and spewing out frequencies and cross-tabs at the same time that I cried my heart out and prayed for the safety of some of the searching young souls I met on what was also my own journey toward becoming an adult woman.

I encountered several interesting challenges during the course of this project. One was to develop ethical methods for interviewing children who were disclosing trauma and describing indescribable violence and sexual pain. I also had to deal with some university officials and court personnel who read my requests for permission to observe female juvenile detainees as subversive. In addition, identifying and analyzing "data" that could adequately represent changes in gender norms was challenging. Most of all, a key struggle centered around making the case that the intellectual and academic endeavor of studying and writing about children (girls, at that), gender, sexuality, and violence should be considered serious, viable, fundable, respectable, and theoretical urban sociology.

Because this study develops interpretations across cultural practices (as opposed to lining up a neat typology), I include, in addition to the words of young women, examples of poetry they crafted, photographs they took, art they made, letters they wrote, and images from magazines we looked at together. My intention is to draw the reader closer to the worlds of girls in trouble. The original artwork in this book was created by young women in locked facilities. The photographs on the cover were taken by girls in an art project that allowed them a rare opportunity to use disposable cameras while in detention to photograph images that had meaning for them. (The young women were instructed not to photograph anyone's face.) The letter following this preface was written by a young woman to her sister. Images from magazines and advertisements are offered as cultural education. These folkloric documents contextualize their narratives and provide the reader with a sense of the study participants' sadness and limitations as well as of their bountiful potential. I selected poems that convey what young women wanted me to share about their lives; I located them between chapters to remind the reader that even though the participants in this study are being adjudicated as delinquents, they are much more than what is written in their case files.

It took tons of Chinese take-out and red wine with the pbs—Elizabeth Bernstein, Jackie Orr, Lucinda Ramberg, and Will Rountree—to pour over every detail of early drafts. For that I am eternally grateful. I did receive funding from the Berkeley Sociology Department and a grant from the Woodrow Wilson Foundation, but my main funder, my VISA card, will, at this rate, be collecting my gratitude *en perpetua*. In California, my friends, family, and our children sustained me over the years: Tiona Gundy, Becky Jenkins, Cary Littell, Alan McKay, Julie Posadas-Guzman, and Lucinda Ramberg; special love to Ruth Apraku, Bianca Jarvis, and Marta Torres. Michael Jarvis, in the truest sense of "for better or worse," remains ever my heart's desire.

My colleagues at the University of Illinois at Chicago (UIC) were with me every step of the way of this project. I had the best writing partner in the world, Ann Feldman, along with two writing groups replete with smart and loving people: Tanya Anderson, Sara Hall, Amanda Lewis, Irma Olmedo, and Beth Richie. I was honored with a faculty-scholar year-in-residence at David Perry's remarkable Great Cities Institute, where I was able to complete my research and much of the writing of this book. I am grateful for funding support from the UIC Office of

Social Sciences Research as well. Other colleagues at UIC have been generous in their support and encouragement; I wish to thank William Ayers, John D'Emilio, Lisa Frohmann, Judy Gardiner, John Hagedorn, Mindie Lazarus-Black, Matthew Lippman, Greg Matoesian, Amie Schuck, and Sarah Ullman for helpful advice along the way. In Chicago, I am also lucky to have the best group of friends, including the We Love Our Book Group book group. Joanne Archibald, Salome Chasnoff, Elena Gutierrez, Sara Hall, Amanda Lewis, Gayatri Reddy, and Beth Richie tried valiantly to take my worried "Is everything going to be OK?" phone calls day in and day out.

Most of all, I thank the young women who agreed to participate in this research project for their courage and honesty. Their reading of various drafts and their commenting on them kept me buoyant and on track. Although I cannot name them here, I am inspired by their strength and in awe of their spirit. I am indebted as well to the adult participants who shared their time and ideas so generously. I encountered the finest editors in the business at Rutgers. The initial acquisitions editor, Kristi Long, gave me superb in-depth suggestions for which I am very grateful. Series editor Myra Bluebond-Langner and the final acquisitions editor, Adi Hovav, guided this project to a gentle landing. I was lucky to be given a clear, thoughtful, and generous copyeditor, Pamela Fischer. Clare Corcoran gave crucial copyediting advice in the early stages. These women took this work seriously and gave me wise guidance for which I am grateful. I thank the many students who worked on this project as graduate and undergraduate research assistants, independent studies researchers, and summer interns: Josefina Alvarez, Ebony Evans, Lauren Graves, Corrine Louw, Janna Thomure, and Haley Volpintesta, to name a few.

All my life, I have been a part of many families; my name could be Laurie Apraku Fielder Jarvis Jenkins Konrad Levine Montes Rountree Shipley Torres Schaffner. My brothers, Billy and David, and I love each other with all our hearts. I wish I could say that everyone lived happily ever after, that I am now rich and skinny, and that the whole world is at peace. I am definitely personally happier than I have ever been, but I haven't "ended up" anywhere yet. Young women still face the same challenges of racism, poverty, and patriarchy—whether through the intensely demeaning messages about themselves with which they are bombarded in the media; through their limited access to abortion, health care, housing, and education; or when men senselessly send bombs to drop on their heads. But the good news is that the struggle continues and that we are part of a long history of millions of human beings from every nation who have always spoken out for peace, freedom, equality, and justice. I know which side of that struggle I will end up on, and I offer this text as an educational and organizing tool to help us on the way.

A letter home from detention. *Credit: Anonymous detainee; research collected with informed consent; used by permission.*

Girls in Trouble
with the Law

Introduction

Girls Trouble
the Law

Popular moral panics often focus on girls' and women's behavior. In the corporate news media and Hollywood films, images of girls and women in crises, such as the unwed pregnant teenager, the welfare cheat, the uncaring, crack-addicted mother, the teen girl in need of an abortion, and the abducted innocent girl child, stimulate civic discourse and outrage. The irony is that most academic studies (as well as policy development and program funding) focus on the situations and experiences of boys and men. In general, sociology is the study of men's troubles.[1] Most books about juvenile law and delinquency (textbooks, ethnographies, theoretical overviews, and federal statistics) contain one chapter, section, or paragraph that addresses issues related to females. Although canonical narratives reveal much about processes of gender, these texts, like others in their fields, rarely made their debut as research on masculinity. Men's and boys' experiences are the unspoken standard to which girls' and women's lives are compared. The results of the research reported in *Girls in Trouble with the Law*, however, point to the importance of understanding the conditions, situations, and experiences of the female half of the population in order to generate not only socially relevant theory but effective public policy.

The concerns of female juvenile offenders have hovered below the radar of media headlines and of the sociological research agenda. The lack of research on girls' experience has exacerbated ill-conceived notions of gender as well as misinterpretations of both the statistical data and the accounts of girls' decisions. A spate of work now, however, features the history of girls' delinquency and troubles.[2] Feminist researchers working in criminology, psychology, and law have quickly amassed reliable social science documenting the experiences of girls' troubles with

1

the law. This work is aimed largely at interrupting current popular and cynical narratives, such as those concerning the surge in girl-on-girl violence, and at developing instead contemporary theories that reflect girls' and women's realities; this ethnography aims to join that body of work.[3]

Because of an overreliance on incarceration in the last decades of the twentieth century, the situation for girls in the U.S. juvenile legal system deteriorated. Arrests of adolescent girls skyrocketed, and, increasingly, girls were charged with violent offenses. In order to comprehend this crisis, we need a new conversation with girls and about girls, trouble, and the law. We must begin by listening to the voices and experiences of young women who are going through the court system and to consider them as contemporary girls, not as a special kind of boy in the delinquency system and not as if they were girls in the 1950s. We must also keep in mind that the category *court-involved girls* is neither uniform nor static.

When we do hear young women, we can identify various processes at work in their lives. First, the vast extent of emotional injury in the form of sexual and violent assault that young women in this population report experiencing cannot be understated. We can trace the dire social consequences of this unattended psychic trauma, such as their own later sexual and violent offenses, in many of the accounts of court-involved girls. Second, we can trace a pattern relating to young women's responses to the hyper-sexualized, consumerist culture they inhabit. Third, listening to girls allows a unique view of the conditions under which they are adjudicated delinquent for violent offenses. In the media and among some social scientists, girls' violence has been framed as an example of how girls violate such gender norms as being nurturing, relational, and internally focused. Girls' narratives of their involvement with violence indicate a much more complex set of factors at work in their lives. The main argument in *Girls in Trouble with the Law* centers on the significance of the experiences of low-income girls of color who have been neglected or exploited and who are situated in a larger cultural and political environment that variously ignores, minimizes, derides, or criminalizes their plight.

We have been prevented from listening to girls who are in trouble with the law because much of our accepted wisdom about young women—both academic and popular—obviates our hearing them. On the one hand, conventional studies of what is rather colloquially termed *juvenile delinquency* reveal the necessity for an interdisciplinary inquiry. Except in explicitly feminist texts, criminological work has often omitted girls; studies from adolescent psychology have pathologized girls' responses to patriarchy and racism; the sociology of gender has missed incarcerated girls; the anthropology of children has focused mostly on

children's "culture"—apparently, a culture that excludes court
ment; and the sociology of childhood focuses in the main on pro
youth socialization in schools. On the other hand, our conventional popular myths—for example, that "boys are violent" and "girls are sexy"—
preclude us from seeing the realities in the lives of court-involved girls.
Young women in trouble are victims of an a priori discourse that theorizes their experiences without detailed empirical scrutiny. For example,
I submit that most people are unaware of the fact that in the entire United
States in 2004 fewer than 1,500 arrests for prostitution were of girls under the age of eighteen, while close to 14,500 arrests of female minors
were for aggravated assault. What are we to make of these data? In this
sense, it is the girls who trouble the law.[4]

Girls in Trouble with the Law presents results from a multiyear
qualitative study of court-involved girls and the adults with whom they
interacted. Although I engage in an interdisciplinary discourse, I begin
with a qualitative sociological approach. This study brings the voices of
young women, aged thirteen to eighteen, to the heart of current discussions about female juvenile offenders and the system that responds to
them. As we adjudicate girls in the juvenile court systems around the
nation today, we must do so with a sophisticated notion about contemporary meanings and portrayals of gender. Here I propose a new window
through which to see this particular population's struggles and offenses.
Girls in Trouble with the Law unpacks prevailing—and shifting—social
and cultural norms for masculinity and femininity, race and ethnicity,
relationships and sexuality, emotions and violence. In essence, the book
constitutes an ethnography of a system of both formal and informal social controls at work in the worlds of court-involved girls.

Historically, sociolegal and delinquency literature ignored gender as
a category of analysis. When considering gender as a variable, commentators tended to rely on antiquated notions of masculinity and femininity for understanding girls' transgression of the law. Current conventional
framings fail to consider the profound shifts in gender norms in the century since the inception of the juvenile court, such as the overall trend
among youth to participate in sexual activities at younger ages, an increased normalization of aggression and violence in everyday life, and
the overreliance on incarceration of girls as a legal solution to social
 problems. So, for example, observations of young women's interactions
in the programs that form the delivery of so-called gender-specific interventions reveal tensions between interventions being offered by system
personnel and community advocates as redemptive strategies for the
young women and programs the young women themselves consider helpful. However, listening to young women brings into view the immense
promise of these programs.

From listening to the accounts of young women, we see that girls' offenses are expressions of the power of the powerless: attempts to defy the overwhelming odds that disadvantaged young women face. Their accounts reveal several cultural gender myths: that girls are mostly in trouble for sexual misconduct, that boys are the only youth who are aggressive, and that all youth are heterosexual. No one girl's narrative tells the whole story; no one "type" of girl comes to the attention of the authorities to the exclusion of all others. That is part of the problem: secrets and chaos imbue young women's accounts with an abiding complexity. However, patterns emerge amid their emotionally laden, albeit short, life histories, and these patterns are taken up in detail in subsequent chapters.

Chapter One begins on the streets, in the middle of the night, with young women. The site of many of their troubles, the streets are where many girls come to the attention of authorities. In this opening chapter, we learn how girls get locked up and what being in the system is like from the perspectives of two young women, Claudia Sereno and LaShondra Wolfe. I present an ethnographic tour of a typical detention facility, giving the reader a sense of the inner workings of the juvenile centers where participants were interviewed and observed, with photographs taken by girls of the inside of a detention center. I then describe the terminology used to separate the girls from the women (and the boys), if you will, and give a sense of the history of the juvenile legal system as it affects girls. A brief description follows of knowledge about girls in trouble; it focuses on literature from a variety of disciplines that have theorized female adolescent conflict. In this chapter we also meet the study itself. I provide a brief overview of the study design and acquaint readers with the demographics of the participants, who hailed from dozens of facilities in four states.

In Chapter Two, through the accounts of Mylen Cruz, Carina Menendez, and Anastasia Rudnik, I theorize how emotional, physical, and sexual injury and exploitation, which is gendered as well as racialized, contribute to girls' coming to the attention of authorities. This point cannot be overemphasized: violence against women animates women's violence. In this chapter, I propose that we unmask the now rather flat term *abuse* and reinvigorate it as traumatic ground that provides explanatory links to girls' pasts, presents, and futures. The social consequences of the emotional injuries that girls in this population have sustained have been inadequately theorized, partially because these topics tend to segregate by academic discipline and social practice. Important features of this trauma have not been afforded the primacy they deserve if we are to understand the distinct experiences of court-involved girls. Precisely here, I argue, the psychic and structural are inexorably intertwined. A sociology of emotion allows us to theorize how the social is imbibed, mapped onto the body, in psychological ways. The abuse and harm of young girls comes to be seen as a process, not an event. And although this harm may take place in private, as individual or personal events, altering girls' very sense of self, it contributes to drastic public behavior with social consequences. The injuries sustained, invisible to the (social scientist's) eye, cannot be understood as simply phenomenological events to be recorded or analyzed as variables. This harm must be articulated and theorized in order to be apprehended. These human experiences are not uniform, regardless of age, race, or gender, and especially not, as this chapter illuminates, for low-income girls of color in troubled urban communities. We hear in their accounts exactly how court-involved young women work through these processes of injury in their adolescence.

A correlation can be drawn between young women's early experiences of harm and exploitation and later problems with juvenile authorities. Chapter Two highlights the research on this topic and introduces a sociological link between these intertwined experiences, these embedded locations where structural damage such as sexism and racism is heaped on the emotional life of individuals. Detailed in this chapter are the conditions and experiences in the lives of the three young women, all of whom had witnessed and experienced considerable victimization in their lives. They were now being adjudicated—one for fighting back when a boy physically assaulted her in a sexual manner in school, another who, in an earlier incident, was charged with assaulting her brother with a steak knife during a family argument and was now being adjudicated for an armed robbery, and the third for beating up another resident in her court-ordered group home placement. These narratives illuminate how impossible it is to comprehend girls' offenses without considering their prior victimization, but not in deterministically causal, defensively excusing, or quantitatively measurable ways. In order to theorize girls' offending, we must consider the distinct significance of the experiences of harm for unprotected, low-income girls of color who are then punished for the response mechanisms they invent.

In Chapter Three, new views of families, sexuality, and trouble are explored. Girls wander in what I term *empty families*: absences caused by parental incarceration, ill health, substance dependence, and death leave system-involved girls unprotected, parenting themselves, and open to romantic involvement in harmful ways. According to system-involved girls, many of their sexual practices are not problematic, in the sense that their romantic and erotic experiences fall within contemporary youth norms. Many young women devise what I have come to view as sexual solutions to nonsexual problems. Unprotected in empty families;

parentified in order to take care of their parents and siblings; enduring a hypereroticized popular culture that emphasizes subordinated femininities; facing challenges in education and mental health care as well as physical and medical issues; surviving unsafe and unstable housing conditions; and navigating childhoods in impoverished neighborhoods lead a disproportionate number of court-involved girls into the arms of "older boyfriends" who later appear in the accounts of girls' offenses.

In Chapter Four, I describe another key arena in which girls are disproportionately punished: when they express themselves aggressively in ways that specifically violate gender norms for emotional behavior. When court personnel do "see gender," girls' violence is characterized primarily as a violation of conventional norms of female expression and behavior; this view places the system's position at odds with a contemporary popular culture that glorifies violence and aggression. Some court-involved young women frame their aggressive and violent behavior as an inevitable part of living in contemporary violent environments. Many do not necessarily see their violence as problematic because, to them, it is often an unavoidable outcome of many of their problems.

Dominant gender norms in contemporary U.S. culture set standards of behavior for girls: that they be heterosexual and monogamous, nurturing and relational, and obedient and (apparently) chaste. Chapter Four centers around narrative accounts of three girls whose violent offenses were framed as transgressing what authorities believed to be gender conventions, especially for girls' compliant subordination. According to the young women, these expectations were in direct opposition to their righteous rage or to unavoidable domestic and community violence.

Chapter Five describes one solution to girls' problems in the system: gender-responsive programming. "Get tough" policies in juvenile justice since the 1980s have resulted in an overreliance on incarceration of girls as well as a disproportionate representation of girls of color in the juvenile system. Developments such as gender-specific programming promise redress of these problems. Gender-specific policy and programs are funded by the Office of Juvenile Justice and Delinquency Prevention in the U.S. Department of Justice and focus on female minor offenders and their unique pathways during adolescence. Chapter Five details the etiology of gender-specific policy and presents quotes from adults and girls in detention facilities where I observed the programs being delivered.

Gender-specific projects work because they bring young women together in girl-only spaces to focus on their lives as girls. These projects also bring together adults from differing perspectives who can agree that young women's lives are important. However, some projects that are gender-specific present in their workshops somewhat anachronistic notions of femininity; for example, they constantly urge young women to consider so-called healthy relationships (meaning abstinent, heterosexual monogamy), to reassess their ideas of images of beauty in favor of conventional representations of middle-class femininity, and to stop what is popularly termed their *relational aggression* (as opposed to the term for boys: *instrumental aggression*). Girls resist many of these workshops, which are presented from the perspective of program providers and often impose (well-meaning, middle-class) adult values. However, when gender-specific policy is designed to challenge gender, racial, and sexual stereotypes and gender myths, it can provide skills that girls can use to navigate their adolescence successfully. Crucial to this policy is the teaching of critical consciousness about shared oppression and how to access the sisterly solidarity that will lead to increased resilience and empowerment.

In the concluding chapter, Chapter Six, I present a summary of the girls' suggestions for the interventions they need in order to get out of the system, and I make recommendations for further consideration. I point out that listening to young women who were being adjudicated in the juvenile court system uncovered the harsh and impoverished emotional and material conditions of their lives in their families, neighborhoods, and schools before they came to the attention of the authorities. Through the girls' narratives, I learned that, overwhelmingly, their daily worlds were filled with abuse and exploitation, hypereroticization, as well as an increased level of socially sanctioned violence—that is, violence that they experienced but in which the state did not intervene. Young women growing up amid social disenfranchisement and concentrated disadvantage imbibed racist, misogynistic, and consumerist messages with their "daily bread," as did those authorities with whom they later came into contact. Along with limited material resources, such as a lack of secure housing, sufficient health care, educational opportunities, and assurance of economic safety, I argue, these sociocultural messages mapped onto girls' psychologies and influenced their strategies in ways unique to young women. The girls' histories illuminated the point that we must consider their lived experiences as we plan interventions that divert them from the juvenile legal system.

Chapter Six ends with recommendations for the care, treatment, and support of young women struggling with court involvement. Young women's offenses should not be seen as acceptable. But these data reveal that in order to address their complicated situations and rehabilitate them, we need to begin by considering the conditions—material, cultural, and emotional—in which young women develop sexual and violent strategies for living through their childhoods.

Girls in Trouble with the Law argues that even though a project may focus on girls, in order to maintain theoretical rigor as well as redemptive qualities it must challenge damaging stereotypical norms in the dominant culture. If not, theories and subsequent policy are in danger of reinforcing the underdeveloped ideas and conditions that bring girls to the attention of authorities in the first place. For intervention, prevention, or treatment programs to work, they must recognize the realities, meanings, and effects of troubled girls' experiences and seek to empower girls by challenging stereotypes and encouraging them to work in concert.

1

New Troubles

for Girls

Two police cars arrived at the corner in a poorly lit neighborhood almost simultaneously.[1] Cutting the sirens but leaving on flashing blue and red lights, both officers pointed their bright headlights at the group of girls embroiled in a fight. It was 2:15 a.m. on a Friday night in 1999. Officer Robinson, the young African American woman I was riding with, jumped out of the car and sprinted toward the melee. Several young women had already started scattering in all directions. Springing out of the other police car—an unmarked Chevy—two young men, one white and one Latino, immediately began separating the two remaining girls. "OK! OK! Knock it off! OK!" shouted the police officers as they disentangled the young women locked in struggle. Empty bottles of the cheap liquor Mad Dog 20/20 were in the gutter nearby. As Officer Robinson explained afterward, the first thing that police do when they come upon such a scene is to separate and handcuff everyone involved so they can begin to sort out what was going on. While checking the combatants for weapons and drugs, an officer found a box cutter in the pocket of one of the girls, Claudia Sereno. Officer Robinson, musing later that night, supposed that the officers had caught this fight right at the beginning, before Claudia had taken out the blade and used it.

Claudia continued struggling. "I'M A KICK YOUR ASS! TE CORTO! TE CORTO [I will cut you]!" she was yelling while kicking her legs at the arresting officer's partner. One of the officers was holding her arms from behind, and she was kicking at the other officer coming toward her from the front. Claudia was a tough, small, round-faced, seventeen-year-old Latina, known to the juvenile law enforcement officers as a "fighter." Her front tooth was chipped from fighting with somebody in her neighborhood: "I love to fight! I cracked my tooth in a fight when a guy hit me with a milk crate!" she told me later.

Claudia had long dark brown hair, parted in the middle and usually tied in a ponytail in the back, but her hair was flying all over the place as she fought being handcuffed and deposited in the backseat of the police car. She continued yelling and kicking the doors from inside the back of the car. "*Te mato, cabrón! Verás lo que te hago*! I'ma kill all y'alls!" Claudia was spitting and jerking around in a terrible fury, crying and screaming all at once. "Claudia, my name is Officer Rodriguez. *Tienes que calmarte*. I need you to calm down and tell me what happened," one of the officers said to her.

Officer Robinson was speaking with the other girl, Dominique Alexander. "She jus' came at me! We was walking over to Maria Elena's place. We weren't doin' nothin'! We were jus' kickin' it man, you know. Man, these girls came outta nowhere and that bitch jus' jumped on me!" Officer Robinson put her in the backseat of our car. Dominique begged the police officer, "Please don't wake up my grandmother. She'll kill me! Go ahead and take me in, but, man, please don't call my grandmother!"

The police officers conferred for about twenty minutes, talking to the young women, checking their stories, and looking for their names on "Known Gang Members" lists. "It's the one thing I hate the most, is when these kids lie to me," one of the officers told me. "I don't care what they are doing out here, just don't lie to me about it, like I'm stupid." I learned later that the officers like to take their time once everybody is cuffed. They figure that if they let the girls' adrenaline dissipate as they simmer in the backseats of the cruisers, the young women may begin to realize the serious trouble they are in. According to these officers, strategies for working with juveniles included letting them settle down, making sure they are not carrying weapons, assessing that they are not "too high" or overdosed, and getting them to focus on the dangers of being on the streets late at night.

As we drove Dominique home, Officer Robinson left the lights flashing and kept Dominique in handcuffs. We pulled into the run-down public housing apartment complex and walked Dominique, handcuffed, right into her living room. Dominique's grandmother and mother were standing there, looking disheveled and upset. Both women wore housedresses over nightgowns and slippers on their feet. Dominique's mother's hair was in curlers, her grandmother's hair was in a hairnet; both women had obviously just been awakened. In front of the mother and grandmother and a sleepy little boy standing wide-eyed slightly behind his mother, Officer Robinson uncuffed Dominique and addressed them all. "OK, Mrs. Alexander, I know you are doing all you can to take care of your daughter. And, Dominique, I know you are a good girl, but I don't want to see you out there at night like this ever again. I know everybody in this neighborhood, and now I know you. I won't bring you home next time; I'll take you in and book you if I see you out late like this again."

I learned later that Officer Robinson uses the drama of the lights and handcuffs to underscore to the youth and parents the seriousness of being out late, drinking and fighting. This was an example of community policing—a relatively new strategy that emphasizes community engagement over crime fighting. Officer Robinson told me that whenever possible she takes girls home and talks with them and their families.

But Claudia had been taken by the other officers, first to the adolescent psychiatric facility for an evaluation, and then to be booked into the temporary detention facility. When I saw Claudia a few days later in the secure detention facility, I learned she was being adjudicated for weapons' possession and aggravated assault.

Dominique's and Claudia's accounts typify experiences of contemporary court-involved girls. Girls—physical and fighting back; on the streets; sexually active, pregnant, or parenting; angry and feeling ill-used; hungry and living in poverty; many of African American or Hispanic descent—are the fastest growing juvenile prison population in the United States. In 2003, female minors constituted 29 percent of all juvenile arrests, an all-time high. At every stage in the juvenile legal process, a disproportionate number of the girls are African American and Latina. As of 1997, more than half of girls in residential placements nationally were girls of color. Court-involved girls face challenges beyond their problems with delinquency. A study of the Cook County (Illinois) juvenile system found that roughly 20 percent of the girls were pregnant or parenting.[2]

When I went to the field to begin this research in 1995, I thought I would meet young women in trouble mostly because of their sexuality: girls working in the pornography industry, young women on the strolls, strippers, lap dancers, and peep-show girls—all oppressed by bad men. According to both popular myth and research, "boys are violent" and "girls are sexy." But to my surprise, over the years, I met, observed, and interviewed more girls in trouble for assaultive and violent offenses than for any other category of offense. Many young women were locked up in detention centers and psychiatric facilities for aggravated assaults with deadly weapons, attempted homicides, and murder.

This chapter opened with the description of the arrest of Claudia Sereno and continues with a brief discussion of the different ways by which a young woman might come to the attention of juvenile authorities; it gives as well an overview of today's juvenile system. We then meet LaShondra Wolfe at intake and in her detention facility. After describing what might be called a typical day in secure detention, with photographs of a girls' unit taken by detained young women, the chapter proceeds with a discussion about the crucial role that language has in shaping the juvenile "corrections" system. The next sections present a short history of the court system for girls and ask the reader to consider cultural shifts in gender norms for girls over the past hundred years. What is "trouble" according to contemporary juvenile authorities and according to young women? I suggest that contemporary girls transgress new norms, as we will see in the following chapters, which present an ethnography of a system: the worlds of girls in trouble with the law. The chapter concludes with a description of the study and of the young women and adults who participated in it.

Girl Perpetrators and Other Unexplained Trends

Popular representations in the media and literature as well as social science often frame juvenile delinquency as male-only behavior. Until the 1990s, young women were typically portrayed as being in trouble because of prostitution, erotic dancing, or other sexual misconduct. Girls who came before the court were called "wayward" and were described as illicit and immoral delinquents. However, those depictions have never accurately represented young women who were locked in juvenile correctional facilities around the United States, especially during the last decade of the twentieth century.

Table 1.1 presents total estimated arrests based on FBI reports for selected offenses for juveniles for 1990, 1995, 2000, and 2004. Because reporting is uneven across jurisdictions, by offense, as well as over time, our best guesses consist of calculated estimates.[3] As Table 1.1 shows, although the total number of arrests of girls for violent offenses is high, it is small in comparison with the total number of arrests of boys for similar offenses. Over two hundred thousand arrests were of boys for assaults, both aggravated and simple.

According to the 2000 census, there were about nineteen million girls aged ten to nineteen in the United States. Even though the total numbers of arrests of young women are rising, of all young women in the total population, few are arrested. Even so, in the United States in 2004, over 662,000 girls under eighteen were arrested. About 17,000 of those arrests were for violent offenses—murder, forcible rape, robbery, and aggravated assault (see Table 1.1). The total arrests of girls under eighteen for prostitution in 2000 was nearly thirteen hundred, while over fourteen thousand arrests of girls were for aggravated assault. Despite these large numbers, we know little about girls being processed in the juvenile legal system and less about girls adjudicated for violent offenses.[4]

Table 1.1

Estimated Juvenile Arrests, Selected Offenses, by Gender

	1990	1995	2000	2004
Boys				
Total violent crime	101,082	127,296	80,765	73,701
Aggravated assault	54,752	67,266	50,450	46,275
Simple assault	115,571	155,892	163,777	166,847
Prostitution and commercialized vice	716	648	598	516
Girls				
Total violent crime	13,408	21,818	18,101	17,086
Aggravated assault	9,718	16,368	15,369	14,345
Simple assault	35,209	59,358	73,241	83,441
Prostitution and commercialized vice	847	605	724	1,304

Source: Author's calculations from Federal Bureau of Investigation, *Crimes in the United States*, Washington, DC, http://www.fbi.gov (accessed October 29, 2005), tables 24, 34, and 35 for 1990, and tables 29, 39, and 40 for 1995, 2000, and 2004.

Note: Crimes in the United States does not provide estimates for each offense by age and gender. I divided the total estimated arrests (table 24 for 1990 and table 29 for 1995, 2000, and 2004) by the total reported arrests (tables 34 and 35 for 1990 and tables 39 and 40 for 1995, 2000, and 2004) for each category. I was then able to calculate weighted estimates for each offense by gender for each year. Violent crimes are murder, forcible rape, robbery, and aggravated assault.

For a variety of reasons, the exact dimensions of court-involved girls' experiences with perpetrating violence have not been clearly established. Past research focused almost exclusively on the violence of boys in gangs because a relatively small proportion of girls had been in trouble for violent offenses. Since the inception of the juvenile court, boys have constituted the majority of detained minors. A lack of social science research that grapples with the unique interplay of youth, gender, and public policy also contributes to the paucity of theory and data about girls' involvement in the juvenile legal system.

In the 1990s, while studies and news reports focused on girls and running away, girls and drug sales, girls and prostitution, and girls in troubling families, scholars and advocates began to notice disturbing and underreported factors. Given the popular media coverage of youth, sex, and violence at the time, I would have thought that most arrests of girls would be for sexually related misconduct and that boys' and girls' involvement with authorities for violence would be incomparable on any measure. But, as Table 1.1 shows, girls' arrests for aggravated assault completely outstripped their arrests for prostitution. By 2004, there were more arrests of girls for simple assaults than there were arrests of boys for total violent crime, which includes murder, forcible rape, robbery, and aggravated assault.

This is not to say that more girls were arrested for violence and assaults than boys. According to Table 1.1, boys' arrests for murder, forcible rape, robbery, and aggravated and simple assault combined approached 242,000, while girls' arrests for the same offenses only came close to 100,000. Of all arrests of juveniles, only 29 percent were of girls. But, by looking at rates of change in the numbers of arrests by gender, we get a clearer understanding of the trends in girls' arrests from 1990 to 2004. Table 1.2 compares the proportions of change in selected categories of girls' and boys' arrests for those fifteen years. The table shows, in all offense categories for girls, a large increase in the proportion change compared with the proportion change for boys. While arrests for aggravated assault declined by approximately 15 percent for boys between 1990 and 2004, girls' arrests in this category increased nearly 50 percent. And we see the astonishing proportion change in girls' arrests for simple assaults, 137 percent compared with 44 percent for boys. Girls' arrests for all violent offenses rose 27 percent as boys' arrests for these offenses declined by 27 percent. So, even though in actual numbers girls' arrests for fighting were nowhere near boys' numbers, we see that, of all arrests for girls, the proportions for violence were on the rise, much more so than the proportions of all boys' arrests for the same categories. Still, this is not the whole story.

In order to contrast differences in the reasons for which young women and men come into the juvenile court system, I compared the top ten reasons for which girls were most often arrested to the top ten reasons for boys. These offenses are presented in ranked order for girls and boys in Table 1.3. For the 2004 data overall, the ranks of offenses were quite similar between genders. As Table 1.3 displays, larceny/theft ranked first for girls and second for boys. For both boys and girls, simple assault was the third most common reason for arrest. A great many arrests of juveniles are for trivial, minor, or status offenses. But aggravated assault (which did not rank in the top ten offenses for which boys were arrested) formed 2 percent of all girls' arrests—yet only 3 percent of all boys' arrests. That they shared similar proportions intrigued me, given the 1990s media and news hype about sexy girls and violent boys. Simple assaults constituted a slightly higher proportion of girls' arrests (13 percent) than of boys' arrests (11 percent). So arrests for violence were beginning to rank higher for girls than they did for boys. That they even ranked *similarly* to boys' ranks struck me, given, as this book will demonstrate, the presentation at the time in the cultural and news media of girls as mainly sexy and boys as largely violent.

In 2004, we saw a sharp rise in arrests of underage girls for prostitu-

Table 1.2
*Percentage Change in Juvenile Arrests, Selected Offenses, by Gender,
1990 to 2004*

	% Change	
Offense	Girls	Boys
Total violent crime	+ 28	−26
Aggravated assault	+ 48	−15
Simple assault	+137	+44
Weapons	+ 91	− 4
Prostitution and commercialized vice	+ 54	−28
Sex offenses	+ 13	+ 4

Source: Author's calculations from Federal Bureau of Investigation, *Crimes in the United States,* Washington, DC, http://www.fbi.gov (accessed October 29, 2005), tables 24, 34, and 35 for 1990, and tables 29, 39, and 40 for 2004.

Note: Violent crimes are murder, forcible rape, robbery, and aggravated assault. Sex offenses do not include forcible rape and prostitution. Weapons charges include carrying and possessing.

tion. However, only approximately thirteen hundred girls under the age of eighteen were arrested for prostitution in the entire nation. In a decade replete with moral hysteria over trafficking of child prostitutes, pedophilias, and predators, the numbers of girls coming to the attention of authorities for sexually related misconduct remained relatively low. It also struck me as odd that authorities identified fewer than one thousand underage sex workers in 2003. The persistence of the fiction about girls' offenses derives essentially from outmoded notions of gender. Popular cultural myths about masculinity and femininity—that males are aggressive, assaultive, tough, individualistic, and violent and that females are passive, sexual, nurturing, relational, and emotional—prevented us, first, from seeing new trends develop among juvenile arrests and, second, from interpreting them.

Overall, after skyrocketing in the 1980s and 1990s, arrests for violent crime by juveniles began a steady decrease in the late 1990s. Nevertheless, in 2004, as can be seen in Table 1.1, girls accounted for 24 percent of all juvenile arrests for aggravated assault and one-third (33 percent) of juvenile arrests for simple assaults. These data raise important questions about the experiences of girls in the larger culture. What is the meaning of the trend of rising arrests of girls for violent offenses? What is the social logic to girls' violence? By listening to young women, what can we learn about helping girl children to thrive in adolescence? The answers to these questions are located in the voices and experiences of court-involved girls. The following chapters explore the shifting trends

Table 1.3
Rank and Proportions of Selected Offenses, by Gender, 2004

Girls

Rank	Offense	Of all girls' arrests, % (#)
1	Larceny/theft	21 (137,299)
2	All other minor offenses[a]	16 (106,026)
3	Simple assaults	13 (83,442)
4	Runaway	11 (70,036)
5	Disorderly conduct	10 (66,662)
6	Liquor law violations	7 (46,242)
7	Curfew and loitering	6 (42,965)
8	Drug offenses	5 (33,594)
9	Vandalism	2 (14,899)
10	Aggravated assault	2 (14,345)
	Other offenses[b]	7 (47,974)
	Total	100 (662,496)

Boys

Rank	Offense	Of all boys' arrests, % (#)
1	All other minor offenses[a]	18 (277,897)
2	Larceny/theft	12 (190,029)
3	Simple assaults	11 (166,847)
4	Drug offenses	10 (161,253)
5	Disorderly conduct	9 (139,662)
6	Curfew and loitering	6 (95,682)
7	Vandalism	6 (89,084)
8	Liquor law violations	5 (84,385)
9	Burglary	5 (72,028)
10	Runaway	3 (48,777)
	Other offenses[c]	15 (233,020)
	Total	100 (1,558,664)

Source: Author's calculations from Federal Bureau of Investigation, *Crimes in the United States,* Washington, DC, http://www.fbi.gov (accessed October 29, 2005), tables 29, 39, and 40.

[a]Excludes traffic violations.

[b]For girls, none of the total arrests for each of the following other offenses alone numbered among the ten most common reasons for which they were arrested: murder, forcible rape, robbery, burglary, motor vehicle theft, arson, forgery, fraud, embezzlement, stolen property, weapons, prostitution, sex offenses, gambling, offenses against the family, driving under the influence, drunkenness, vagrancy, and suspicion.

[c]For boys, none of the total arrests for each of the following other offenses alone numbered among the ten most common reasons for which they were arrested: murder, forcible rape, robbery, aggravated assault, motor vehicle theft, arson, forgery, fraud, embezzlement, stolen property, weapons, prostitution, sex offenses, gambling, offenses against the family, driving under the influence, drunkenness, vagrancy, and suspicion.

in girls' arrest rates, bring the young women's voices into our discussion, and demonstrate what being processed through the juvenile system is like for girls.

Juvenile Corrections Today

The first juvenile court opened its doors in 1899 in Chicago as a Cook County institution. Juvenile legal jurisdictions continue to operate at local levels. Although there is a federal system for juveniles who commit federal felonies, there is no unified, national juvenile justice system. Thus, in each state the system may have a slightly different structure and style. Depending on the size of the population in a given jurisdiction, juvenile legal systems may be formally divided into distinct branches: a detention facility with its own administrative system, a court legal system with attendant support staff, and a juvenile probation system that oversees children who have been court-ordered to serve a probationary sentence. For example, in 2000, the Office of Juvenile Justice and Delinquency Prevention estimated that there were 277,784 cases where youth between the ages of thirteen and seventeen were adjudicated delinquent with probation as their disposition; 28 percent (77,758) of them involved girls.[5] Juvenile court systems may draw on the resources of state or county long-term secure facilities, sometimes referred to as "ranches," as well as a network of community-based social service agencies such as after-school programs, group homes, and adolescent psychological and mental health treatment facilities. According to the Census of Juveniles in Residential Placement, in the United States in 2001 almost fourteen thousand girls aged thirteen to seventeen were living in public, private, and tribal residential facilities that house juvenile offenders.[6]

Each of these bureaucracies may have a mission that conflicts with those of other branches. For example, in some jurisdictions, the primary purpose of secure detention facilities is to provide a safe and secure environment for minors in custody as they await a hearing, transport to other facilities, or retrieval by family members. Juvenile detention centers can be tense hotbeds where conditions are volatile, and youth brought in from the streets or from other facilities are typically unsure what is going to happen to them next. Juvenile detention staff may be trained in techniques for managing assaultive behavior, and often the central concern of detention center workers is to protect detainees as well as themselves. Employees at some secure facilities are called correctional officers, while at other secure facilities they are called youth counselors.[7] But a correctional-driven philosophy may be at odds with, for example, the court's task of establishing the facts of a case and administering justice or with a probation system that focuses on youth accountability and psychological rehabilitation, one that perhaps sees its mission as being "a primary and effective resource for positive change in the lives of youth and their families."[8] At various locations in the system, both probation officers and detention staff may work side by side in areas such as intake units and serious habitual offenders units. Differently trained and oriented in the profession, these adults' professional missions may be at odds with each other—and confusingly indistinguishable to the youth in their care. Petty turf wars can be common among workers in these systems because personnel become entrenched in their civil service positions, squabbling over scarce resources.

From the viewpoint of the juveniles, in the space of a few short days in detention, they may see a social worker trying to give them a psychological assessment, a juvenile public defender trying to put the best spin on the case, a detention officer trying to keep them from hurting each other, a judge trying to determine "the truth," a juvenile prosecutor trying to land them in a long-term facility, and a probation officer seeking information from them in order to find programs that might benefit them. It was common for me to hear young people refer to all these adults as "the enemy."[9]

Not all juvenile jurisdictions share definitions of juvenile court activities, nor do they report these data evenly. Minors are usually handled in child, juvenile, or family court systems. Increasingly in the 1990s, juveniles, charged with a variety of felonies at earlier ages, were transferred to adult courts. In 1997, twenty-three states had no legal age limit specified in statutes, allowing "discretionary" transfer of children to adult court. In Kansas and Vermont, the legal age for possible transfer to adult court was ten. As of 2001, three states legally defined all sixteen- and seventeen-year-olds as adults, lowered from the international standard of eighteen.[10] Youth of that age in those jurisdictions are handled automatically in adult court. Most states have several juvenile jurisdictions, and each state has public welfare codes and local, county, even city statutes that determine formal transgressions, such as curfews and loitering ordinances. In addition, in metropolitan urban systems, each branch of the juvenile system may issue its own set of statistics and reports.

All these variations make the gathering of national data problematic. For example, the stages of juvenile court processing—variously termed *booking, petitions filed,* and even *detention*—can mean different things in different jurisdictions and may be reported differently and unevenly from each juvenile jurisdiction to federal offices. Many local juvenile halls, county-funded, have outdated computer systems. Detention data often represent one-day counts. So, for example, a child who is temporarily detained while awaiting the arrival of her parents to retrieve her may be counted next to a child who is serving a long-term adjudicatory disposition. Criteria for detaining children in public facilities may vary from criteria for detention in private facilities. Definitions of the activity of juveniles assigned to placements in group homes, juvenile halls, out-of-home placements, ranches, diversion centers, voluntary-treatment facilities, shelters, unlocked placements, and locked-down cottages vary from county to county and state to state.

The Gendered Nature of Juvenile Justice

Everything about the juvenile system is gendered—the process, the administration, the programming, the logic, the organization, the data collection, the discretion of state's attorneys and judges, the personnel—but the ways in which masculinity and femininity are constructed and controlled are not explicit. Gender, race, and class play out in the juvenile court through the work of the personnel, the decisions that are made around the nature of punishment, and the struggles of the youth in confinement.[11]

The handling of status offenses is one area in the juvenile legal system that disproportionately affects girls. Status offenses are offenses that would not be considered criminal if the child had reached majority age. Examples of status offenses are truancy, running away from home, sexual conduct, curfew violations, and drinking alcohol. Only by virtue of status as a minor does such behavior become legally actionable. In the year 2000, over 58 percent of all status offenders were girls.[12] Societal assumptions include the notion that girls may need more protection than boys: when boys do not come home at night, mothers may be less likely to call police and report them as runaways.[13] When girls are considered incorrigible or out of control or when they are out with their friends on the street at night or not able to attend school, families and law enforcement tend to interpret these behaviors as status offending.

Young people may come into secure detention facilities without ever having committed a delinquent offense. Before the Runaway and Homeless Youth Act, which was enacted as Title III of the *Juvenile Justice and Delinquency Prevention Act of 1974,* status offenders could be locked in secure detention. But the 1974 Congressional reform barred authorities from securely detaining children who have not committed a delinquent act. However, children who are picked up for curfew or truancy or runaway violations may be held until a guardian comes to collect them. Youth can also arrive in secure detention as status offenders when they are charged with violating a condition of their probation order. For example, in court, a judge may make it a condition of probation that a young girl attend school every day. Then, when she misses a day of school, she is in violation of one of the conditions of her probation. Even though no crime has been committed, a probation violation is a detainable offense. Thus do minors come into lock-up even though they have committed no delinquent offense.

Because law enforcement officers use their discretion when deciding to bring children into detention facilities, any data collected about youth in the juvenile system will necessarily reflect attitudes toward gender. For example, as part of his community policing strategy, Officer Rodriguez, one of Claudia Sereno's arresting officers, told me he "usually brings the girls home" when he encounters them out at night, on the streets after curfew, but he brings the boys into the station "to give them a little wake-up call." Judges also can remand children to temporary and long-term detention. A woman judge in an urban courthouse told me she preferred "to see these young ladies start to act like young ladies." Girls' court files contain an inordinate amount of gendered and sexualized references ("she is a very loud" or "big" or "defiant" girl, or "she has many sexual partners"). As we will see in later chapters, judges have the power to include gender-specific interventions in the probation conditions they order. Thus, powerful social actors—police officers, judges, probation officers, district attorneys—draw not only from their own interpretations of the law but also from their behavioral expectations for law-abiding boys and girls. These assessments are reflected in arrest, detention, and adjudication determinations. In these ways, the facts and statistics produced about the juvenile system and by the system reveal that the supposedly neutral decisions that are made on behalf of girls actually are mediated by many factors, including gender. Contact with the system is always emotionally fraught, as LaShondra's story illustrates.

How to Get Locked Up: LaShondra Wolfe at Intake

Hands shackled, unable to sit still, LaShondra Wolfe peered grimly into the camera. "Face forward," intoned the bored guard. As she turned for a profile shot, her pregnant belly came into view. LaShondra, a sixteen-year-old African American girl, was being processed for a felony weapons charge in a juvenile facility in 1998. "Mmm, I'm fittin' to go off here in a minute, these [her handcuffs] is too tight! And I have to pee!" The guard unlocked her handcuffs. "I am TOO hungry! What y'all got for me around here?" "Have a seat," he grumbled, trudging down the dimly lit cement-colored hall toward a circular central station. "Hey! I'm HUNGRY! I'M TALKIN' TO YOU!" The young woman shot up off the bench. "I don't got to go so long without food, you know—I KNOW MY RIGHTS!" Agitated, she threw jabs into the air and took a few steps toward the central desk area. From out of nowhere, three men appeared and wrestled her back into restraints. Her yells echoed down the dingy halls as the counselors escorted her to a temporary holding room. "All I wants is somethin' to eat! You don't got no call doin' all this! I'ma kick all y'alls ass up in here!" Even though she was pregnant, detention officers were taking no chances with everyone's safety.

Girls come into the juvenile legal system through a variety of pathways. Police officers, using their discretion, may bring them into a precinct station after parents, teachers, or neighbors call for help. From there, girls may be transported to intake at a detention center. Girls may come into an emergency room because of medical or psychological trauma, or if they have overdosed on a drug, have been seriously wounded, or have made a suicide attempt, juvenile authorities may be notified. From triage, girls may be booked into detention. Girls also come in from the streets to temporary facilities when they run away from home; typical reasons girls cite for running away include negative family dynamics and physical or sexual abuse. While in the streets on the run, young women may become involved in the street economy: for example, through drug use, drug sales, sex work, providing sex for favors, or sexual assault. And, at intake units across the United States, disproportionately high numbers of girls report having been victims of violence. Thus drawing the attention of law enforcement, psychiatric, or emergency-room personnel, young women enter the juvenile system.[14]

Girls sent to secure facilities usually have serious felony charges. At screening and intake, facilities have some kind of system for determining who gets locked up and who can go home. Through a screening assessment and other methods, probation officers working on intake units make crucial decisions. Some young women are moved onto the locked-down units solely because detention personnel are unable to locate suitable legal guardians to retrieve them. It was common for detention personnel to remark that "the saddest thing I've ever seen is a girl whose mother will not come get her." Because of concern over disproportionate minority representation in all phases of the U.S. justice system, many facilities nationwide have adopted some kind of screening instrument in order to systemize the decision to place a youth in secure detention. Some jurisdictions use a scoring sheet. The sheet in Text Box 1.1 is based on a system whereby fifteen points gets a child into secure detention. A youth automatically receives fifteen points for being arrested for a violent felony, five points for felony possession of narcotics, and three points for six or more court referrals in the previous twelve months. Arrests for automatic transfer to adult court and violation of juvenile electronic monitoring earn fifteen points and an authorization for immediate secure detention.

```
Screen Date:      Screen Time:      A.M./P.M.      Screener:
YOUTH OFFICER: _____  District: _____
MINOR RESPONDENT: _____  D.O.B. _____Age:_____
Sex:  M  /  F   Race:  WHITE / BLACK / HISPANIC / ASIAN / OTHER  YD: ___
FACTOR  IR# _____            FAMILY FOLDER NUMBER: _____
  MOST SERIOUS INSTANT OFFENSE: _____
  (Choose only one item indicating the most serious charge)
  Automatic Transfer Cases                                      15
  Violent Felonies
      (Murder, Armed Robbery with Handgun, Home Invasion,
        ACSA, UUW-Gun)                                          15
      Agg Batt – Bodily Harm, Agg Vehicular Invasion, Agg Discharge
      of a Firearm, Agg Battery with a firearm) Other Forcible Felonies
      (Robbery, Kidnapping, Intimidation, CSA, Hate Crime, Agg Batt,
      Vehicle Invasion)                                         10
  Other Offenses
      Felony Sale of Cannabis (Class 1 or 2 felony), Arson, DCS   10
      PCS w/int deliver, Residential Burglary, UUW (not a gun),
        Possession Explosives                                    7
      Felony Possession of Narcotics/Drugs for Sale or Other Felonies  5
      Misdemeanor Possession of Narcotics/Drugs or Other
        Weapons Possession                                       3
  Other Misdemeanors                                             2
  Not Picked up on New Offense (WARRANT)                         0


DECISION SCALE                            TOTAL SCORE _____
  Score 0-9    AUTHORIZED RELEASE (with notice of prioritized date)
  Score 10-14 COMPLETE NON-SECURE DETENTION OPTIONS FORM
  Score 15+   AUTHORIZED DETENTION (for minors 13 years of age
                and older)
ADMINISTRATIVE OVERRIDE  (Supervisory approval is required)
  ☐ NO   ☐ YES   REASON: _____
  Family Folder #:
  FINAL DECISION ☐ DETAIN ☐ RELEASE ☐ RELEASE WITH CONDITIONS
```

Text Box 1.1. Portion of a typical intake assessment form. *Credit: Author's research, used by permission.*

Intake is a location for critical decisions whose results intertwine race and class. Many young women in the juvenile legal system are from poor or working-class families and live in neighborhoods of concentrated disadvantage. Despite the booming economy of the 1990s, 5.6 million children were living in severely distressed neighborhoods in 2000, an 18 percent increase from 1990. Furthermore, girls in the juvenile system are disproportionately girls of color: in 2003, approximately 55 percent of girls thirteen to seventeen in juvenile residential placement were girls of color, while, of all girls this age in the U.S. general population, 34 percent were girls of color. And, as in the adult system, status and privilege prevail. Often middle-class girls are shunted out of the system because their parents show up immediately with private attorneys who arrange for the girls to be released on the spot.[15]

Upon admission into larger facilities, young people are usually housed in a special intake unit, where their orientation to the facility is conducted, clothing is issued, and requisite educational, physical, mental health, and possibly dental health assessments are conducted. Children's belongings are collected and placed in a bag with their name on it for return when they are released. These may be referred to as their "Personals," as in "Please put this piece of artwork I did in school in my Personals for when I get out."

In jurisdictions where drugs may be a problem, girls are observed for drug use at intake. A pattern has developed: fearful when approached by police, children are ingesting all the drugs they are carrying. Girls are falling sick upon being admitted, but because it can take a few hours to determine their health status, I have heard facility personnel say in frustration, "Take 'em straight to the emergency room and let them wait it out there." They do not want to be responsible for an overdose—morally, legally, or financially.

After being admitted, girls are bathed, tested, given orientation materials, and allowed to settle down a bit before they are put on a unit, where they may stay for a few days or weeks, depending on their charged offense, family situation, and health conditions.

Any child who has been in detention will tell you that it is an eye-opening experience. As they put it, "Lock-up is hell!" It is intended to be that way. After all, some would say, we don't want it to be enjoyable for children. Around the nation, facilities differ along many variables such as their size, purpose, layout, architecture, and location. Old or new, detention centers have their own personality. Some are informal and friendly and allow lots of rough-housing, hugs, and contact among staff and youth, even among serious habitual offenders. Others have a military-style, maximum security atmosphere. But, almost without exception, secure detention is considered the last resort for troubled youth, and it sometimes is the first step to an adolescence full of system involvement.

The reason for such wide disparity among facilities is that although federal funds are distributed nationally, no federal office oversees and unifies the juvenile legal system statutorily. States and counties set guidelines, often decreeing that each county or other jurisdiction that maintains a juvenile court should maintain a juvenile detention facility. Some states require citizen juvenile justice commissions to oversee compliance with federal, state, and county regulations; others do not.

Detention centers share enough similarities for me to be able to describe them generally. For example, LaShondra's facility, in California, was known as the Youth Guidance Hall. It held 125 detainees in secure units, but court detention centers may hold from twenty youth up to three hundred children at a time (see Illustration 1.1). Again, according to jurisdiction, youth held in secure detention are generally under the age of eighteen or seventeen, and over the age of eleven or twelve; they may be in secure detention for a variety of reasons. Some are awaiting a hearing in a courtroom in the building; others may be under transport to medical centers or other treatment facilities such as group homes or adolescent psychiatric centers. Children may be awaiting transportation to long-term county placements (often located in remote "ranches" outside of cities) or simply may be waiting for their parents to retrieve them. Some may even be ordered by a judge to spend a few days or weeks in temporary detention facilities. Thus a child awaiting a guardian may be housed with another child who has a long-term sentence for a violent offense. In the facility that LaShondra was in, at that time, the average stay for young women was approximately twenty-one days, but some stayed only overnight, and others had been in and would continue to be in secure facilities for many months. In 1997, in the United States, the Office of Juvenile Justice and Delinquency Prevention estimated that half of juveniles committed to long-term residential facilities had been in placement for almost four months, while half of detained juveniles had been in custody fewer than eighteen days.[16] A detention facility may sit nestled in the center of any urban neighborhood. But for the eerie razor wire topping the chain-link fence surrounding the grounds, secure facilities might look like any ordinary public school.

LaShondra was in a facility that sat on a hill, across the street from a large urban high school. Urban detention centers are often housed in large, multistory, concrete buildings that include a juvenile courthouse containing court personnel, several courtrooms, and other necessary legal and social service offices. The Youth Guidance Hall was built in 1957, and the county had already approved funds to build a new facility because it was overcrowded, in shambles, and shamefully grim, dark, and dingy. Although many detention centers around the nation are over fifty

Illustration 1.1. A typical detention facility. *Credit: Laurie Schaffner.*

years old, others are brand new—prison building was a thriving domestic industry in the 1980s and 1990s. In California alone, as of 2001, there were 130 juvenile halls and camps statewide. As of May 2004, twenty-one juvenile facilities were under construction (either being built anew or having beds added), two projects were "on the drawing board," and forty-nine new construction projects were completed. In Illinois, as of June 2005, there were eight long-term secure correctional facilities ("youth centers").[17]

In order to enter juvenile court buildings, one typically passes through metal detectors and is required to tell an official one's business, not unlike entering an airport or other governmental facilities, especially after September 11, 2001. To visit LaShondra, not surprisingly, I passed through a metal detector and had my bags and briefcases checked by a security guard. I was always careful to leave food and candy, sharp objects, and, of course, drugs and weapons elsewhere. Girls' rooms were regularly searched for "contraband"—food, drugs, and other objects that they often received from visitors. Youth-oriented hip-hop magazines such as *VIBE, The Source,* and *XXL* or photographs of gang-related friends might be seized as contraband. When girls were caught with contraband, they could receive extra hours of what was referred to as "room time." Girls could be relegated to staying locked up in their individual cells after school for three to six hours at a time, taking their meals alone in there as (even more) punishment.

In contrast, newly built, modern, shiny glass and brick secure juvenile facilities are often set on wide lawns, resembling suburban community college campuses. As I approached one new juvenile center, I heard the sprinklers on the grass, birds chirping, and the voices of children playing basketball on outdoor courts. Then I turned and saw a movement—the term for transporting groups of offenders from one area to another. In this correctional facility, movements were completed in military formation, each youth with her left arm straight out ahead resting on the shoulder of the youngster in front, all calling off their steps in shouts.

In LaShondra's lock-up, the lighting was harsh, the air was stale, and the windows did not open. Doors were all locked along wide concrete hallways, and therefore a probation or court employee was required to escort me through with a big ring of keys: I felt as though I were in a time warp, a 1950s movie perhaps. Newer facilities have pass cards that operate doors electronically.

At the turn of the twentieth century, when the juvenile system was first constructed, the popular thinking was to move children out of crowded tenement conditions to more healthy country living. Children were farmed out on "orphan trains" to midwestern rural households.[18] Eventually, the long-term secure facilities came to be known as ranches, and the living areas were called cottages. Some of these terms persist archaically in the contemporary concrete buildings of urban detention halls.

Living areas in juvenile halls are also sometimes called "units" and are located in groups, featuring eerie rows of doors along wide gray halls. Each unit may house up to twenty youth, with ten or fifteen units in a large facility. LaShondra was housed in a unit with 25 beds. Youth are housed in groups that vary depending on the type of facility and jurisdiction; the groups may be age-graded units, maximum security units, gang units, or units separated by gender. Young women may be housed in "Girls' Units"—"G-1," "G-2"—or "The Green Unit," "The Blue Unit," or other such designated areas. Depending on the type of facility (maximum to minimum levels of security), funding levels, and philosophy, girls may be housed dormitory-style in bunk beds lined up in a large room or may be locked into individual cells, called "rooms," as shown in Illustration 1.2, a photograph taken by a young woman in lock-up. At first glance, the typical juvenile detention cell looks like any other prisoner's dungeon. But children can spend months in this bedroom, with no visitors on weekends and no home to return to.

LaShondra did not share a room with anyone at first because the unit was not overcrowded. When she moved from the intake unit to the general population, she walked into an 8-foot-by-6-foot cement room, with a window high up on the wall. Carrying her bedding, she found it jarring to hear the door slamming shut and locking behind her. She looked up, only to see a thin gray light filtering through the sealed-shut window. Located out of her reach near the ceiling, her "window" was only a square-foot piece of glass embedded with chicken wire. A concrete ledge jutting from the wall formed the platform for LaShondra's thin, indus-

Illustration 1.2. A typical room. *Credit: Picture conceived and created by the young women in the Solutions Program, San Francisco.*

trial-grade, single mattress. An overhead light bulb gave off little illumination. When the census count rose, staff would place a plastic cot on the floor for another girl to share the space with LaShondra.

At the entrance to LaShondra's unit sat detention personnel, seemingly relaxed. They called out to girls, barking orders from a central, circular, glassed-in counter, called the "counselor's station." These so-called counselor jobs are union-protected positions and highly coveted in some areas of the nation. Mostly people of color in the urban centers, counselors can earn around fifteen dollars an hour with benefits for a job that may require only a high school diploma. In LaShondra's facility, the counselors earned $19.34 an hour, more than the schoolteachers in the district. In most facilities there may be three or four counselors to staff day shifts, when most activity and movements occur. Night-shift staff, however, may consist of one worker on each unit and, say, one staff member to roam and spell workers.

Various adults are present on the units at any given time. A casually dressed social worker may be sitting at a table in a dining area interviewing a girl to see whether placement in a particular group home is appropriate for her. A few men in suits may be inspecting the physical plant to ensure compliance with governmental guidelines. Juxtaposed against this serious and formal activity, a group of young men with dreadlocks and white cotton garb may be carrying drums and other musical instruments down a hall to perform for the young women's afternoon programming. Because large probation departments may have as many as twenty probation units, a probation officer from a social investigations, intake, or after-care unit may be coming or going to check on a detainee or on something in her file.

The unit where LaShondra was detained featured plastic and metal furniture. In her dining area, the tables were bolted to the floor. Each table had four stools welded to it. Loose chairs quickly become weapons in volatile conditions, as we shall see in later chapters. Generally speaking, there were no doorknobs, towel racks, or any other fittings that might be turned into lethal weapons by the detainees.

At the central station on the unit, where the files or folders for each detainee were stored, a desk was littered with items such as binders with facility rules and regulations, daily logbooks where shift activity was recorded, and incidence logbooks where special movements, events, fights, medical or other emergencies were recorded; the desk served as the central congregating spot for all three shifts at this county facility. Office supplies were limited—county-run facilities have tight budgets.

Other supplies were carefully doled out. Toilet paper was handed out a few sheets at a time. Some facilities count how many sanitary napkins girls get; they are recorded when handed out and counted when returned soiled. In one facility where I spent time, staff wrote the girls' names on the Kotex boxes. To protest their grim situations, girls have been known to block the toilets by stuffing them with sanitary napkins. The economy of attention is such that every little thing that a young woman requests can precipitate a power struggle between staff and detainee. Staff may feel they have to safeguard against hoarding behavior as well. In one facility I observed in Southern California, as part of standard procedure, girls were "allowed" to use their panties as washcloths.

Bathrooms and shower stalls for LaShondra and her sister detainees were in full view from the central station—and all counselors on girls' units were not women. In some older facilities, a few minors' rooms may be wet rooms—that is, they have a sink and toilet. Many facilities provide a large bathroom area with eight or ten toilets, a row of sinks, and a half dozen shower stalls. When LaShondra needed to use the toilet, she banged on her door and called out to a counselor. The policy and procedures manual for the detention facility stipulated that a minimum of two counselors had to be present whenever detainees were unlocked from their rooms. It was considered unsafe for counselors to be alone with an unrestrained detainee. So, when a girl wanted to use the bathroom, one counselor unlocked the door and another watched from the counselor's station. Especially at night, when staff levels were at their lowest, girls might have had to wait awhile to be let out to use the toilet.

This procedure was especially hard on pregnant girls, and one night, because of understaffing, LaShondra urinated in the wastebasket in her cell. Her doing so was reported formally as an incident and was investigated by unit administrators for its "barbarity," but line staff had so many mandates to follow that that they could not meet all health and safety standards at all times.

Showers in public places (like gyms at school) bring up many emotional challenges for young women: body issues, hygiene issues, privacy issues, and, especially for this population, stimulation of frightening memories. In LaShondra's unit, showering was conducted in small groups, by hallway, in morning or evening shifts. Counselors shouted out, "Stand by your doors!" and unlocked doors one hallway at a time. Girls wandered out, some tentatively, some brazenly, and stood in the hall by their open doors. As the girls in the hall filed toward the showers, they were handed a towel and a used chip of soap and given five minutes to bathe. "Hurry it up, women!" was a common call as counselors tried to rush girls through this time-consuming process. Whenever girls were out and about in groups such as for showers, meals, or classes, counselors sensed they had to stay especially vigilant.

Privacy was a luxury that some administrators with tight budgets at larger, old facilities felt they could not afford. Shower curtains were considered a safety risk by facility administrators: sexual victimization could take place behind them. Girls told me that bathing and using the toilet in public was "humiliating" and "scary," especially those suffering from the trauma of sexual abuse. In interviews, they recounted that they felt violated ("invaded") because they could not control who saw their bodies.

Another challenge in many facilities is the extremely poor quality of the hygiene products. Shampoo, body soap, clothing and bedding soap, and hand lotions are all inferior and unpleasant. African American girls, especially, complained because they said their skin got "too ashy" without nice oils and there were no products for black hair care. Teenage girls in detention were forced to put their hair in office-style rubber bands and leave their facial skin blemished, infected, and uncared for.

Clothing is significant for most American adolescent girls in any setting, and so it is in lock-up. During an art workshop for young women in detention, girls received disposable cameras with instructions to photograph objects that had meaning for them. They were not allowed to photograph any faces, but they were invited to gather images that they wanted others to consider important. Not surprisingly, they chose to photograph their clothing. Standard-issue garb may be khaki pants with elastic waistbands, socks, and rubber sandals, and maybe t-shirts and sweatshirts in designated colors (see Illustration 1.3). That way, when they move to gym or church, it is easy to determine their unit. For example, intake-unit detainees might wear blue sweats. In one facility I spent time at, violent offenders wore neon orange. In another, youth who had not admitted to their crimes wore bright red sweatshirts. Girls at extreme high risk for running away might be issued a green jumpsuit so that staff are alerted to keep them in sight at all times. One way of seeing the sandals in Illustration 1.3 is to consider that the girls believe they are ugly and uncomfortable to walk in, and they know that the sandals are designed to be impossible to run in.

An example of how meaningful clothing was to detainees was the way that girls in one facility felt about sharing their underwear and bras. It was standard procedure that all soiled clothes be placed in bins for washing together; thus girls might not get the same panties back from the laundry. Girls complained about wearing old, stained undergarments that other young women had already worn before them. After this procedure became a topic for discussion in one of the community-run girls' discussion groups, the facility responded by implementing a new policy. At intake, girls were issued their undergarments in a zippered net bag with their name on it, and then, for the duration of their stay, the panties and bras that were issued when they arrived were washed and returned to them each time.

Daytime schedules in detention halls vary widely from facility to

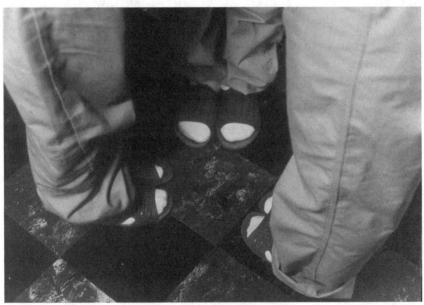

Illustration 1.3. Girls' sandals. *Credit: Picture conceived and created by the young women in the Solutions Program, San Francisco.*

facility. Some detention centers have stringent rules and strict atmospheres. Others feel like day camps with popular radio stations blaring and much informal interaction between personnel and youth. Typically, youth are awakened around six o'clock; they wash up, organize their sleeping areas, move out to a cafeteria, and eat breakfast. Breakfast might arrive from a central kitchen elsewhere to sit in steam warmers for serving. "The food is nasty!" was a common complaint, although most facilities have mandated nutritional guidelines including approximately an extra five hundred calories per meal for pregnant girls. If girls get rambunctious during a meal they may be ordered to stop talking and to eat in silence ("Talking is dead!"). At LaShondra's facility, dead time was not uncommon because fights often broke out during meals, as I will detail in later chapters.

After breakfast, girls were carefully escorted in groups to classrooms to begin their school day. Movement times were often tense because staff had sometimes to coordinate up to fifty youth. Even on a good day in a public high school, some chaos can be expected. But in a locked facility housing severely distressed girls, the prevailing sense was that care must be taken to ensure everyone's safety. Girls were asked to leave breakfast one table at a time and line up against a wall, with their toes aligning with the patterns in the linoleum on the floor. At other times, when youth were moved through the building individually or in pairs, they were sometimes placed in handcuffs for the hallway portions of the movement. The level of security depended on many factors: the mood of the girls, the mood of the staff, the level required to comply with regulations, and, according to some staff members, the necessity of a show of force and power as a means of crowd control.

Some young women stayed in their dormitory areas if they were ailing, although signing up on the "complainer's list" (the phrase used in one facility for the list of girls who had fallen ill and were in need of medical attention) had its own consequences. Speaking to nurses in front of the other girls about one's personal ailments was one of the more humiliating events, according to the girls. Or if they had court dates or other appointments, detainees were kept locked down until their time came to move. It was not uncommon for the day to be interrupted for interviews with social workers, lawyers, trips to medical centers, or placement assessments. LaShondra requested a lot of time away from the classroom because she was pregnant, in ill health, and tired most of the time.

Many facilities run their own schools on site—that is, the public school district maintains a school in the detention building. The teachers are sometimes trained in special education in order to work with developmentally or otherwise disabled youth. However, many teachers are not specially trained to work with this challenging population. In order to receive federal accreditation, detention centers follow mandates to provide, for example, a certain number of hours of schooling per day, as well as a certain number of minutes daily of large-muscle activity. After-school hours may be filled with volleyball, basketball, or other sports (see Illustration 1.4). Such activities may sound adequate in theory, but the reality is bleak. The grim exercise area in the photograph in Illustration 1.4, taken by a twelve-year-old girl in detention, is similar to many outdoor courtyards set aside for large-muscle activity for minors in secure facilities. Being cooped up in airless cement buildings day in and day out may make even the torn-up black-top pavement covered in chicken wire seem desirable. Because, as discussed above, many jurisdictions provide rubber sandals for youth to wear, athletic shoes may be issued at gym time. Counselors at one facility where I spent time observing noticed with irony that the shoddy gym shoes issued by the facility did not compare with the often two-hundred-dollar designer athletic shoes that youth had in their Personals.

Sometimes showering after gym, youth in LaShondra's facility were then locked down for quiet time or maybe allowed to congregate in a recreation area and watch television or play games. After dinner, there were often activities such as those provided by church groups that came

Illustration 1.4. A typical exercise yard. *Credit: Picture conceived and created by the young women in the Solutions Program, San Francisco.*

in to proselytize or by other kinds of groups for youth. Many jurisdictions have begun to hold gender-specific girls' discussion sessions where young women are encouraged to talk about relationships or healthy dating or other topics deemed gender-appropriate.

Final lock-down and lights out typically were scheduled around nine o'clock. After shift change, when the night staff arrived and got settled in, some young women required special attention. This was a sad and lonely time for the girls, and I spent many nights listening to young women cry themselves to sleep in distress, fear, and worry.

Thus might pass a typical day, but one without incidents or altercations. However, a full day with no incidents would be an anomaly. Most facilities I observed logged a fight, episode of suicidal ideation, complaint, or other mishap at least once every twenty-four hours. If an incident occurs—a physical fight among detainees (and staff), a young person throwing a fit (expressing rage), or the discovery of contraband or a gang communication—staff may respond by locking all youth in their rooms while staff members sort the situation out.

Language Matters: Terminology and the Construction of Reality

The kinds of troubles girls face lack their own terminology. When I began this research, no academic discipline existed to turn to, nor was there a lexicon that described and analyzed the experiences of this population. Other advocate researchers studying women's lives have encountered this phenomenon; for example, when social science first set out to study housework, domestic violence, and rape, no definitions set the problems' parameters.[19]

While talking to young women in adolescent facilities, I began to notice the disconnection between writings about delinquency and the realities of young women's lives. It became increasingly evident that we needed to bring girls' voices to the fore so we could begin a new conversation that encompassed the dire situations they faced. Both the invisibility of their lives and the lack of analyses provided by conventional social science contributed to the lack of public policy directed at alleviating their problems and served to maintain the crisis as invisible and chaotic.

The disparate and seemingly unrelated conversations taking place in both the academic and public spheres about youth violence tend to focus solely on guys, guns, and gangs. In many news reports about violent girls, journalists fail to present careful descriptions of girls as perpetrators, and they especially do not highlight how girls' earlier victimization through sexual assault and harassment might be linked to

their later offending. Furthermore, the policy debates over zero tolerance and community violence too often do not include the voices and
experiences of young women.

The term *female juvenile delinquents* originally encompassed girls
under the age of majority—in the past, eighteen years—who broke laws.
That term is no longer adequate because labeling young women as female juvenile delinquents inscribes their choices and experiences with
archaic meanings. First, referring to the biological *female* instead of using the sociological term *girls* contributes to a dehumanization of the
young women, as if they were female animals. The term *female* puts the
focus on their bodies instead of on their behavior, which, we will see,
derives from socially shaped choices.[20] Second, when the focus is on bodies, girls are often considered to be "acting like males" when, in reality,
they are acting like people. As author Simone de Beauvoir aptly noted,
"Man is defined as a human being and woman as female—whenever she
behaves as a human being, she is said to imitate the male."[21]

The girlhoods of young women in detention exist at the blurred borders of varied representations of gender, adolescence, and the law. Girls
live at the edge of gender: Do they act like boys? Girls are at the edge of
childhood: Are they women yet? And girls' behavior cuts at the edge of
the law: Are their acts truly criminal, or is it simply time to revamp the
law?

Although contested, *gender* is the term that social scientists generally use to describe feminine or masculine behavior (sex being used to
indicate physiological difference). The contemporary practices of some
court-involved young women, such as fighting and perpetrating violence,
trouble conventional analytic categories of gender and make traditional
definitions of gender somewhat outmoded because (middle-class) femininity, traditionally, was signaled through displays such as nurturing,
sexual availability (to male desire), or willingness to be a passive recipient of what life hands one. Much of what I heard from the young women
in this study contradicted the strict binary of mainstream understandings of gender. Listening to young women in trouble forced a reinterpre-
tation of conventional definitions of femininity.

The term *adolescent* is relatively new, having entered the popular
lexicon with psychologist G. Stanley Hall's landmark 1904 work, *Adolescence—Its Psychology and Its Relations to Physiology, Anthropology, Sociology, Sex, Crime, Religion and Education*. The ways that
contemporary girls are depicted in any setting depend on who is defining
them: psychologists refer to young women as adolescents, middle-class
families called them teenagers, and the juvenile justice system calls them
minors. But the legal term *juvenile* is increasingly contestable. Are these
young girls at the edge of childhood, of adolescence, or of adulthood?

Life does not follow linear developmental trajectories. As more and more (male) juveniles were tried in adult courts, an (unfortunate) trend developed to dispense with juvenile justice entirely.[22]

The tension between empowering and infantilizing youth became a central theme of the social constructions of adulthood. Should parents encourage their children to explore sexuality, or should society keep sexual material from children? As adults expressed consternation over this debate, so too did young people. Essentially, a particularly political, economic, and cultural battle about the definitions of such tropes as family values and youth crime was being waged—over the lives of a subgroup of disenfranchised young women who simultaneously troubled the law, were troubled by the law, and for whom the law troubled.

The term *delinquent* is also increasingly outdated. The notion of delinquent offenders inscribed a growing population with descriptions that followed them around long after the behavior was past. For the girls in this population, some transgressions (for example, promiscuity) were sanctioned along a new continuum of normative sexual availability and were no longer troubling, in the legal sense at least. Contemporary working-class girls' practices, displayed in film and television nightly, pushed at the boundaries of the meanings of offending.

Legal terminology, however, is distinct from daily language. *Black's Law Dictionary* defines adolescence vaguely as "the age which follows puberty and precedes the age of majority" and juvenile as "a young person who has not yet attained the age at which he or she should be treated as an adult for purposes of criminal law. In some states, this age is seventeen. Under the *Juvenile Delinquency Act* (1974), a 'juvenile' is a person who has not yet attained his [sic] eighteenth birthday. . . . In law, the terms 'juvenile' and 'minor' are usually used in different contexts; the former used when referring to young criminal offenders, the latter to legal capacity or majority."[23]

Comparative perspectives reveal that the U.S. system is not always the leader in humanitarianism. The United Nations *Convention on the Rights of the Child* set the international standard when it defined a child as "a person under 18," adding, "unless national laws recognize the age of majority earlier."[24] Language is crucial because it can make a difference between seeing children as children or seeing children as adults. As of this writing, the United States was one of only a few nations that had not ratified the international children's rights convention.

In the popular imagination, the terms *youth violence* and *community violence* might bring to mind the now prosaic notion of African American boys wearing black hooded sweatshirts and standing on street corners, carrying concealed weapons, and selling crack cocaine. But as I listened to girls in trouble, I heard about new definitions of violence that needed to be incorporated into our understanding of community violence so that community violence includes the violence that girls experience, witness, and perpetrate. In girls' worlds, violence includes being hassled at home to clean up after older brothers who threaten and harm them without chastisement or intervention from adults; being traumatized by repeated sexual molestation, innuendo, and attack, and by fear of rape and assault; and being hassled, threatened, and otherwise bothered while in their neighborhoods and at school. Violence for girls includes seeing their mothers, aunts, and sisters being mistreated and demeaned by men in their families and communities. It is an act of violence to allow girls to be raised with these images and experiences. Girls' experience of violence is sexualized, gendered in its own way, and deeply implicated in their offense patterns.

Thus, I argue, the term *female juvenile offenders* or *female juvenile delinquent* does not even begin to capture the lives of these troubled young people, and such terms are generally reviled by the young women themselves. A more apt description of the young women in this study would be *formerly detained* or *court-involved.* I use those terms, along with phrases such as "girls in trouble," "girls in detention," and "girls locked up," to describe girls who are being processed in the juvenile corrections systems. Indeed, they could be referred to as "unhealed trauma survivors" or "formerly traumatized perpetrators."

Much academic literature as well as the social service industry now use another outmoded term, *at-risk girls*, to describe this population. But the term does not adequately describe the young women in this study because they were already in trouble. A prerequisite for many of the young people in my sample was that they be in the process of or have been adjudicated or treated in juvenile corrections systems. *Adjudicated, adjudicated delinquent, having a petition filed* were terms used in the juvenile court system to mean being processed in juvenile court or having been found guilty in juvenile court, depending on the context. A similar term in the adult court might be *tried as a criminal.* The young women in my sample often carried multiple diagnoses: they had depression or other affective disorder diagnoses, were HIV positive, and suffered from substance dependence. Many were dually labeled with juvenile delinquent dispositions (sentences) and adolescent psychiatric diagnoses. Already-risked, in this sense, was a condition for being eligible to be a member of this project.

At this time, juvenile offenders in the United States were generally twelve to seventeen years old, although policies varied by jurisdiction. Children picked up for problem behaviors who were younger than twelve were usually referred to county child protective divisions or other dependency systems of protection, although several states had no lower limits on the age for juvenile offenders. Throughout this work, I use the terms *girls, children, youth, adolescents, young women, minors, juveniles, and teenage girls* interchangeably to represent the participants in my study, who ranged from thirteen to seventeen years old. I use these terms purposively and thoughtfully to challenge both the assumptions of masculinity beneath phrases such as "youth violence" and the absurd notion that children at age twelve can possibly be considered adults in criminal courts.

Two naming processes are at work. The juvenile legal system has carefully crafted terms to differentiate itself from the adult system. And society has tried to distinguish the guilty offender child in the delinquent court from the innocent victim child in the dependency system. Because each of these three jurisdictions has its own statutes and directives, these naming devices create a cottage industry of social workers, probation officers, and juvenile lawyers who debate the fine points of cases, sometimes ignoring the person involved: a girl child entangled in the very systems themselves.

Even more complex, the entire juvenile corrections system encompasses two further strategies of formal social control of minors: legal and psychiatric. The opportunity for some young women to be restored to psychological health with more humane treatments (in place of adjudication and punishment) has decreased as public mental health facilities lose funding for adolescents. But, even so, girls migrate between the two systems. Young women in detention can be "5150'd"—transferred directly to acute-care adolescent psychiatric facilities.[25] This transfer can occur when a girl in a locked situation behaves in such a physically assaultive manner that counselors fear for their safety and hers. Reserved for the most physically and emotionally out-of-control children, psychiatric care may offer what some consider to be an advantage—the five-point restraint. Not legally available in most detention facilities, five-point restraint consists of a table with leather belts to restrain a youth at the forehead, both wrists, and both ankles. In addition, if girls assault psychiatric personnel, they can be transported back to juvenile lock-up to be legally processed for assault.

I observed the case of a sixteen-year-old girl who was found guilty of simple assault in San Francisco. According to her files, it was her twelfth time coming before the court, and the judge wanted to send her to an out-of-home placement. Because there were no beds in California facilities, experts located a placement for her in a Colorado adolescent psychiatric treatment center. This young woman essentially boarded the plane in California with an assault charge, disorderly conduct, and deplaned in Colorado with a psychiatric disorder, oppositional defiant disorder. As one group of medical doctors begins their study of girls' health, "Female adolescent antisocial behavior is prevalent, whether defined as conduct disorder or delinquency."[26]

Thus are girls shuttled to and fro in juvenile corrections systems. If they have no parents/guardians to rescue them, girls may not emerge from corrections until they are eighteen. I witnessed girls moving back and forth between legal and medical incarceration, trading dispositions for diagnoses. Most everyone I observed and interviewed—judges, counselors, lawyers, parents, and girls—was frustrated with this process. Girls were especially embarrassed to be characterized as crazy. Most agree that the solution—shuttling girls between legal and psychiatric facilities—has become part of the problem.

A History of the Legal System for Girls: Social History Is Sexual History

When the juvenile court was founded in 1899, it constituted a radical reform in the criminal justice system. Until then, children were imprisoned and put to death next to adults. Torture, hunger, and forced labor were not uncommon. Then, as now, public debates raged over what to do about crime. Then, as now, reformers worked to humanize crime policy as politics and economics played a role in shaping the legal system. The juvenile court was founded on the philosophical doctrines that children are not only physically, but psychologically and morally, different from adults; that children should be protected from adults; and that children, because of their tender years, can be rehabilitated. Social worker Jane Addams, one of the founders of the juvenile court and a winner of the Nobel Peace Prize in 1931, was adamant that public policy reflect newly developed social theories regarding childhood and adolescence.

This early juvenile court assumed a paternal role, and its mission was to rehabilitate young people (as distinct from the goal of the adult court, which was to punish adults). The juvenile system, by design, used distinct terminology to distinguish it from the adult system, such as "juvenile court" in place of "adult court," "delinquent" in place of "criminal," "adjudicated delinquent" in place of "person found guilty." But calling a guard a counselor and a cell a room could not completely mask the racialized sexism and often brute force of state intervention into the lives of poor, immigrant, or otherwise suffering families and their children.

Girls and young women were brought to the attention of authorities at the turn of the twentieth century for talking to men, hanging out at night with men, or "flirting" with men. Standards for girls' behavior reflected then-popular proper, Victorian norms. Twentieth-century state interventions in female juvenile delinquency tended to sexualize girls' offenses.[27] Addams and others with newly minted women's college degrees warned of the immoral temptations for working girls in the dance halls. In their important work on delinquent women, sociologists Sheldon and Eleanor Glueck devoted an entire chapter to "illicit sex convicts." A 1912 Chicago study found that 80 percent of the 2,440 young girls who passed before the juvenile court during the court's first decade were brought there because "their virtue is in peril, if it has not already been lost." Historically, the law (and popular culture) focused on the idea of the sexy bad girl (see Illustration 1.5). On the covers of 1950s' pulp fiction novels, bad girls were constituted as sexy and seductive. In Illustration 1.5, we see a "reform school girl" with "scarlet secrets," a cigarette dangling from reddened lips as she adjusts her garter beneath a bright red dress. The anachronism of the sexpot as deviant and shameful persists, even though, as we see throughout this book, today, as a bad girl, she is an anomaly.

One goal of the early juvenile corrections system, however, was to improve girls' morality and reform their sexual behavior. In fact, the history of girls' delinquency is a history of the social control of the sexuality of mostly working-class, ethnic women in urban settings. The court's work was characterized as keeping newly arrived, working immigrant girls off the streets, out of the dance halls, and away from sailors, soldiers, and other working men. In general, the law was utilized to control girls' erotic behavior that occurred outside of middle-class marriage and family norms.[28]

Institutional interest in the moral and sexual behavior of young women was evident in the establishment of the juvenile legal system. In the era from the 1890s to the 1920s, the doctrine of *parens patriae* (the state as father) organized the rehabilitative principles of the juvenile reform institutions. *Parens patriae* postulated that if parents could not adequately raise decent, law-abiding citizens, the judiciary could intervene and act *in loco parentis*—in place of the parents.[29] In an astonishing display of disrespect and invasion of privacy, during the Progressive era all teenage females referred to Juvenile Hall in Los Angeles were given mandatory pelvic examinations to ascertain whether they were sexually active because adolescent girls often entered the juvenile system by way of an adult identifying them as having "morally dubious behavior" or as being "sex delinquents." Even as late as the 1970s, girls' primary offenses were "being ungovernable," which could be translated as being promiscuous.[30]

Incorrigibility now more likely signifies some kind of violent offense, and, by the 1980s, the data reflect a shift away from a criminalization of girls' sexual misconduct toward a focus on girls' violent crimes. And the state's concerns about girls have shifted from their

Illustration 1.5. The "old" "bad" girl. From the cover of *Reform School Girl,* by Felice Swados, 1948. *Credit: Pulp Image copyright 1995 Jeffrey Luther/PC Design. www.pulpcards. com. All Rights Reserved.*

being immoral to their being trafficked. Contemporary mainstream expectations for girls' sexuality, emotions, and aggression have shifted as well; these expectations are made visible by placing them within the history of the ways girls' troubles have been constituted.

Contemporary Girls Transgress New Norms

A formerly troublesome sexiness has now been routinized, accepted, and normalized: the ubiquitous bare-midriffed GapGirl stares down from billboards. For a time, an urbanite couldn't ignore Calvin Klein advertisements featuring gaunt preadolescents modeling underwear. Middle-class, white high school girls displayed belly-button rings. Bikini thongs were, for a time, marketed to preteens by the popular chain store Abercrombie and Fitch. In 1999, one Barbie doll in toy stores sported a tattoo; the 2003 doll line Bratz featured shrunken sweaters and tiny, midriff-baring t-shirts stretched across overdeveloped chests. Girls' dolls were explicitly sexually mature. As a result of changing expectations for women's behavior, certain events, such as unwed pregnancy, extramarital sex, and commercial sex work, were by the early 2000s less alarming than they had previously been both to the general public and in the eyes of the law.[31]

One national report noted that teenagers were initiating sexual behavior at earlier ages and were being exposed to sexual messages more than ever before. Over half of young people in this report confided that they had "been with someone in an intimate or sexual way."[32] Intimacy no longer implied heterosexual intercourse. Researchers reported that sex among teenagers declined precisely as children reported that they do not consider oral or anal sex to constitute sex. Despite—and because of—parental controls, the internet hosted thousands of sites where youth could pursue sex, love, and romance. Shifts in mainstream standards regarding gender and sexuality since the mid-1960s show how cultural change driven by market growth contributed to a routinization of sexiness for girls and women (see Illustration 1.6). Although the origin and meanings of the changes are contested, shifts did occur.[33] In supermarkets around the nation, the covers of popular magazines feature images of the current standards of beauty for which mainstream girls and women are to strive. Ironically, the new "beauty move" that the magazine cover in Illustration 1.6 suggests is to wear a red slip, much like the one featured in the image of the seductively clad white woman in Illustration 1.5. It is now common for young women to dress provocatively, and indeed it is expected—the mainstream press exhorts the cosmopolitan girl to "sexify your look" as a matter simply of looking stylish in a new, hip, contemporary way.

Illustration 1.6. The "new" "good" girl. From the cover of *Cosmopolitan* magazine, August 2001.

Societal expectations for girls and women revolve around more than just sexual behavior. The stereotype of girls as passive and relationally receptive contains implications for normative emotional behavior as well. I observed young women who were locked up expressing themselves violently to dispel their fears, anxieties, and disappointment. I eventually came to see that a shift was underway: acting out sexually did not bring as much attention from adults as acting out violently. In this sense, girls' fears and hatred toward each other, for varying reasons, need to be taken seriously as forms of community violence, as the system widened its net to criminalize girls for violent as well as sexual behavior.

Emotional responses among adolescents have begun to come to the fore as a factor in violence. Court-involved girls are mistakenly constituted as "acting like males" by legal-system personnel as they discuss girls' fights and crimes. Troubled girls' lives and the anger they express about their personal histories and interactions with others lay bare the center of this cultural moment of changing gender norms for girls' expression not only of sexuality but of anger as well. Girls' violence developed amid myriad concurrent shifts in norms of femininity: fashion, sexuality, and emotional expression. Young women described to me attacking others, sometimes in self-defense, sometimes for less apparent reasons. This violence is based in socioemotional patterns, such as memories of early injuries. A social logic at the epicenter of girls' violent behavior emerged as I listened to them relate their life narratives. Given the gendered opportunities from which urban disadvantaged girls have to "choose," their choices, while not always legal, began to make social sense because girls experience violence in specifically gendered ways. I came to see that community violence linked seamlessly with family violence in their lives. Even using those terms glossed over the everyday harshness, anger, fear, and physical abuse, the sexual taunting in the street, and the gendered inequities at home that girls faced, witnessed, experienced, and perpetrated.

The Study and Its Participants

The purpose of this study was to address the absence of empirical work that focused on young women who were involved in the juvenile corrections system. My first intention was to explore with the young women their perceptions of their experiences and interactions. This work was inspired by theory and research that focuses on the study of human lives and that privileges an interpretive framework of sociological inquiry (for examples, see the work of Mitchell Duniere, Irving Goffman, Arlie Hochschild, Dorothy Smith). In addition to bringing the voices of the young women to debates over theory and policy, a second intention of this study was to root their accounts in the cultural and material forces at work in their lives. My effort was not to produce a set of generalizable findings about all girls, but rather to attend to contradictions in the narratives and realities of a group of young women who were being adjudicated delinquent in the late-twentieth-century United States.

Meet the Study: Who Will Make Knowledge, and How?

Every step of this research required the charting of new territory.[34] Conventional methods used to study incarcerated boys and men did not always apply to the study of detained girls. For example, traditional interview training rarely included instructions for what to do when interviewees spend hours describing sexual assault or incest. Because boys' prior sexual harm has not been constituted as causal for their delinquency, stories elicited when interviewing them give rise to narratives of bravado and daring, not victimization from incest and rape. Thus, boys' interviews inspire different kinds of research design than do girls'.[35]

Research designs, like research questions, are also driven by theory and politics. Ultimately, research findings either challenge the status quo or apologize for it. A researcher's question, design, and methodology express her world-view. The challenge has been framed in this way:

> Integrating [participatory action research] methods into our discipline will require flexibility and reflection. It will require us to reconsider what constitutes valid forms of knowledge generation, and to acknowledge the inherent political nature in all the work we do. It will demand greater involvement and commitment on our parts to our own communities and to addressing issues of social justice around the world. At the same time, it will allow us to place our skills and training [in our disciplines] in the service of our personal and political values, giving our work new energy and meaning. For those of us committed to addressing social issues in an open and democratic fashion, it provides a way to integrate our politics and our [discipline]—to the benefit of both.[36]

Choosing design, methodology, and sampling, often presented as neutral and scientific, asks us to consider what we will accept as "objectivity," "the truth," "good science," and "knowledge." In this section I discuss the design, methods, and demographics of the samples utilized in this project.

My focus was on adolescent girls in the correctional systems and the adults who work with them. The young women ranged from thirteen to eighteen years old, and they had been processed or adjudicated delinquent by police. I observed them in courtrooms, in out-of-home placement facilities and group homes, in juvenile psychiatric wards and detention facilities, as well as in state youth authority systems.

This study used both qualitative and quantitative data-collection techniques. Secondary data from the Federal Bureau of Investigation's *Crimes in the United States* were analyzed to present estimates of numbers of arrests nationally. The qualitative data were collected between 1994 and 2000 in three states: California, Colorado, and Massachusetts. Between 2001 and 2005, I followed up that research and interviewed and observed at juvenile facilities and community-based organizations in Illinois.

In order to contextualize the lives of study participants, I immersed myself in the worlds of girls in trouble, youth advocacy, and popular youth culture. I toured twenty-two youth-serving community agencies such as the Boys & Girls Clubs; drop-in centers for homeless or runaway children or children living on the streets; and a YWCA girls' mentorship program. I attended, observed, and participated in nine formal training sessions on various aspects of juvenile health run by community organizations such as adolescent health clinics that offered in-depth training on "dually diagnosed" youth (those who share both a mental health and a substance abuse diagnosis). Other trainings were in the field of juvenile justice; they were offered by judicial or legal agencies, such as licensing boards for county group homes. Training sessions lasted from half a day to a week and covered topics such as how to deliver gender-specific services, how to best work with pregnant and parenting girls, and how to manage assaultive behavior in secure facilities. The tours and trainings allowed for cross-disciplinary views of the same children, who were variously constructed as sick or bad, damaged or about to be hurt, or in need of punishment or therapeutic attention.

I observed, presented at, and participated in twenty-four community-based service agencies' roundtables, committees, and task forces where advocacy for court-involved girls' was discussed and planned. From commissions on the status of women located in county governments to think-tank task forces organized by police departments and universities, academics, advocates, and social service providers have been coming together around the nation to address this topic. The questions on everyone's mind were: What exactly is the problem with girls? What is the cause of their offenses? What programs best prevent juvenile female offending? My findings began to point out that those were not always the best questions to be asking.

I conducted formal interviews and took ethnographic notes in eight detention halls, six schools and after-school programs, five long-term secure residential facilities, four adolescent mental health and psychiatric facilities, and five out-of-home group placements for court-involved youth. Two of the public schools I spent time at were "probation schools." The facilities were publicly funded, but the students were court-ordered to attend and were on probation at their time of enrollment. The results presented in this study represent findings from interviews with one hundred girls and forty-two adults who worked with them, as well as observations in the settings mentioned above.

After procuring university approval for research involving human subjects and community access, I sought out a variety of youth facilities, after-school programs, adolescent health clinics, and other social service agencies, as noted above. The sites were selected for specific reasons besides convenience and geographic range. One site had unusually high rates of incarcerated youth (California), one had undergone dramatic reform in its juvenile system (Massachusetts), one offered a unique and consistent option for girls (Colorado), and one was the location of the oldest juvenile system in the nation, as well as one of the oldest gender-specific intervention program in operation (Illinois).

After obtaining access, entry, and parental/legal guardian permission, I invited girls to be interviewed for a study on girls in trouble. I explained that the project was to listen to girls to find out their opinions of, ideas about, and experiences with juvenile corrections and in their lives. I invited them to participate but let them know that participation was not connected to (that is, would not help or hurt) their probation or therapeutic outcomes. I explained that their participation was voluntary, confidential, sometimes anonymous, and that they could terminate the interview at any time.

A few young women ended interviews prematurely. Three interviews were left unfinished halfway through (one after hearing the introduction to the section of questions on childhood harm and two immediately following that section). One participant terminated abruptly after reading the informed consent document, and two interviews were interrupted by staff. In northern California and the Chicago area, participants, both juveniles and adults, received a list of phone numbers of local community services for girls. Girls ended up by saying that they "really enjoyed talking with me" or that they were glad I was doing the study. Others couldn't believe it: "You spend all your time going around talking to *girls*?" one young woman asked incredulously.

Young women used the interviews for different purposes. Some used them to construct a kind of perfect self. They warmed up to developing a narrative to account for their actions, such as deploying techniques of neutralization to argue that "I didn't really do anything wrong," "I didn't harm anyone," and "I don't even smoke cigarettes!" (that is, "I am so good and innocent"). I heard them search for a vocabulary of motives as they explained who they were and communicated how they felt about the world. Others used the opportunity for a kind of cathartic therapy, to discharge pent-up emotions or perhaps to elicit some nurturing. A few girls asked for a copy of their interview (which I declined to place in their Personals, explaining that it contained too much information about them in writing). Some asked for their interviews back (at which time we immediately tore them up into little pieces to be thrown away later by me outside the secure facilities). Interviews concluded with my asking how they thought their accounts should be shared with those in power in order to make changes.[37]

Whenever possible, I used a life-history approach to the interviews; our conversations were long (averaging two hours), and I visited them in their institutional settings several times. The interview schedule assessed a broad range of risk and strength factors in their life events, experiences, and resources including details about family background and relationships; their own and their family's involvement in the legal system; educational history; use and abuse of drugs and alcohol; history and nature of physical, sexual, or emotional harm; experiences with medical, dental, and psychological health care; gynecological and obstetric health care; sexual experience and preference. The interviews concluded with a discussion of interests, strengths, and other characteristics that would stimulate resiliency. Wherever possible, I spent time in each facility, eating on the units with detainees, observing the day-to-day routine. I stood back as probation personnel broke up fights, transported youths, booked and released detainees. I stayed on the units overnight.

A total of 191 U.S.-born or immigrant girls participated in this project through various kinds of interviews, participation in focus groups, or agreeing to be observed. I entered data from one hundred youth interviews into the Statistical Program for Social Scientists (SPSS) to determine the demographics of participants and to conduct cross-tabulations (age by school drop-out, race by offense, history of sexual abuse by type of crime, for example). Originally, I had intended to contrast and compare young women's experiences by jurisdiction. However, because no identifiable differences emerged in girls' experiences by region, I eliminated irrelevant information in the presentation of their case studies here and thus strengthened the guarantee of confidentiality for them. In the first coding round, I sought to identify main narrative patterns in each of the areas discussed in interviews. I then coded the key themes that emerged using a quantitative content analysis. Throughout the following chapters, the prevalence of the central experiences is noted along with excerpts from participants' interviews.

For comparison purposes, I conducted two focus groups with a small subset of twenty-three "good girls"—middle-class college-bound teens from an urban high school and a group of minority students who were participating in a "summer bridge program" to prepare them for entering university the following fall—and with a group of thirteen boys in a "serious and habitual juvenile offenders" (SHO) unit.

Talking intensely with vulnerable young people created emotionally intimate contact, itself one of the most challenging tasks of the research. I had to interrupt the fieldwork at one point in order to learn techniques for handling traumatic disclosure during interviews. I became particularly concerned with preventing coercion of and assuring protection to this multiply-vulnerable group of "human subjects." Many of the young women, struggling with survival economies such as drug dealing and other street work, were wise beyond their years. They were minor girls, mostly of color, mostly from no-/low-income families, some in detention, some with substance abuse diagnoses or double and triple diagnoses of mental health problems complicated by toxication at birth or exposure to HIV.

Research with court-involved populations requires care and attention to detail. I had to take special precautions not to record in field notes any identifying details that could be traced back to an individual girl. I took the threat of subpoena seriously. I did not directly ask young women if they had committed their offenses and reminded them that I would not safeguard their confidentiality if they disclosed that someone was currently harming them or if they intended to harm themselves or others.

Which girls are not in this study? First, girls who were free of the widening net of juvenile corrections. Furthermore, the group of young women who participated in this research was not located using statistically random sampling methods. The sample does not pretend to represent all court-involved girls. For example, white, middle-class girls' parents typically can get their daughters released quickly and often can get them admitted "voluntarily" to private treatment facilities rather than allowing them to be placed in publicly funded detention centers and psychiatric hospitals. Girls suffering chronic, severe, or acute mental health problems are typically too immobilized to get out of the house to the streets or into the general population on a unit, where they might agree to an interview. These were not girls whose mothers drove them to weekly, private psychotherapy appointments. They were not white suburban cheerleaders or the girlfriends of sports jocks or preppies. Most girls in this sample proudly self-identified as playettes (the feminine version of players or playboys) or as hip-hop, ghetto-style, round-the-way, gang-banger, street, or punk girls.[38]

Meet the Girls: The Youth Sample

The girls in the study were often bright and tuned in to what they considered the duplicity of adult society, yet they had already dropped out of school. They were typically parentified survivors of abuse who said, as La Shondra did, "My mom is more my girlfriend than a mom. We get high [on drugs] together." They were active, out on the street, and in the world. Although many young women were clearly troubled, most were bold, sharp, clever, daring, and loud. Severely learning-challenged and emotionally disabled girls were not generally out in public enough to be perpetrating offenses. The following tables highlight key demographics of the youth sample.[39]

As Table 1.4 shows, on average, girls who come into the court system are fifteen; they are slightly younger than boys who enter the system (sixteen). The age at which a girl can be arrested, locked up on the delinquency side of the juvenile court, have her case heard in juvenile court, or be transferred to adult court varies by state. Some states (Kansas and Vermont) have lowered the age at which girls can be sent to adult court to ten years. Many others have no specified lower age limit, which means that a girl as young as eight can be tried as an adult; in such discretionary transfers the prosecutor or judge can recommend that a case be heard in criminal court. As discussed previously, most very young children who get into trouble with the law are referred to the dependency side of the court. The average age for young women in this sample was similar to the national average age of court-involved girls, fifteen.[40]

To talk about girls who are locked up is to talk about racism and race relations in the United States. Girls in the juvenile justice system disproportionately come from communities of color.[41] The juvenile system is a reflection of the adult system in that respect. Disproportionate minority representation has been identified by the Department of Justice's Office of Juvenile Justice and Delinquency Prevention as one of the key problems plaguing the juvenile court system,[42] and the complete imbalance of the racial and ethnic heritage of the young women in this study when compared with their proportions in the general population

Table 1.4

Age of Participants, Youth

Age	Number
13	6
14	23
15	26
16	23
17	20
18	2
Total	100
Range: 13 to 18 years old	
Average age: 15.3 years old	
Modal age: 15 years old	

Table 1.5

Self-Reported Racial/Ethnic Background, Youth

Background	Number
African American	37
Latina	35
White/European	13
African American and Latina	5
Asian American	4
Native American Indian	3
African American and Asian American	2
Asian American and Latina	1
Total	100

Note: African American includes children who said "black" or "African." Latina includes children who said "Chicana" or "Hispanic" or who said their families were from Guatemala, Nicaragua, Puerto Rico, El Salvador, or Mexico. White includes children who named European countries (including Russia) or who said they were Jewish. Asian American includes children who identified their national heritage as Filipina, Chinese, Japanese, Vietnamese, Korean, or Cambodian.

supports that claim (Table 1.5). Only 13 percent of the young women I interviewed who were in the system were white, while 37 percent were African American and 35 percent were Latina/Hispanic with heritages from countries such as Puerto Rico, Mexico, El Salvador, and Guatemala. Asian Americans, including first and second generations from Vietnam, China, Korea, and Japan, accounted for 4 percent of the total. Only 8 percent said they were mixed race or bi-racial.

Almost one in five (18 percent) of the young women I interviewed preferred to speak Spanish, probably because I speak Spanish and asked whether any young women wanted to speak in Spanish. In addition, facilities in both northern and southern California housed a large population of girls from families of Hispanic immigrants and from Spanish-speaking communities. One girl I interviewed in Spanish was in Massachusetts (Puerto Rican), and one young woman in Colorado also spoke *mitad mitad* (half English, half Spanish).

Monolingual staffing posed problems for the young women—problems that I did not find discussed in staff meetings, conventional correctional literature, or among gender advocates. If a young woman did not speak English, she had no one on staff to speak to if she was on a unit or ward where there were no bilingual staff members. Of the forty-one interviews I conducted with Latinas, I found it alarming that three of them began by asking me in Spanish, "What am I in here for?" or "Where is my baby?"

For certain staff, speaking Spanish constituted a social danger deserving of correction. When two young women were speaking Spanish to each other, I would overhear guards say, "Hey! Cut that out! English only in here!" They explained that it was a "safety issue." However, in other settings, being bilingual is considered a strength and is a skill young women are encouraged to pursue. In many other settings, girls' heritages, cultures, and histories are a source of pride and well-being on which advocates build.[43]

Interviewees' offenses fell into five categories according to the charges for which they were being adjudicated as noted in their files at the time of the interview:

> 4 percent sexually related offenses (although 14 percent admitted to having traded sex for money or having worked in the commercial sex industry, including stripping and lap dancing)
> 6 percent minor offenses and probation violations
> 24 percent property offenses such as petty theft and shoplifting
> 29 percent drug or alcohol charges
> 37 percent violent offenses

To my surprise, the largest category of charges against the girls was violent offenses. More than one-third of the sample were being investigated for, charged with, or adjudicated delinquent for violent offenses including car jacking, armed robbery, arson, and assault (both simple and aggravated). Six percent were involved with attempted homicide or homicide charges. In this sample, more girls were charged with homicide than with prostitution. These findings did not jibe with much of the research literature about delinquency or about adolescent girls.

Although the few demographics presented here only begin to bring the psychosocial, political, and economic worlds of girls in this net of juvenile corrections to the bright light of sociological inquiry, I offer them as an introduction to a complex look at their various concerns. I develop analyses across in-depth accounts of types of interactions rather than across quantified and static variables. As discussed previously, this effort reflects a commitment to bringing the voices of girls to the fore of our policy and sociolegal discussions. Allowing time, energy, and space for researched subjects to tell their own stories in their own rhythms, with the gaps in their narratives that they choose to leave or clarify, requires a political and ethical stance for a sociologist that is fraught with controversy and methodological dilemmas for which I continually sought both methodological advice and legal counsel.[44]

Meet the Caregivers: The Adult Sample

Probation personnel, social workers, and other professionals who work with young women have much to teach. Many youth advocates interviewed were city or county civil servants and had over thirty years of experience working with young people. Dedicated and passionate about their work, adult participants expressed an urgency about the need to bring juvenile legal systems up to date. But too many had limited education and little understanding of the issues that contemporary girls face. Most knew what gender-responsive programs were but couldn't define the term *gender.* Some didn't care.

A total of eighty adults who worked with juvenile corrections and adolescent health were formally interviewed for this project. As described above, I observed and did community advocacy work with a wide variety of parents and social service providers, worked on task forces for girls in juvenile probation systems, and taught gender studies to youth in detention. I met with girls and adults as they gave and received services in community-based agencies and nongovernmental organizations such as adolescent community health care facilities, mentoring programs, after-school centers, and group homes for girls in out-of-home probation placements.

During the fieldwork phase of this project, I announced at public coalition and collaboration meetings that I was in the process of conducting research. I passed out statements approved by university review boards and handed out a "Community Services for Girls" list to both adult and youth participants in the study. The list of local agencies that serve girls and their families was prepared as a "research-benefit" handout. I used the same interview format for forty-two adult interviews, and I report the demographics of those participants in this section.

The adult interview protocol included questions assessing work experience, formal training, and personal demographics. Adult participants were invited to assess changes they had witnessed in young women over time, to describe differences between males and females in their care, to define terms such as *gender, gender-specific,* and *culturally competent,* as well as to suggest the key problems in this area and solutions to them.

Of the forty-two adults interviewed, 80 percent were women. That finding is not surprising, given that many were working in girls' coalitions and gender-specific projects. In interviews, men said, for example, that they "needed a female partner" in order to work with girls. Most interviewees were in their thirties; the average age was forty-one; and their ages ranged from nineteen to over sixty (see Table 1.6). The range of ages of adult caregivers, probation personnel, and service deliverers was inspiring and hopeful; adults from older teenagers to postretirees recognized the importance of a career focused on working with youth.

Over half of the forty-two interview participants were white, but most staff and line workers in juvenile facilities appeared to be persons of color. Neither the facilities nor their websites offered breakdowns of

Table 1.6
Age of Participants, Adults

Age	Percent	(#)
Below twenty	2	(1)
In their twenties	10	(4)
In their thirties	29	(12)
In their forties	14	(6)
In their fifties	19	(8)
In their sixties	7	(3)
Age unknown	19	(8)
Total	100	(42)

employees' race or ethnicity by job category. Table 1.7 displays the racial and ethnic backgrounds adult interviewees reported. In addition, 89 percent claimed to be born in the United States with the remainder stating that their nation of origin was located in Latin America or Africa.

The adult participants I interviewed had experience and expertise in their work. On average they had ten years of experience; most had at least six years working in the same field. In all, the forty-two people interviewed shared 381 years of experience working with young people. Table 1.8 displays the breakdown by job category for the adults interviewed. The employees who participated in this study were well educated. Over 80 percent had bachelor's degrees or postgraduate degrees; 15 percent had completed the terminal degree in their fields.

Throughout the next chapters, I hope to deepen our understanding of the challenges, triumphs, and overall dedication that the adults who work with young women reported. Theirs is a story of empathy, conflict, and perseverance in the face of funding cuts to their agencies and programs, increased violence in the community, so-called tough-on-crime mandates, antifeminist and racist backlash, and myriad cultural shifts.

Table 1.7
Self-Reported Racial/Ethnic Background, Adults

Background	Percent	(#)
White	52	(22)
African American	23	(10)
Latina/o	12	(5)
Latina and white	2	(1)
Jewish	5	(2)
Unknown	5	(2)
Total	99[a]	(42)

[a]Less than 100 percent because of rounding.

Table 1.8

Adult Participants' Occupations

Occupation	Percent	(#)
Lawyer/prosecutor/defender/judge	21	(9)
Psychiatric worker/psychologist	14	(6)
Assistant director/staff	14	(6)
Executive director of community-based agencies	12	(5)
Probation officer	12	(5)
County agency administrator	10	(4)
Social worker	7	(3)
Nurse/adolescent health worker	5	(2)
Teacher	2	(1)
Exact occupation unclear	2	(1)
Total	99[a]	42

[a]Less than 100 percent because of rounding.

Ethnographic Observations

I invited ten girls to allow me to spend more in-depth time with them outside of formal facilities—eight agreed to participate. (See Table 1.9 for their ages, races/ethnicities, and offenses.) This was a challenging portion of the data-gathering strategy because, after gaining permission from their parents/guardians and the girls themselves, I found them difficult to track down in any systematic way. The young participants lived in chaos and disarray; it was never a matter of just picking up the telephone and seeing whether I could come over. As they put it, they "stayed" at their mothers or their aunties, moving around. Operating pagers, cell phones, public pay-phone cards, and answering machines was an intricate part of their daily social and emotional lives.[45] Their cell phones and pagers were all turned off, turned back on, and changed frequently. Often, I would find that the girls had been picked up on a warrant or had been involved in some kind of incident and were back in detention, or worse.

I spent most of the time devoted to this method of data collection chasing them down and visiting them at home, school, their job, or just out on the streets. They did respond to talking on the telephone, sometimes for hours at a time. I amassed CDs and song lyrics from their favorite songs, and collected poems, letters, and testimonials that they wrote. I subscribed to the magazines they told me they read and listened to the stations they programmed on my car radio.

Inviting young women to participate in the more in-depth, long-term ethnography offered another challenge. I was seeking permission to spend long periods of time day and night with people who were accustomed to being ignored, roaming free of adult supervision, and living with secrets.

Table 1.9
Names and Demographics of Girls

Name	Age	Race/Ethnicity	Current Most Serious Offense
Portia Barlow	16	African American	Prostitution
Mylen Cruz	15	Filipina American	Aggravated assault
Elizabeth Martin	16	White	Assault with deadly weapon
Carina Menendez	15	Nicaraguan	Armed robbery
Claudia Sereno	17	Latina	Weapons possession, aggravated battery
L'Teshia Williams	16	African American	Drug possession
Cora Winfield	15	White	Domestic battery
LaShondra Wolfe	17	African American	Weapons possession

The young women often distrusted adults, noticed adult hypocrisy, and frankly reported that they felt betrayed by almost every adult in their lives who they believed was supposed to protect and provide for them—their mothers, fathers, teachers, kin, neighbors, lawyers, judges, social workers, and probation officers. Why should they trust a researcher? Among other reasons, I suggested that it might feel good to be heard by a caring listener, especially one who was not going to divulge their names or fill out forms and submit records on them, and that we would work together to bring their perspectives to the attention of adults in powerful positions.

Knowledge of teen girls' worlds coupled with their sharing of their internal processes uncovered a rich and intimate psychosocial life important to understanding their gendered and emotional strategies. For example, girls were inundated by advertising and messages from the music and fashion industry. Many young women listened in their earphones to droning refrains from masculine voices, intoning edicts such as "Is there any room for me in those jeans?" They played these messages endlessly, as loudly as they could, whenever they could, without necessarily critiquing the subtler meanings or cultural ramifications of the refrains. I am not arguing that, for example, the media/music industry causes girls to be "boy/sex crazy," but we cannot remove young women in trouble from the cultural and emotional environments pressed on them by adults and then wonder why they behave as they do.[46]

Throughout this book, the accounts of young women and the adults who worked with them form the data and facts from which I draw my conclusions. As much as possible, wherever possible, I read the young women's files and spoke with their parents, probation officers, and social workers. That effort was the basic mission of this project: to bring forth, and take seriously, the words of the people who were experiencing the phenomenon under study. Although I am biased in favor of efforts that make life better for girls and young women as well as endeavors that increase social justice, I did not, by any means, necessarily feel affection for all study participants. Many of the young women I met had committed serious and violent offenses involving brutally harming other individuals. During one interview, one young woman threatened to beat me up. As an older white woman, albeit someone who had personal and family experience with the criminal legal system, many times I did not "connect" with study participants. But I did not embark on this project in order to make friends with young women, prove that all girls were good, or attempt to free the wrongfully convicted. My hope is that an analysis of the narratives of the lives of young women in struggle with racism, poverty, and injustice will move readers toward working for the amelioration of the conditions of girls' lives that lead to their coming to the attention of juvenile authorities in the first place.

Conclusion: An Ethnography of a System

Social control is maintained in juvenile justice by twin structures: formal (juvenile corrections) and informal (gender, sexual, and emotional norms and cultural messages). Because court-involved girls can go from police contact to a courtroom, a detention or a probation facility, and then back to their same neighborhoods, families, and peer pressures, this study necessarily presents an ethnography of a system. In order to capture the meaning-making work of troubled girls, I needed to "see" such illusive data as gender norms, emotional struggles, and power interactions with their families, schools, and juvenile corrections personnel. As with studies of boys and men, the reflexive and self-perpetuating nature of the system is best revealed by listening to how the girls themselves make sense of their struggles in their emotional lives, their families, and their communities. The following chapters offer a look at what the girls had to say about the state's response to troubled girls one hundred years after the opening of the first juvenile court.

2

Injury, Gender,

and Trouble

Mylen Cruz was Filipina American, sixteen years old, and in detention for stabbing a boy at her school. "I was in the office at my school, and this boy come up to me jus' to fuck with me. He was all, 'I'ma get me some of this shit, man.' He touched my butt! He thought we gonna be kickin' it or some shit! We got into a violent fight. I did a violent act. I don't know. I was mad. I couldn't deal with my anger; I couldn't hold it. I'm not a killer, but I would be able to do it. I hoped he wouldn't die, but I didn't want to go home. I wasn't scared to come to Juvey."

What did Mylen mean by "but I didn't want to go home"? It turned out that she was under brutal attack in her own house. In her file, I read that her mother was often homeless with Mylen and her little brother. Mylen continued: "My mom is there for me sometimes. She's always busy 'cause she has a lot of problems: the rent, money. We used to be close, but her stress affects me. I never ran away, but we always got evicted." One time her family was staying with another family, and her mother "had to serve the other family's father coffee and take a lot of shit, like she was the slave! I watched him treat her like shit!" Mylen was deeply affected by watching her mother be demeaned. She mentioned it in the interview and again when I went with her and her mother to an Ala-Teen meeting the following week.

Mylen became very upset during that first conversation and started crying. She said she felt that so many things were wrong with her life she couldn't figure out how to begin to fix it. "One of my mom's boyfriends molested me. It was the grossest thing in the world. Everybody knew and nobody would help. When I was twelve years old, I started hanging out with [a] guy from by my street, and he used to hit me all the time. He made me do gross shit to him, and then he even hit me!" Mylen also said she hated school and knew she shouldn't have gone the day she stabbed the boy. "I knew I was gonna go off on somebody."

Mylen's narrative was representative of the stories of most of the young women I met who were in detention facilities charged with violent offenses. They were simultaneously victims and perpetrators, and it was hard to know whether to console them or punish them. My contention in this chapter is that in court the biographies of Mylen and girls like her should play a significant role in determining their best interests—not as an excuse for physical assault, but as an aid to the court. The abuse that Mylen endured was sustained, chronic, and acute. The experience of abuse is gendered. For boys, abuse goes against what they are taught to expect from their position of superiority. Abuse of girls confirms their place in a gendered hierarchy. A distinct process needs to be enacted in order for girls to heal and to regain or achieve a sense of safety and psychological integrity. Thus, gender deeply affects how childhood abuse is processed and how recovery occurs. This chapter argues several related points. Sexual violence is fundamentally gendered and racialized; it is experienced differently by girls than by boys, and among girls. Abuse plays a special role in the lives of many girls who come to the attention of authorities. This role must be theorized because its meaning cannot be determined empirically. Finally, the definitions of community and youth violence must be broadened in order to begin to capture the prevalence and significance of sexual violence in girls' lives.

Violence Against Girls Provokes
Girls' Violence: Reconfiguring "Abuse"

Growing up female today includes sorting out and facing delicate sexual dilemmas. Pubescent and adolescent girls must learn to navigate the world of being feminine and attractive without getting raped. Girls constitute the majority of children who are traumatized in childhood both sexually and physically. Psychologists note that emotional responses to sexualized trauma unconsciously guide behavior. Girls in detention spoke of how, at home, their mothers' boyfriends, their fathers, and their stepfathers sexualized relationships with them. Girls recounted incidences of sexual degradation by neighborhood men and by cousins, brothers, friends, and strangers. Studies link girls' early sexual debut, as well as unhealed childhood injuries from sexual trauma, to unhealthy practices such as self-medicating with drugs and alcohol, striking out in aggression and violence, and seeking parental-type attention from adult men through romance and sexuality. Indeed, the range of choices that were available to young women were inextricably connected to and controlled by these varied sexual and gendered interactions.[1]

As we will see below, poverty and socioeconomic class influence girls' outcomes. Fewer alternatives and opportunities and thinner decisional avenues are available to poor girls than to their more affluent counterparts. Young women from disadvantaged communities are more vulnerable to predation by neighborhood men hanging around on street corners, are less likely to be protected by the law, and enjoy less access to resources that would help them heal from the trauma that occurs in their young lives.[2]

Child abuse—its study, measurement, prevention, treatment, and the punishment of offenders—has become a veritable cottage industry. Social work, psychiatry, psychology, and criminology have developed definitions, coursework, even diplomas. Legal experts make their cases and government officials win elections by focusing on attendant popular moral outrage. Meanwhile, young women across our nation are quietly dying from exploitation and injury. During the course of this research, I found it increasingly disturbing to witness celebrity indignation designed to increase Neilsen ratings and political rhetoric designed to boost voting popularity regarding prostitution, trafficking, and child abuse while vulnerable young women continued to be punished for the defense mechanisms they deployed in response to this onslaught against them.

Amount of Sexual Abuse

Family researchers and social service providers consider sexual abuse of children one of the most serious social problems of our times. In one U.S. study, 8 percent of women reported their first intercourse to be nonvoluntary. Of all Americans who do report episodes of nonvoluntary sexual intercourse, women were more likely than men to report having had this experience, with just under one half of all nonvoluntary experiences among women occurring before the age of fourteen. National reports indicate that sexual offenses against children declined from 1992 to 2000 but were still widespread. Girls are sexually abused and raped more often than boys. Eighty-six percent of all child victims of sexual assaults in 2001 were girls. Indeed, girls are seven times more likely to be raped than boys. In the 2003 Survey of Adolescents 13 percent of the girls reported having been sexually assaulted. Most abuse (90 percent) is committed by men and by persons known to the child.[3] Indeed, one scholar framed sexual coercion of girls and women as so prevalent that it constitutes a new norm:

> Appraisers of the current sexual "scene" rarely discuss sexual victimization. Yet intimidation, coercion, and violence are key features

of sexual life in America today. We may profess to view coercive sexuality as deviant. But, actually, it is in many respects the norm. To be sure, we are not all rapists, sexual harassers, or child abusers. However, these behaviors are extremely widespread and may well be increasing. They are not isolated departures from some benign patterning of our sexual activities. On the contrary, they constitute important indicators of where our current values, priorities, and socioeconomic structures are leading us sexually.[4]

Indeed, the victims of one in four persons incarcerated for sexual assault in the United States are their own children or their stepchildren. Convicted adult sexual assault offenders revealed that over 75 percent of their victims were under the age of eighteen and that almost 85 percent of their victims were females. These data point to deep chasms in prevalent myths about how morally righteous a nation the United States is.[5]

The Price of Sexual Abuse

Sexual abuse of girls takes its toll in many alarming ways, from psychological problems, ranging from depression to suicide, to problems with the criminal justice system resulting in incarceration. As girls in general are disproportionately victims of abuse, so too are girls in trouble with the law. Owen and Bloom's 1997 study of young women in the California Youth Authority found that 85 percent indicated some type of abuse in their lives. In an assessment of girls in the California juvenile corrections system, 92 percent reported sexual, physical, or emotional abuse; many reported combinations of multiple forms of abuse and experiencing abuse on multiple occasions. Almost 68 percent of adult women in the U.S. criminal justice system reported having been beaten, abused, molested, or burned when they were young girls.[6] Mylen Cruz's involvement with an abusive boyfriend is typical for young women who suffer childhood harm. In my study 53 percent of the girls reported that they had experienced physical injury, 53 percent reported sexual injury, and 71 percent reported that they had been neglected emotionally.

Survivors of sexual injury develop common psychological effects such as intrusive thoughts and memories, anxiety, low self-esteem, loss of trust, and difficulty establishing intimacy. Researchers note a variety of problems: complex posttraumatic stress disorder, feelings of hopelessness, feelings of angry aggression, disassociative behaviors, self-mutilation, and suicide attempts are common for survivors of sexual abuse. Substance dependence has been linked to sexual abuse. Unplanned pregnancies resulting in abortions or unwanted children, as well as bulimia, anorexia, eating disorders, and self-loathing related to being over- and underweight, manifest among adolescent girls as responses to abuse or emotional neglect.[7]

Many girls are not formally diagnosed. For some, their emotional conditions are not recognized by parents or authorities as results of sexual and physical victimization. Adults sometimes characterize these kinds of female troubles as part of teenage angst or raging hormones. Girls reported to me and others feeling that nobody was listening to them or was taking the time to notice and proactively help them. Socioeconomic differences matter as well. Poor girls are less likely to be seen by medical and psychological personnel. Girls from no-income and low-income families have less access to the most highly skilled therapists and their expert guidance in the use of psychopharmaceuticals. Research has also revealed that girls respond differently to victimization based on their racial and ethnic family backgrounds.[8]

Furthermore, young girls previously innocent of sexuality and sexual activity who are introduced forcibly to sex most likely would not "naturally" have developed an interest in or paid attention to sex per se for another decade or so. Early sexual assault can result in a sexualization of girls' awareness, their psyche, and may force a premature introduction to a sexual sensibility, giving girls a sexualized lens through which they begin to view other social interactions. One study found that victims of sexual abuse were likely to have more sexual partners than other adolescents and that "indiscriminate sexual behavior may be one way in which some survivors cope with the emotional pain associated with child sexual abuse."[9] Even the ubiquitous threat of sexual assault creates fear, which keeps young women focused on their safety from male predation. Although precocious sexuality is no longer considered a valid explanation for girls' delinquency, much of the sexual activity that young women in the past were blamed for might have resulted from factors other than reaching puberty at early ages. Here I would like to distinguish what might be termed healthy sexual exploration, play, and activity among young people from coercion and sexual injury. However, even though not all childhood sexual attention and activity is "bad," forced childhood sexual activity should constitute a serious crime. Experts and victims know that the harm endures—that is to say, memories do not disappear.[10]

Studies suggest other correlations between early sexual injury and later troubling practices. In one study of homeless youth, 75 percent of the homeless young women who traded sex for money had been sexually abused. The authors noted that "another study revealed that of runaways in Southern California, 36 percent left home because of physical or sexual abuse and 44 percent ran from other severe long-term problems. Nearly all the street youth whom we have seen in our clinics have histories of significant abuse and neglect, and well over half have been involved in intermittent or full-time prostitution."[11]

Girls' sexual exploitation and injury have been linked as well to their "risky behavior" later in their teens.[12] It has been suggested that subsequent decisions injured girls make appear to the girls to solve their sexual abuse problem or to heal prior hurt and injury.[13] Living in a culture that often emphasizes the urgency of the moment, they devise impetuous or numbed solutions such as risky sexual practices or violent actions. Going with an adult boyfriend at twelve years of age may have been Mylen's attempt to escape her parental abusers. This connection may well be part of the social logic to what Mylen was trying to relate: she had been sexually assaulted and subsequently committed an extremely violent act.

I began to ask, Do girls have a right to *not* be sexual? because I found that girls who were locked up offered their sexiness as an excuse so often and in so many ways. Here are examples of their statements:

> "I'm good to go." "Oh, I want to do him!" (indicating a girl's eager readiness to engage in sexual activity)
> "I'm just out there looking good" (meaning that she was simply a sexy-looking person and not really doing anything wrong)
> "He didn't rape me—he's my boyfriend [now]" (indicating her reconstitution of assault as just bad first sex)

Even the girls who hadn't had sex yet had strong opinions about why, when, and where they would have it. In many interviews, I noticed that the few girls who did not have much to say about sex, love, or romance were new arrivals in the system. They were preoccupied with pressing, immediate crises such as dealing with their family's response to their arrest, finding where their babies were being cared for, or locating their court officials to discover what they were being charged with.

Dropping out of school and running away can be first responses to sexual abuse. While on the run, girls may get involved in survival behavior in the street economy, such as drug dealing, trading sex for money or favors, or making pornography. They often find themselves in situations where they need to protect themselves physically, or they get so angered at being injured that they fight back. Or they report just feeling generally demoralized and debased, so they just "do things." Often, at this point, girls come to the attention of the juvenile legal system. It is a plausible hypothesis that the many young women charged with status offenses— being where they are not supposed to be, not being where they are supposed to be—may be fleeing, and otherwise responding to, childhood sexual and physical injury.[14]

In general, therefore, we can see that the price of abuse and subsequent anger often is aggressive behavior:

> Feelings of rage and murderous revenge fantasies are normal responses to abusive treatment. Like abused adults, abused children are often rageful and sometimes aggressive. They often lack verbal and social skills for resolving conflict, and they approach problems with the expectation of hostile attack. The abused child's predictable difficulties in modulating anger further strengthen her conviction of inner badness. Each hostile encounter convinces her she is indeed a hateful person. If, as is common, she tends to displace her anger far from its dangerous source and to discharge it unfairly on those who did not provoke it, her self-condemnation is aggravated still further.[15]

Mylen's life history makes correlations among factors such as early neglect, sexual abuse, witnessing violence, later involvement with older men, and aggressive offenses abundantly clear.

Who Pays? Comparisons of Girls and Boys, Middle Class and Poor

These factors differ greatly from the rhetoric and language employed in conventional (male) delinquency theories. In introductory criminology texts, factors that are most often mentioned as reasons for boys' offenses include their fathers' being in the criminal justice system and their learning behaviors such as gang fighting, stealing cars, and committing burglary from other delinquents. Boys' heterosexual practices are not problematized; if anything, they are valorized. Promiscuity is not often linked to boys' court involvement, nor is sexual abuse noted as a dominant precursor to male juvenile offending in the mainstream delinquency literature. Girls, more than boys, drop out of school for what are cryptically called "family problems."[16]

To get at another view, I met with a group of college-bound middle-class minors in an urban high school. In response to the survey questions "What is the worst thing you've ever done?" and "What is the worst thing that ever happened to you?" they wrote:

> "Climbed out a window in the 5th grade."
> "Drove without a license."
> "My friend Belinda was killed by her step-father."
> "Parents divorced."
> "Cat died."
> "Getting fired from a job."
> "Cheating on my boyfriend."

Although the urban girls on their way to college were not completely immune to family and community violence ("my friend Belinda was killed"), most listed status offenses (being where they were not supposed to be) or emotional/romantic dilemmas—what commentators might consider typical female-gendered concerns, meaning privileged or white middle-class daughters' concerns.[17] Girls from affluent neighborhoods had broader life experiences than corrections-involved girls. They drove cars, worked and got fired, and had pets, whereas many of the young women who were locked up worried about where their babies were or whether their men had been arrested as well or soberly faced overwhelmingly uncomfortable memories and haunting emotions. Well-off girls got molested and ran away too. But they had ATM cards; private psychotherapy; social networks of families and friends with homes, spare bedrooms, and food; and other opportunities to protect and heal themselves and propel themselves forward toward college, marriage, and other middle-class goals. All young women face the possibility of being harmed in childhood, but poor girls face as well the brunt of poverty; lack of adult attention because of overwork, ill health, and disability; untreated substance dependence; death and incarceration of their parents/caregivers; and lack of protection from other harsh conditions such as inadequate health care and unsafe environments.

The Price of Sexual Harassment

Girls in my study reported being "hassled by guys" in public, especially at school. Although often unsuccessful, girls attempted to fight back. When girls fought, they were labeled violent offenders by officials who did not "see" or witness the original sexual harassment or who viewed it as inconsequential ("a little teasing").[18]

Sexual harassment is defined in federal law (Title VII of the *Civil Rights Act of 1964*) and commonly in state statutes.[19] In its landmark 1999 decision in *Davis v. Monroe County Board of Education*, the U.S. Supreme Court held federally funded public schools responsible for monitoring sexual harassment: "Persistent sexual advances . . . created an intimidating, hostile, offensive, and abusive school environment that violated Title IX of the Education Amendments Act of 1972, which in relevant part, prohibits a student from being excluded from participation in, being denied benefits of, or being subjected to discrimination under any education program or activity receiving Federal financial assistance" (p. 1).

In one California probation school where I observed, the "School Harassment Complaint Form" clearly stated: "Sexual harassment, sexual advances or other forms of religious, racial or sexual harassment by any pupil, teacher, administrator or other school personnel, which create an intimidating, hostile, or offensive environment, will not be tolerated under any circumstance." In theory, yes, but apparently not in practice. I met girls in detention for "kicking a boy's ass"—fighting back against sexual offenses—with no adult intervening. In addition, I observed sexually tormenting incidents when I visited young women in their schools.

Sexual harassment was not a term that girls often used, although they were frequent victims. They called it "gross," they said boys "hassled them," they said boys were "assholes," they said "a boy grabbed my butt," but the idea of school as a site of sexual harassment seemed to be just coming into their awareness. One time, while I was interviewing Christina Gaffney (seventeen years old, probation violation: truancy), a boy looked at her, looked at me, looked back at her, stuck out his tongue, and wagged it back and forth in a lewd gesture. This, right in front of an adult (me). The young women varied in their responses; here Christina just shook her head, looked down, and said in disgust, "That's just how they are." Whatever we call it, one expert on the sexual harassment of girls at school reminds us that "whether it's the criminal version of sexual assault or the civil version of sexual harassment, school is a very violent place for girls."[20]

Being verbally abused by boys, being grabbed and fondled sexually, and even being shot at by boys were topics that girls brought up when talking about school. Attention to the topic of sexual harassment in schools has generated many studies measuring the number of sexual attacks occurring at school. In one landmark survey, 85 percent of young women reported experiencing some form of harassment, ranging from looks and jokes to being grabbed and touched in sexual ways, categorized as "unwanted and unwelcome sexual behavior."[21] Sexual incidents in New York City public schools—including sexual grabbing, rape, and sodomy—occurred at the rate of ten per week, nearly four times the national average.[22]

Girls reported that they carried pocketknives and pepper spray in order to feel safe. One young woman said, "Unless we gonna have police follow us everywhere we go, boys are going to be rude. We need to carry some mace and maybe a pocketknife, but then *we* would be in the wrong" [emphasis mine]. Nearly half of the teen women surveyed in a 2001 initiative said they wanted to carry a weapon "at least sometimes," and a majority reported that they had been the target of sexually threatening behavior.[23]

In my study, the girls' violent acts were sometimes preceded by sexual harassment. As at Christina Gaffney's school, where girls were regularly called homophobic names, degradation and objectification were often followed by angry and assaultive outbreaks by girls toward boys. Accounts from girls in detention about their school experiences were similar to the following statement from fourteen-year-old Djovani Timmings, of San Francisco, who was charged with fighting on school grounds: "I was suspended from school because this boy put his hands on me and I tried to hit him back. Now I'm sittin' up in here! Shit!" This young woman tried to defend herself at school and ended up in detention herself.

Ironically, much of the rise in the use of detention in juvenile facilities for girls' fights at school can be attributed to the growth of zero-tolerance policies for violence on school property. These policies allow students who violate school rules or break the law to be expelled or suspended from school quickly. The notion arose as part of the law-and-order response to the media-created panic over a spate of school shootings during 1980s and 1990s. The popular media and government reports constructed school violence as a gun issue. In a 1998 report on school safety from the U.S. Department of Education, graphics and bar charts display the proportions of serious violent crimes against students, percentages of students carrying guns and weapons to school, percentages of street gangs at schools, and the like. Even so, the report notes that schools are not particularly dangerous places: children are more likely to be victims of violent crimes "in the community or at home than in school."[24]

But official documents such as these often miss the ongoing unsafe and violent environment for girls at schools; the issue is not guns but gender: mostly girls are harmed by mostly boys in gendered and sexually tormenting ways. Sexual assault and harassment are much more prevalent on school grounds than shootings. For example, in the 1990s, about a dozen school shootings were highly publicized and caused widespread concern. However, a less-publicized 1997 study released jointly by the Departments of Justice and Education reported approximately 4,200 rapes and sexual assaults per year on school grounds.[25]

Zero tolerance for violence in school, if it is to exist at all, should reflect zero tolerance for the ways that girls experience violence at school—through gender harassment, sexual harassment, homophobia, and misogyny.[26] However, gender scholar Nan Stein cautions against using punishment to combat sexual and gender violence. Stein refers to deploying the zero-tolerance policy in the punishment of sexual harassment as "the hijacking of the legal victory in the *Davis* case . . . used in the service of student surveillance, punishment, and control amid [the] law-and-order/school safety discourse that so consumes our nation."[27]

Besides fighting, another response to sexual harassment at school was to simply drop out. Over half (53 percent) of the young women in my sample had already quit school. That such a high proportion of girls in juvenile justice also faced challenges in school settings points to the importance of listening to what young women who are locked up have to say about their schools. One common way for girls to come into the system is through a process termed *bootstrapping,* in which probation departments cause girls to be locked up simply for violating a condition of probation, even if the original offense was relatively minor. For example, juveniles cannot be placed in locked confinement for status offenses, such as truancy. However, when girls appear before juvenile judges for any reason, one typical condition of their probation is to attend school daily. Then, if the young women become truant, they can be detained in confinement for probation violation. I met girls who spent years in the system and had not ever committed a criminal offense. It was not unusual to meet young women who were in detention for not attending school—and they were not in school because they had been suspended for fights involving self-defense against harassing males. Although we know that, in a generalized way, school problems are an important factor in girls' delinquency, listening carefully to young women's narratives uncovered specific links among sexual harassment at school, truancy, and involvement in the juvenile legal system.

In the past, juvenile justice reports on school violence rarely noticed or linked violence to gendered forms of sexual harassment. The incident I witnessed when I visited Christina Gaffney at her school was not ever addressed by the school officials present. That girls were targets and recipients of sexual assault and harassment remains hidden in criminology reports about community violence. Without this knowledge, girls' violent acts appear unprovoked, and it can seem that young women are becoming more violent, as some have argued, or that they simply suddenly initiate aggressive behavior.

Voices in Girls' Narratives

Throughout interviews, I noticed unique patterns in girls' representations of themselves and their experiences. Often they deployed a passive voice when describing their victimization: "He got stabbed" instead of "I stabbed him," or "She was raped" instead of "I SAW MY MOMMY GET RAPED— IT TOTALLY FLIPPED ME OUT!" And the flat, disassociative boredom expressed in parts of their interviews indicated that some of the young women had begun to take their horrific experiences of torture and harm for granted. They would list events—"My grampa raped me, I ran away, I turned tricks"—as if talking about someone else's experience. Such a disassociative voice is common among trauma victims; psychologists describe disassociation as a vital defense mechanism in response to crisis.[28]

Young women in detention often told their life histories in fragments, jumping from an event that happened when they were three years old to an experience they had last week. I think that they connected events in their minds and in their hearts in ways not chronological or linear. They were protecting themselves from feeling too much and revealing too much. I share this observation as a caveat: if their stories seem jumbled, it was because their experiences were jumbled. But an odd rhythm can be heard when one listens thoughtfully.

Carina Menendez: To Witness Violence
Is to Be Victimized by Violence

Carina Menendez was born in 1982 in northern California to Nicaraguan parents who were fleeing war at home. She liked to read (she said she was reading a book entitled "The Story of a Little Girl Addict" at the time I met her) and spoke Spanish and English. Carina had many friends and was usually social and outgoing, but when I met her she was in great distress. She told me that she had called the police on her dad for domestic violence against her mother. She said, "I don't know how many times I called the police on my dad. He's still in jail for DV on my mom." Carina grew up witnessing intense physical brutality in her family and sat in detention on her own charges of assault when I interviewed her. Carina estimated that her father had been arrested about four times for domestic violence against her mom. Once, she said, the police even came to his restaurant to arrest him.

Carina was raised in a traditional patriarchal family with her Latino father as head of household and recipient of assumed respect. When I met her family, Carina's mother hovered behind her husband as Sr. Menendez came forward to shake my hand. He smiled confidently at me. He smelled strongly of men's cologne, and he had little razor cuts on his neck from his morning shave. Owner of a local franchise of a well-known, popular "Mexican" restaurant chain, Lolita's, Sr. Menendez was a handsome, portly, successful businessman. He seemed quite accustomed to being revered and obeyed by his wife, daughter, and employees: waitresses, busboys, and dishwashers. "Carina is a good girl but here in America we have to watch the girls closely," he confided, seemingly searching for paternalistic agreement from me.

Carina worked the cash register on Tuesdays and Saturdays at her *papi*'s restaurant—when she was home. She said she had run away from home five times already. Carina barely went to school anymore: "I go there and I get so bored. All this stupid algebra—I don't have a clue what they are talking about. Then I get irritated. Then I just say, 'Fuck this shit!' and leave. All my friends have gone anyway. Nobody cool goes anymore! Fuck it!" According to Carina's file, "She runs away, becomes belligerent, loud, rude, angry." Carina was already on electronic monitoring when she broke a girl's nose at school. She was awaiting a disposition hearing on a petition for a charge of armed robbery. Her victim was a woman in her seventies. Carina's file read: "If she were an adult she would do 6–12 months for this."

How can we make sense of Carina's story? She says:

> I know I have trouble obeying my father. See, when I was little, my *papi* used to come home from the restaurant really tired and worried. *Siempre quejando* [always complaining] about money. He drink so much then, and lots of nights we would be so scared we wouldn't want to move in front of the TV. He would be yellin' at *mi madre* and saying all kinds of scary things. . . . Then he would just . . . like . . . blow up, and we would all start crying and *habia muchos gritos y platos tirando* [there was a lot of yelling and dishes flying], and we just wanted to die. Me and my brother just wanted to die. It's like my dad be trying to kill my mother, so much blood. I couldn't do nothin' to stop him. He was *un loco*! It was hella fucked up. . . . I ain't never be able to forget [*sic*] him for this.

Carina was an emotionally injured girl. Her father had been frightening her—and more—all her life. He terrorized her family. Violent and aggressive behavior was modeled for her at a young age. She saw her father manage anxiety, worry, fear, and sadness by turning on her mother and her and her brother. I became convinced after listening to Carina's accounts that she was responding violently in much the same fashion as had been demonstrated for her in her family.

For young people watching their parents or other adults hurt each other can be terrifying and have lasting effects. Carina talked about her memories: "I used to have to hug my pillow and cry from my bad dreams. *Mi madre* . . . I felt soooo bad for her, and I couldn't understand why our *familia* was always fightin' and yelling. I can remember going into the bathroom to hug my mom around her legs, I was so scared. I remember feeling kind of frozen and shit. . . . I still have nightmares about it, even in here! I wanted it all to stop, and I wanted to go far, far away."

Her relationship with her older brother was violently oppressive. Describing an earlier offense, she said:

> My mom called the police and turned me in for another thing. I did hit her, though. I hit my brother too. I'm tired of him slapping me around! But that time, I was in here on a charge—I only accidentally stuck my brother with a knife while I was doing the dishes! Shit, he accused me of threatening him with a golf club and throwing a coffee can at his head. He was beating *me* up! He wants me to get sent to placement! My brother is such an asshole. He's a freeloader in our house. *Mi madre y yo trabajando*—workin' at the restaurant and doin' everything, and he jus' sits on his ass 'cause he

thinks he a man, or somethin'. He probably gets it from *mi papa.*
Mi papa lets him get away with murder!

Carina survived unprotected in a violent family. Her father attacked
her, her brother attacked her, her mother called the police on her, probably to get her out of the house and save her life. As in other accounts I
listened to, Carina struck out in angry, aggressive ways, responding directly to immediate danger or inspired by earlier-experienced and later-
revealed ungrieved losses and unhealed wounds. The girls believed they
were righteous victims, but they were constituted by authorities as perpetrators, paying the consequences for their violent behavior in juvenile
corrections system. Although we know that factors such as family violence, marital discord, authoritarian parenting strategies, and the like
correlate with delinquency, Carina Menendez's aggression was an example of a link among factors: witnessing violence, experiencing violence, and then later perpetrating violence.[29]

Anastasia Rudnik: To Witness Violence Is to Learn Violence

Anastasia Rudnik grew up in a chaotic house in California. Her
mother emigrated from Russia while Anastasia was still a baby. When
she was young, Anastasia lost a younger sibling in a devastating apartment fire. Anastasia was lanky and light-haired and sat hunched over
her own body. The other girls told me her arms were "covered with scars"
from cutting herself, and her files confirmed that they were. Anastasia's
mother had been in a long-term relationship with a man who was physically violent with her often, and Anastasia witnessed the abuse. Anastasia
moved around a lot, and her file noted, "When her mother can't handle
her, she seems to 5150 her a lot" ("5150" is the California police term
for a call regarding a person who appears to have a mental health—read
aggressive—problem).

Anastasia says she has "too much problems—I have to care for all
my brothers and sisters. My one sister is in a psych hospital. She is slow
because my stepdad beat her and molested her. Then she got raped."
Anastasia related these details in a deathly quiet monotone, as is we
were talking about the weather.

> I know I'm a crime committer, but I'm human too. I just did it
> 'cause I have so much hatred for my stepdad, well my mom's boy-
> friend or whatever he is. Basically my only family was my PO [pro-
> bation officer], but he retired. My new PO just leave me rot in here.
> I'm in here for assault and battery.
>   When I was little, I got teased by all the kids and older people. I
> was in a psych ward when I was five [years old]. My brother died in
> a fire when I was seven—I almost died too! *Ooh* I'll never forget

that smell of the fire. God! I was soo scared! We cried so much. I sort of remember.

I was raised up in a not so good house. That asshole was always pushin' my mom around and making her cry. One time he pushed her so hard she fell down! I hate him so much, I'd like to hit him with a 2 × 4! He's a pig!

My mom is pregnant now. Her boyfriend is a bad man. I got put in the ward for beating kids up. I am very violent. I been in trouble since I'm eight. I don't communicate a lot with girls because they talk too much, and I have to beat them up. I have a temper. I'm in here now 'cause I beat this girl in my group home.

In Anastasia's situation, her own assaultive behavior mimicked the family violence she witnessed. When she turned her hurt and fear outward and toward others, her aggression was an emotive response to the many stressors confronting her.

Broadening the Definition of Violence

Not until blood was spilled or police were called could the young women in this study "see" the community and family violence surrounding them. More than half—53 percent—of the young women reported being physically or sexually injured directly, and when asked whether they had ever witnessed their parents or other combinations of family and household members in physical battle, 71 percent answered in the affirmative. However, when asked whether they had ever witnessed abuse or whether they felt that there was violence in their homes, only a small portion framed abuse and fights as violence. A relationship between witnessing violence and subsequent offending was certainly suggested by these findings, but it was as if young women did not see the connection, and if they did, it was not that bad.

At first, the young women did not seem to have been disturbed by the chaos and violence they reported witnessing. Only when my follow-up questions signaled to the girls that I thought their feelings were crucial did they begin to unfurl details of powerful events that had made up just four—or five-word phrases in their files (and lives): "gfa [grandfather] raped her mo [mother] in her room one night," "was kidnapped and forced to watch pornographic sex acts before being released," and "was raped with a gun inserted into her vagina." After prompts such as "So, how do you feel about what happened that night?" "What do you think that means to you now?" girls reported feeling frozen with fear, terrified at seeing their mothers and siblings being hurt and unable to do anything to stop it, and panicked when recalling harm. Even though at least some of our discussion might have been prompted by my questioning, that to become disturbed about violent mistreatment would need probing was interesting in itself.

Some of the girls who insisted there was no connection whatsoever between their exposure to trauma and their current troubles seemed to disassociate themselves from the terror while they were recounting it. Many appeared a little bored by telling their stories over and over again to yet another social worker, which I believe is how I was often perceived. For example, one young woman related in a monotonous tone an account of watching her mother get raped by some men who stopped to "help" them when they had a flat tire on a Colorado highway one night. She knew it was an extraordinary experience, but I got the sense that it had become so normalized, made into a notation in her file, that she did not think it was of much importance or such an out-of-the-ordinary experience anymore. The girls' accounts in this research exemplify why definitions of community violence need to be broadened to include the abuse youths (meaning girls as well) see, face, and deal with all the time at home, at school, and out on the streets.[30]

Children are now considered invisible victims of domestic and community violence: "More than half of the police calls in many communities are for domestic disturbances, many of which are witnessed by children. Countless numbers of children whom one never hears about, and for whom the police do not receive calls, are exposed to physical and verbal abuse between their parents or caretakers several times a week."[31] In 1999, the California legislature signed into law a bill that provides for state assistance to victims and "derivative victims" of sexual abuse and domestic violence. Derivative victims include primary caretakers of minor victims of sexual or physical abuse and surviving family members of a victim who dies as a result of domestic violence. If witnesses in the family are later identified as in need of psychological counseling, state funds cover these expenses. In line with the reports of the court-involved girls in my study, the California policy demonstrates that witnessing family violence can have a long-term impact on the entire family structure.[32]

Although not expressly gendered, media exposure to violence can desensitize youth. Researchers claim that the average child is exposed to eight thousand television murders and more than one hundred thousand other violent acts by the time he or she enters seventh grade. Studies have found that Saturday morning programming for children contains twenty to twenty-five violent acts per hour. Exposure to violence in the media may result in young people becoming less sensitive to the pain and suffering of others, being more fearful of the world around them, and possibly behaving in more aggressive or harmful ways toward others.

Directly witnessing or being a victim of violence has even stronger effects.[33]

Girls in juvenile corrections revealed that they witnessed an inordinate amount of violence on a regular, routine basis. They saw brothers, friends, cousins, fathers, and boyfriends being kicked, beaten, punched, knifed, shot, and killed. They witnessed their mothers being devalued and hurt physically by fathers, stepfathers, and boyfriends. Well over half the girls in my sample reported witnessing physical, sexual, or emotional abuse of others. Almost every girl could recount such events. Most recounted multiple events. Many intertwined tales of abuse and mistreatment with the regular stories of their daily lives:

> My mom drinks two cups of vodka every day. My dad was arrested for beating on my mom. They have six kids, but only my brother is my real brother. I used to put my head under my pillow when I was little so I wouldn't hear my brother cry when he got hit. (Ilsa Davis, fourteen years old, simple assault)

> My best friend's brother hanged himself. I found him there. . . . I'm stressin' now because my friend Benito got killed in Bayview, and they wouldn't let me go to the *funeraria*. See what happened is, um, *chiflaron y salió mucha gente. Luego lo mataron* [they whistled and a bunch of people came out of the house and then they killed Benito]. (Claudia Sereno, seventeen years old, assault, stringing various events together)

> I got cut off home detention 'cause I didn't go to school. I need to stay at my boyfriend's [apartment] 'cause he lives nearby my school, and I can just go from there. My mom's always goin' to jail.
> *For what?*
> For partyin'—I don't know what you call it. She freaked out because my cousin got shot so my brother shot the people who shot him and then *he* got shot. Me and my mom aren't getting along ever since my brother died. I probably want to go to NA for crank [Narcotics Anonymous for taking speed]—I been doin' like six lines a day to forget about my problems. (Cheyanne McDerby, seventeen years old, probation violation)

> My daddy gets in jail a lot for drinking. I run away from home because it is loud and noisy there—the music. It's hard to concentrate. I've run from placements and hospitals too! My mom and her boyfriend hit each other and hit me too. They give me bloody lips. But I went to a hospital for cutting my arm. [File reads: "Body covered with scars from cutting herself."] (Anastasia Rudnik, fifteen years old, assault with a deadly weapon).

I came to consider the young women in this population as unnoticed, mute witnesses of front-line violence in day-to-day urban life. Girls in my study reported living in worlds tainted daily by aggression and assault. Many adolescents experience power struggles with siblings and parents, but for these girls common household conflicts such as not being able to use the telephone or go out with friends, or discussions over their chores turned into physically violent disputes.

For some people in some situations, violence becomes normalized, even utilized as an emotional strategy and a psychological response to troubles and frustrations. In my study, a certain routinization of violence in girls' everyday lives was embedded in their decision making. Carina would talk about throwing coffee cans, stabbing her brother, seeing her mother get hit, and whacking a woman on the head in the street for her purse all in one breath. She would explain how she would just go off—lose her temper, let her frustrations build up, and then pour out violent expressions, as if that were normal. The social logic to her expressions of anger was that, unfortunately, they were a normal and natural part of day-to-day interactions.

Data from my interviews and observations made clear that factors such as witnessing sexual and physical trauma were salient when interpreting girls' violent offenses. Girls' troubles with juvenile authorities must be theorized within the contexts of the violence they suffer, including listening to fighting and watching brutal assaults.

> My dad was an abusive alcoholic, and the divorce helped him straighten up. But since their divorce, when I was eleven, all went downhill from there for me. I grew up in a bad household. I seen my dad pound on my mom. I can't blame it on my mom and dad but ever since my mom and dad got their divorce, I haven't got through it yet. I never thought it could happen to our family. Now I'm in here for jumping this girl and beatin' on her—I stole her chain too. It's jus' all bad for me. (Doris Montoya, fourteen years old, assault and battery)

> I even had to call the police on my own dad. He used to fight with my mom, with my uncle, even our neighbors! Fights: my dad taught me "If someone hits you then hit them back!" I don't know how many times he's been in jail for assault and battery! He taught me how to fight pretty good, well, not that good [laughs]. I lost the fight I'm in here for. (Joanne Billingsly, fifteen years old, assault and battery on school grounds)

Although girls' aggression and anger, as well as their parents' marital discord, were consistently related to offending behaviors, many criminology studies fall short of exploring the ways girls who grow up seeing their mothers beaten respond by being aggressive themselves. Research cannot definitively prove that witnessing or being victimized by brutality in childhood directly causes later offending behaviors, and it cannot predict which witness will become an offender, but plausible links among factors such as exposure to violence, girls' anger, and subsequent offenses, especially girls' involvement in violent crimes, became easy to verify by hearing the voices of girls who were locked up for violent offenses.[34]

Children are born into families where they learn their culture and family history, values, and how to love and work. Young people gravitate to safe and loving places in which to grow up. As one group of feminist scholars found in their work with urban girls, "'Homeplaces' can be broadly defined to include comforting, safe spaces in institutions such as schools or in social groups such as clubs, social movements, or gangs. Listening to young women's critiques of schooling, domestic spaces, gender relations, racial hierarchies, and social violence, we have learned that homeplaces, broadly defined, can also become constricting places from which they often try to break free."[35] As we saw, Anastasia's experience typifies how families can simultaneously offer girls and young women a home to grow up in but one sadly filled with violence, neglect, and abuse.

Conclusion: From Private to Public Injury

When we dig into the girls' accounts we see how their private anguish affects us as a public. In their families, friendships, neighborhoods, and schools, they were provoked into making an astonishing number of aggressive assaults. Their injuries were connected to their sexual misconduct as well. Their narratives revealed neither a simple structural determinism as a result of being poor or discriminated against nor any facile psychosexual dysfunction or pathology. Instead, girls' involvement in juvenile corrections resulted from the interplay among these forces and others, mediated often by an unprotective culture and punitive social stance.

Girls related relatively freely their sexual experiences as victims. Many court-involved girls sense that they may gain sympathy by sharing accounts of their victimization. Although the girls were comfortable presenting themselves as sexual objects, they seemed less comfortable sharing experiences of sexual agency. They were much more recalcitrant when it came to some aspects of their sexual choices—sex work, trading sex for favors and money, loving older men, and having desire for other girls. These narratives were difficult for them to share. They sensed that they had much to lose and could get into even more trouble if they told adults about much of their private lives. In addition, as the following chapter illuminates, the dual effects of growing up in families devoid of positive encouragement coupled with a hypereroticized popular culture led young women into problematic and, at times, illicit relationships.

I See the Sky Fall Down

I see the sky fall down once again
night's here and I'm off
another hit or another puff
no matter what, I need my stuff
I leave my house late at night,
mom cries and starts to shout,
"Erica, why do you do this to me?"
In return I yell, "Fuck, why can't I be free?"
Free to me is to do what I want,
but in reality I'm just another prisoner
in the game of dope.

—Erica

3

Empty Families,

Sexuality,

and Trouble

The matron buzzed Portia Barlow through the locked gate, and the thin African American girl walked slowly toward me, looking around curiously as she dawdled along the dark, cement hall. "What I'm doing is not beneath me!" she protested immediately— before I had said a word to her about commercial sex work. Portia's short hair stuck out wildly in all directions, a little bit of it captured in the back with a dirty rubber band. Her patchy skin ("ashy," as she described it), was badly in need of her beauty and hygiene products. The California Penal Code she was detained for violating was "disorderly conduct: any person who solicits, agrees to engage, or engages in any act of prostitution."[1] The sixteen-year-old consented to talk with me as a way for her to "kill some time" while she was in Juvenile Hall.

> Oh I quit school when I was fifteen—it wasn't really workin' for me up in that school. I got kicked out of Belmont Springs Academy. I have a learning disability—I have Attention Span [sic]. I usually take Ritalin, but I don't got any in here. I need for my mom to bring me my stuff, but . . . my mom is so mad at me. . . . My whole family thing is all fucked up. You see, I'm adopted. My big sister is nineteen, and my little brother is adopted too. What happened is, I got mad and left my mom's house and went to Oakland. I had a friend there and that's where I met Jimmy [her twenty-nine-year-old boyfriend].
>
> I prefer to live with my boyfriend. He loves me; he is always there for me. He is not my pimp, but he understands me. I got the

idea about prostitution when I met him in Richmond. It was cool down there and then . . . well . . . I spent five days in Oakland Downtown [adult detention facility].

According to system-involved girls, their sexual practices are not problematic, in the sense that their romantic and erotic experiences are representative of contemporary youth norms. Portia's pimp is her boyfriend, and he loves her and takes good care of her.

In this chapter, we hear more from Portia and her family and learn that some young women wander in what I term *empty families* throughout their childhoods. According to the accounts from the respondents in this study, almost all the young women who spent any considerable time in detention seemed to hail from living situations where family members disappeared and reappeared in erratic fashion. Parents, siblings, guardians, cousins, grandparents, aunts, and uncles, often through no fault of their own and not on purpose, would come and go because of ill health, their own problems with the criminal legal system, unemployment, divorce, homelessness, substance dependence, and even death. The court-involved girls in this study, often without stable and reliable sources of protection and guidance, lived in such empty families. Many of the young women talked about having families, but I came to see the word *family* as an empty term for them because their so-called families were devoid of the meaning and substance that protection, nurturance, guidance, and conflict—yes, conflict, but successfully resolved conflict—were supposed to provide. The young women, set in these abandoned families, then wandered in an increasingly misogynist popular culture that exhorted them to enjoy being demeaned and made into sexual objects available to the heterosexual male gaze and touch. I describe in this chapter the commodification and sexualization of teen girls' concerns, a process that complicates many of our common sense assumptions about young women in trouble, including their relationships with their older boyfriends. Girls' solutions to their pressing economic problems and adolescent needs produce tensions between young women and the adults who protect and punish them.

Young women's sexuality and sexual practices are linked to girls' troubles in both familiar and new ways. By focusing on the contrasting narratives of Portia, LaShondra, L'Teshia, and Christina, I answer the question that this chapter raises: How are shifting gender and sexual norms, troubled girls' material experiences, and girls' rule-breaking behaviors interrelated? I locate their very real structural constraints (including the overreliance on criminal solutions to social problems) inside a late-twentieth-century, popular, consumerist culture that commodifies adolescent girls' sexual interests. These forces—material, cultural, and emotional—combine to produce a picture of a small number of youth living in dire circumstances, in concentrated disadvantage, unprotected and punished, with few alternatives.

Young women devise sexual solutions to nonsexual problems, a well-worn strategy noticed by other scholars. For example, a girl may get a new boyfriend as a response to needing somewhere to stay, or she may go out partying and looking for a lover when problems with home life, money, school, or family seem unresolvable. When adults devise sexual solutions, it is seen as a coping strategy for dealing with the tension in their lives. But adults have access to a wide set of resources and tactics for problem solving. Because young women's access to those resources is limited, using their sexual capital in their (albeit shortsighted) eyes becomes their greatest asset.[2]

After all, girls have been coming to the attention of the law for uniquely gendered sexual practices since the inception of the juvenile system. But during the 1980s and 1990s a decrease in the provision of public material support for poor young women and their families was coupled with a normalization of sexual and violent images in the news, entertainment, and consumerist popular culture. Increasingly relying on incarceration as a solution for social problems, government decreased spending on quality-of-life infrastructure such as streetlights, sidewalks, and parks, while increasing budgets for juvenile detention facilities.

These political and economic decisions affected African American neighborhoods disproportionately—not coincidentally the areas where most arrests of girls take place. Simultaneously, an unprecedented volume of hypererotic and violent images of women being demeaned bombarded popular consciousness, unfettered by corporate or governmental intervention. A ubiquitous consumer culture, an ominous development in the late twentieth century, emphasized misogyny and subordinated femininities. These pernicious economic and cultural processes combined to differentially influence the shifting beliefs, attitudes, dreams, and choices of young women.

The data in this chapter point to a dialectical interlinking of these material processes. With children depicted as criminals and as oversexed, popular support for their care, welfare, and education decreased. At the same time, problematic behaviors increased, as did popular support for funding punitive solutions, such as community policing and additional detention facilities.

For the young women I interviewed in secure facilities, getting an older boyfriend or girlfriend to help them out solved many of their problems, such as procuring housing, transportation, and food. For them, growing up meant surviving in families that offered no protection, turning into "little parents" for their own mothers and siblings, being embedded in a hypererotic and racialized popular culture that fed on demeaning images of young women and especially young women of color, and learning to define adulthood in patriarchal and racialized gendered ways.

Sexed and Gendered Survival Strategies

When I first met Portia Barlow, she had been arrested for sexual misconduct and was locked up in a juvenile detention facility. Contrary to popular myth, prostitution was an unusual charge for young women in the late 1990s and early 2000s. Of the 1,475 prostitution-related arrests of girls and women in San Francisco in 1996, only 10 were juveniles under the age of eighteen. Similarly, in a 2000 study, only 35 of the 5,651 prostitution-related arrests in metropolitan Chicago were of girls below seventeen. Nationally, in 2004 only 2 percent of all arrests for prostitution were of female juveniles. In 2004 nationwide, only an estimated 1,304 arrests for prostitution were of girls under the age of eighteen.[3]

Racism plays a crucial role in how young women are represented and labeled in the system. African American girls aged ten to seventeen represent roughly 7.5 percent of the national population.[4] In my sample of court-involved young women, they accounted for 44 percent of participants. Yet 100 percent of the girls in my sample who were arrested for sexual misconduct were African American. I attribute this disturbing fact, in part, to the dehumanizing processes of the hypererotic (and lucrative) popular-culture industry. That cultural dehumanization, coupled with disproportionately limited material avenues available to young black girls, produces a situation in which young women endure, clients enjoy, and arresting officers utilize their discretionary power. Furthermore, as I demonstrate in this chapter, listening to the experiences of girls who participated in the sex trade updates our understanding of young women's motives and provides a realistic picture of what adults like to call "girls' options."

This was Portia's first time in juvenile detention, but not her first time being picked up for prostitution. Originally, for this charge, she told police that she was eighteen years old, and they sent her to the adult facility, 850 Bryant (San Francisco City and County Jail). "See, in the TL [the Tenderloin] they just give you tickets [jaywalking, public nuisance, and loitering citations instead of charges of prostitution]. I went in to pay them, and they wanted me to do three months over there! So I told them my mom's real name and my real age, and here I am in Juvenile. They said I could go home now and stay at my mom's and abide by her rules and go to school."

At this point in the interview, Portia asked me, "What do you think

I should do?" She seemed concerned that she would not be able to be a "good girl" at her mom's house:

> This [juvenile hall] is worse than jail at 850. But I don't want to be a square; I want to look good.
> *What is a square?*
> Square means "not bad."
> *What are you?*
> Not good. I'd say I'm in the middle trouble zone.

Portia talked about how she felt about prostitution: "They came in here last night with some group for us girls and said that what I'm doing is beneath me. It is not beneath me—I don't even do it all the way with anybody!" She eagerly explained that she does something called "trick-fucking": "See, I take him and lube him up with Vaseline and kind of stick it tight, uh, high up between my legs. He so high anyway he don't know the difference." "See," Portia said about her sex work, "I'm just faking it anyway, and faking oral sex too." I suggested to her that this was a dangerous strategy, one likely to result in having an angry, possibly not-so-drunk client on her hands. But Portia was doing all the talking and not much listening at this point.

Her everyday frank talk of sex and the negotiation of male desire was considered taboo by most middle-class adults who were trying to "help" her. Portia's quotidian experiences, language, and beliefs differed from those of mainstream middle-class girls. Ironically, some of her ideas about sexuality reflected new sexualized norms for young women. She did not understand the counselors' shock and distaste for her ideas. She considered the former prostitutes who ran the workshop for girls as "square" and believed they simply did not understand that Jimmy was her boyfriend and that she was really doing the right thing for herself. Locked up for turning tricks, she described herself as being only in a "middle trouble zone." Portia was articulate, straightforward, and un-apologetic about her sexual survival strategies. "They say, 'But, you're out there selling your body!' I say, 'Hey, I'm just out here lookin' good!'"

Portia had a lot to say about how she was not really doing prostitution and that it was not even really wrong but was the right decision for her to be making at this time. "I don't pay any taxes. It's all take-home money. I set my own charges—whatever I want. Hell, I get $50 for a blow job and $100 for all the way. If I was at McDonald's, I'd be making, like, $4 an hour and then after taxes, well, hey!" Portia may have been exaggerating her prices considering the corner on which she was working. But, limited yet logical, this sixteen-year-old framed her alternatives as getting a minimum-wage job or dealing drugs: "Selling drugs is a felony! And at least I'm pleasing somebody, not trying to kill somebody with a gun over a bag of dope."

Toward the end of the interview, Portia told me: "In the future, I want to save money, and invest it into real estate so it will double back up on itself. I want a nice house, money to fall back on, and a nice car. I want to go to Spelman's [sic]." I was struck by the contrast between her present situation and her dreams of attending Spelman, the prestigious, historic black women's college. Portia asked me the meaning of the word *emancipation*. We had a friendly talk and laughed together. In our last exchange in lock-up, Portia made a plaintive plea in the small voice of the lost child who was also a part of her: "Do you ever take girls home? Can I come home with you?"

For Portia, her boyfriend wasn't her pimp, she wasn't really a prostitute anyway, and at least she wasn't participating in the violent drug-trade sector of the street economy. According to her, love powered Portia Barlow into the arms of her boyfriend/pimp. Sex provided her/them with a way to generate cash. Portia struggled to minimize and even deny her sex work, neutralizing her guilt. The social logic to her decision making was largely transparent. Given the choices that Portia believed were available to her, for her to move toward the boyfriend and the seeming financial security made sense. Her grim bravado during the interview hardly reflected what sociology has referred to as girls' "impulse to get amusement or adventure." Her sexual choices served instrumental purposes. Portia coolly claimed she turned tricks for a chic modern reason— money—and she did. But I also saw that emotional nourishment and care were available to her, in her eyes, only from her so-called boyfriend. By focusing on her budding sexiness within the constraints of a patriarchy only too willing to sexualize black females, Portia devised a sexual solution to survive that part of her adolescence. Many of the narrative accounts of court-involved young African American women reveal this precise enactment of the new racism of sexual politics.[5]

Inestimable damage is done to society's humanity, and particularly to African American young women's sense of self, by the "controlling images" of a dominant media that present young women of color as over-sexed or always ready for sex. Numbed by a barrage of hip-hop video images of "booty-shakin' mamas"—with little critical analyses or adult intervention—some young women who are relatively unprotected from misogyny experience popular culture uniquely. Everybody learns cultural messages from the images: the boys learn that it is acceptable to demean women, and the girls learn to accept being demeaned. In one girls' group focused on violence against women, one of the young participants observed, "Look at all these videos out nowadays. The girls are so sexy and willing—they send the message that they can't be raped because they *always* ready!"[6]

But the problem is not that "young people have too much sex" or even simply that African American girls are hypereroticized in popular culture. It is that black girls have few dominant alternative images, avenues for engagement, and material resources. Nationally, highly visible pro-girl, antiracist campaigns aimed at funding schools, building housing, creating jobs, and the like are largely nonexistent because of the steady backlash against the gains made in the 1970s by second-wave feminists. Building national girls' movements has become the work of girls' coalitions and girls' organizations worldwide; these groups believe that if children are bombarded with images of families, communities, and youth joining together with the material resources in reach to build positive, healthy futures full of peace and prosperity, the devastating effects of the narrowing misogynistic popular culture will be minimized.[7]

When Portia said, "He's not my pimp—he's my boyfriend," it seemed like Shakespearean protesting too much and led me to speculate that he was pimping her. Disclosures such as hers reveal what young women do to get love into their lives and how they reconstitute their sense of being cared for as the product of romantic sexual relations even though those relationships involve older men who prey on them in the streets. Portia's case file read: "P. has bonded with an older male (her 'boyfriend'). She refuses to see that his drug use and involvement in other illegal activities have a bad influence on her. Her mother is overwhelmed and, given that her mother feels she can't control P., a group home placement may be best for her. Her back-talk gets her into a lot of trouble with staff. It is unlikely she would stay long in that setting."

Grown and defiant, disobedient and autonomous, Portia challenged her family and the juvenile corrections system in ways that neither was equipped to handle. The notion that Portia's choices constituted a feminine delinquency strategy is anachronistic. When we meet Portia, in a way, we are introduced to a classic "old-style" bad girl: a sexy, immoral temptress in need of rescue. At the turn of the twentieth century, it would have been a clear case: the state punished and reformed this kind of behavior. Moral reformers and social workers, mostly white, upper-class Protestant women with new degrees from newly founded women's colleges, worked among working-class ethnic, Catholic, and Jewish "unadjusted" immigrant girls to punish, guide, control, and rehabilitate them. But one hundred years later, by the turn of the twenty-first century, popular culture, media advertising, and television prime-time programs had normalized the commodification of the image of a defiant, sexy teenage girl and marketed that image largely to heterosexual adult males.[8] When the daughters of more affluent families become too defiant and sexual for their privileged, middle-class soccer moms to handle, they pile them into Volvos and drove them to psychotherapy appointments, such as we saw in the 2003 film *Thirteen* and read about in pop-psychology advice books. But overwhelmed inner-city mothers like Portia's are forced to forfeit their daughters to the system, even to out-of-home placements.[9]

"Empty" Families and How They Come to Be

We walked across the street to Portia Barlow's concrete apartment building from the Ella Baker Tutoring Center, where Portia went on Thursday afternoons. Hip hop blared from the metal-rimmed windows, almost drowning out children's playful voices. Bits of paper and trash blew in the wind around our feet. Portia had been released from detention and was court-ordered to serve her probation in her mother's one-bedroom apartment with her mother, her two little cousins, and her younger brother. Her probation conditions included getting back into a high school, observing a home curfew, and attending a girls' Saturday program in a nearby church basement.

Portia's mother, Sadie, came out as we approached and was already talking before we reached her. "I can't control *none* of these kids! They sure don't listen to me! They never mind me no matter what I say! I got to go to the doctor's 'cause my leg be *killin'* me, and these here kids won't mind me at all, sittin' in the doctor's office just playing with everything all *over* the place!"

Pushing open the screen door, we entered an empty, small, drab front room with a pile of laundry in one corner and a big, beat-up lounge chair against another wall. With no other furniture in the room, two young boys squirmed and tumbled over one another, playing and laughing loudly on the chair. "My cousins—that's how they are," Portia explained dryly. The walls were bare but for a lonely Certificate of Achievement earned by Portia at Belmont Springs Academy for sixth-grade reading, which was thumb-tacked high up near the ceiling in the center of one wall.

Sadie immediately dominated the conversation with her problems, worries, and ailments. It was clear that she was exhausted and overwhelmed by her circumstances; it was also difficult to distinguish her as the adult in the home who was caring for all the children. Like many low-income, single mothers who stay indoors with children all day and night, Sadie was hungry to talk to adults—in this case, me. But her energy inappropriately pulled the attention toward her and her woes, taking up all the emotional space in the room and leaving little in which her daughter or little nephews could flourish. She seemed as needy as Portia and the elementary school–aged children in the family. Conditions such as these provided the rationale for service providers who work with girls in trouble to insist on working with the entire family to locate mother-support services.

Girls in the juvenile system do have families, but their families' grave challenges often derail parents' abilities to guide and protect their daughters. Divorce, overwork, substance dependence, incarceration, mental illness, ill health, homelessness, and death were events that young women in my sample identified as reasons for the absences and ineffectuality of their mothers, fathers, grandparents, aunts, uncles, cousins, and siblings. These factors, not necessarily mutually exclusive, accounted for why girls wandered in empty families. Empty families are peopled, but the people are worn down, fighting their own battles, with little access to social, cultural, and economic capital, and simply unable to provide the protection and guidance their daughters need. In most of my interviews, it was not only that families were poor or that families were fighting among themselves. Families simultaneously and without relief faced severe, chronic, and multiple challenges—no income, no furniture, no food, involvement in the criminal and juvenile justice systems, alcohol and substance use, undiagnosed mental illness.

In addition, I came to see that the phrase "poor parenting skills," which was used by juvenile justice officials, often reveals differences in class attitudes toward parenting itself. In an ethnography of families, Annette Lareau found that middle-class parents identified the notion of "concerted cultivation" as necessary for raising healthy children. Parenting was best achieved, according to the more privileged parents, when it included exposure to a wide array of activities and direct experiences for their children. Lareau pointed out that working-class and less-advantaged parents accomplished a "natural growth" in their children by issuing directives. But for many families of girls who cycled in juvenile corrections systems, neither of these child-rearing styles were options. In many cases, because of situations beyond their control, many parents of the young women in this sample were tragically not physically present to exert any kind of sustained parenting. It was not so much that parents lacked the skills or the right attitude as much as they lacked the ability to control where they were at all.[10]

Family disruptions were painful events in the lives of the young women in the study, especially low-income girls of color, who were largely unprotected by other social institutions. Table 3.1 displays the self-reported living arrangements of the young women I interviewed in juvenile corrections. While 91 percent of the young women I interviewed reported growing up in homes where there was at least one parent or family member, the saddest answers I heard to the question "Who mostly raised you?" were "Nobody" and "I mostly raised myself." Only 22

Table 3.1
Family Arrangements

"Who mostly raised you?"	Number
My mother (and stepdad/boyfriends)	38
Other family members (grandmothers, aunts)	24
Both my parents	22
Nobody; I mostly raised myself; raised in placements	9
My father	7
Total	100

percent of the young women in my sample were raised by both parents. As of 2001, over fifteen thousand court-involved girls were living in residential placements outside their homes of origin. This figure does not include those in facilities for drug or mental health treatment, but a sense of the "homelessness" of this population is revealed in these figures.[11]

The extent of disintegration among the families of young women in juvenile corrections cannot be overstated. In my sample, 38 percent of the girls said they lived with their mothers only; nationally, in 2004 about one-fourth (23 percent) of children lived with their mothers only. Not surprisingly, almost 80 percent of the young women said that their parents were divorced or separated. But, surprisingly, one or both parents of 12 percent of the girls I met in the system were deceased. The loss of a parent to death has been documented to have long-term disruptive consequences for children, especially children who live in already-unstable families. Rarely do delinquency theories underscore the devastation to a child of losing a parent.[12]

Parents, absent for various reasons, many beyond their control, left some female youths adrift. It was not uncommon to meet young women who had been in out-of-home placements for most of their childhood and then spent most of their adolescent years with boyfriends twice their age. These were the children who had lost their grandparents, aunts, and all the other "back-up people" that we imagine are raising them. Quite a few young women spoke in stark terms about their family arrangements. One girl did not even know who lived in her own house:

> I thought that guy was just visiting. I didn't know he lived with us! I mean, he's my mom's boyfriend, but hey . . . (Julie Woods, fifteen years old, grand theft: auto)

> My mom had an affair and I felt like, "Fuck you, Mom!" and "Fuck you, Andy!" My dad just cried. (Mariana Lincoln, fourteen years old, diagnosed with "oppositional conduct disorder")

I can't blame my problems on my family, but ever since my mom and dad got their "divorce," I haven't got through it yet. Ever since, I got hurt because I never thought it could happen to our family. (Norma Guzman, fifteen years old, possession of marijuana)

I was upset because my dad left on my ninth birthday. We caught him with another lady, and so he left us. I didn't want to listen to my mom after that. I thought, "Why should I do good for you?" I didn't love myself. (Wendy Chew, fourteen years old, assault with a deadly weapon: knife)

Mom is *always* at work! She works at night, she works in the day. She is *never* home. She has, like, eight jobs or somethin'! (Deenah Low, fifteen years old, possession of drugs for sale)

Families of incarcerated girls are confronted with material as well as psychological battles: their problems aren't necessarily caused by "poor parenting skills." Research from a variety of disciplines reveals that families of girls in trouble have to deal with an inordinate proportion of the national crises in health care, education, and jobs. One group home manager from Southern California whom I interviewed suggested that parents, not children, are in the greatest need of empowerment. "These girls don't need to live in public facilities; their families need more support services: jobs, education, psychological help, political organization."

Adult health care. The absence of parents or other family members because of ill health or mental illness was a topic that young women returned to in their interviews. For example, girls frequently said that they had to live with somebody besides their mothers because "My mom got sick" or "My mom went to the hospital." An Illinois study found that "the daily stress associated with living in a neighborhood where danger, trouble, crime, and incivility are common apparently damages health."[13] In addition, both the prevalence of untreated mental health problems and therefore the injurious effects of poor mental health are more extensive in poor families of color, families from which the girls in this study emerged.[14]

Substance dependence. Data from the U.S. Department of Health and Human Services regarding the use of alcohol and drugs reveal that almost twenty million Americans, or a little over 8 percent of the population age twelve or older, were current illicit drug users in 2003. Rates of drug use varied little among major racial and ethnic groups: 8.7 percent for African Americans, 8.3 percent for whites, and 8.0 for Hispanics. Almost 20 percent of unemployed adults over eighteen were illicit drug users, according to the government report. Young women in my sample reported that 44 percent of their mothers and 61 percent of their fathers drank or used street drugs on a daily basis. An estimated 119 million Americans regularly drink alcohol; 54 million participate in binge drinking; and almost 22 million are classified with substance dependence or abuse, according to the 2003 national report.[15] It would be impossible to estimate the damage caused by this type of absence of parents on children, but it is likely that many of the children of the adults who are besieged by drug and alcohol addiction are the children who come to the attention of juvenile authorities.

Children's health care. When parents are not able to be present, they cannot care for their ill children. In addition, the percentage of all children under age eighteen with private health insurance coverage decreased from 71 percent in 2000 to 66 percent in 2004. During the same period, the percentage of children with Medicaid increased from 20 percent to 27 percent. Eleven percent of children in the United States have neither private nor public health insurance.[16] Youth in juvenile detention facilities are likely to be uninsured—plausibly the children of uninsured parents. In most of the juvenile facilities I studied, girls received mandatory medical and dental checkups. One girl stated that she did not remember ever seeing a dentist before. Another young woman in the dental clinic asked whether she could bring her sister in to see the dentist too. The nurse had to explain to her, "No, honey, we do not want you to bring your baby sister in here. This is a jail."

Families in crisis/schools in crisis. Parents of girls who come to the attention of the system have a difficult time keeping their daughters in school. Because poor families are often forced to move around quickly, school records get lost. If home life cannot be organized around the school schedules of the children, they do not get enough sleep, wake up late, do not have clean clothes to wear, or miss their buses. Girls in the study revealed that, for these and other reasons, they fell behind, became frustrated, and lost interest in going to school. Locate these everyday experiences within a debilitated national public education system in crisis, which is reflected in factors such as a shortage of teachers and supplies and poor physical conditions at the schools, and it is easy to see that mothers of incarcerated girls face multiple challenges keeping their daughters focused on getting a high school education. It is simply not that "their mothers didn't raise them right," a refrain of some of the officials I interviewed, but that the nation's funding priorities had not raised these girls right. Rhetoric aside, in the 1990s, the U.S. public education system already trailed in critical academic areas, and U.S. eighth graders lagged behind students in less affluent nations. The United States devoted fewer of its resources to education than ever before. Spending on public education has been in decline since the 1970s. These misplaced priorities resulted in some shocking statistics—for example, U.S. middle schoolers had lower science and math achievement scores than their counterparts in Hungary, Bulgaria, and the Slovak Republic.[17]

Joblessness and poverty. Joblessness and poverty contributed in unique ways to the emptiness in the families of the system-involved girls I interviewed. Girls came disproportionately from families of the poor: 48 percent of my sample reported that they lived in no-income families. Over one-fifth of the girls reported that their mothers and 10 percent said that their fathers did not work or received some kind of federal benefits. In a variety of studies, poverty is correlated with juveniles being processed in the system. Children form the largest group in the United States of people living in poverty. As of 2003, almost one in five children under eighteen in the United States (16.7 percent) lived below the poverty line. Families of color are disproportionately represented in the rolls of the poor: while 11.2 percent of children in families living below the poverty level are white, 27.8 percent are Hispanic, and 33.1 percent are African American. Studies show that children who live in poverty are more likely to become teen parents and have trouble in school, are less likely to be employed as adults, and earn less as adults when they are employed (compared with children who do not live in poverty). Service providers who work with girls from troubled families also notice the effects of poverty and the problems these young women face. One of the most popular gender-specific interventions for young women in the system includes workshops on skill building in order to enhance girls' employment possibilities. But when asked what kind of work they are interested in, girls typically reply, "Oh, any old thing," "Passing out condoms," or "Warden." Many simply do not know about jobs and about working.[18]

Given the struggles involved with the injustices highlighted above—lack of access to health care, addictions, lack of good schools and jobs—it is no wonder that many of the young women in this study mistrusted adults who worked in the system, and although they had siblings and parents, foster parents and stepparents, they seemed to come from empty families. According to these young women, the public systems designed to provide them with equal access to the American dream—education, health, and welfare—had let them down and left them out. By listening to the accounts of young women and contextualizing their experiences in demographic indicators of well-being, I saw that the crises in empty families could not be reduced to personality problems, value systems, or the parenting skills of the mothers. In addition to narrating what life is like while being raised amid concentrated disadvantage and depleted institutional support, young women who were locked up talked about their missing family members. But for court-involved girls, family members' absences were not random, accidental, or unrelated to their trajectories into the system.

Poverty, Absence of Kin, and Race

For many reasons, both historic and contemporary, African Americans have been disproportionately hindered in their efforts to maintain family integrity. The overrepresentation of families of color being "served" by county-level governmental departments is a reflection of the racialized effects of poverty. In 2001, 542,000 children lived in the U.S. foster-care system. However, child removal was not evenly distributed across all families. For example, in San Francisco, 78 percent of the youths in foster care in 1996 were African American, yet African Americans constituted only 16 percent of the city population. As of 2001, nationally, while African American youth made up 15 percent of the youth population, they constituted 38 percent of children in out-of-home care.[19] Five percent of the young women in my study came into juvenile detention from group homes, foster care, or other out-of-home placements where they had been living for their entire lives.

The rapid growth of the prison system contributed to girls in my sample living in empty families. Thirty-eight percent of the young women interviewed reported that their mothers had been in the criminal system at some point in their lives. Half said that their fathers had been arrested or jailed at some point. Like poverty, imprisonment disproportionately affects women of color. In the year 2000, 2.2 percent of all children under the age of eighteen had a parent in state or federal prison. But the proportion of African American children with parents in secure custody was 7.5 percent. These were often the parents of the young women caught in the juvenile corrections system.[20]

The devastation to African American families from the explosion in imprisonment in the United States since the mid-1980s cannot be overstated. Although only five out of every one thousand white women can expect to go to prison, the estimates rise to fifteen out of a thousand Hispanic women and to thirty-six out of a thousand African American women. In 1997, an estimated 75 to 80 percent of imprisoned women were mothers. Those women who are most vulnerable to punitive state intervention are also most vulnerable to child welfare intervention policies. Once arrested and detained, poor mothers of color are likely to lose custody of their children. Because women are often the primary caretakers of poor children of color, the result of this state intervention is often placement of the children in the foster-care system as well as termination of parental rights.[21] These children were often the young women I met in detention facilities and adolescent treatment facilities.

In poor families in disadvantaged communities, fathers do not and cannot stay home; mothers want and need to work. In addition, state intervention causes disruptions in families' lives. As a result, as studies have revealed, African Americans have a rich history of devising supportive kinship networks to address family disruption. In particular, because of the current overreliance on incarceration and the criminal justice system to solve social problems, families who have members in the system work to build new support networks to address their particular needs. In my sample, more than one-third of the girls were raised by their mothers alone or by their mothers and a boyfriend/stepdad. More than three-fourths were being raised outside their original nuclear families: by their mother, mother and stepdad, mother and boyfriend/s, other family members, grandparents. Over one-fifth of the girls reported that their fathers were completely absent from their lives, drinking/drugging, in jail, or deceased. [22]

But even when these young women developed emotional mechanisms with which to face their incredible losses, their suffering did not leave them unmarked. The emotional effects of disruption in or complete loss of parental relations have been well documented in the psychological literature.[23] Parental death places children in peril of going into social welfare systems: 12 percent of the girls in my sample had a deceased mother or father. In addition to suffering from the grinding effects of poverty, racism, and other defeating conditions, the young women talked about these family losses in ways that made me realize they had not yet acknowledged, accepted, or healed from this great emptiness and lack of love. This was an already debilitated population of young people. Heaped on top of the actual losses were the facts that they had less access to mental health care and support and less stability in the home to support the kind of grieving and healing that needed to be done after the death of a parent. Sometimes the young women would conflate so many challenges in their narratives that the deaths of their primary caregivers—of grandmothers, aunts, parents, and older siblings—became lost in their general discourse of "I have so many problems!"

Practitioners and service providers I interviewed noticed that these challenges provided the symbolic and material groundwork for the degradation of girls' psychological integrity. One juvenile attorney observed:

> The young women I defend face multiple challenges. Sometimes I think it is insurmountable. The girls need real goals; they need their minds opened. Many are raised by their grandmothers, who are too far removed in age (or are in denial) to see what today's girls are facing. The girls' attention is kept focused on the day-to-day survival in their lives. They don't [imagine] things like "I could be a

doctor or a politician. I could buy a house or travel." They complain of being so bored. How can they have a positive mentality when all they are offered to think about, to get relief from their problems, is hair, nails, sex, money, and babies? (Lorena Gutierrez, Family Law Project, East Pasadena, California)

In the ways noted above, poverty, absence of kin, and the pernicious effects of living in a racist society intersected in the lives of the young women in my study to produce empty families.

The Parentification of Unprotected Girls

Many girls in empty families reported that they felt they needed to take care of their mothers and younger siblings. These girls figured out ways for some kind of parenting to occur in their families, even if they had to do it themselves.

LaShondra Wolfe was pregnant when I met her in a Los Angeles detention facility. By not listening to her and by not taking her concerns seriously, the adults around her had allowed her to sink like a stone to the bottom of the system. Sixteen, African American, LaShondra grew up in a large, working-class, multiethnic neighborhood in a big wooden house that had rooms rented out to different families. "I'm sixteen now, but when I was eleven years old, my grampa molested me. After I got out of the hospital, my mom's boyfriend moved in. I been in foster care, whatever. . . . I started bein' bad, and they put me in a group home. But the doctors told me I was still a virgin, even though what my grampa did to me."

Bright-eyed and round-faced, LaShondra said she wanted to be a singer like Chaka Khan. This cinnamon-skinned young woman with green eyes had her hair cut short, "down to the good stuff," she laughed. To get a sense of how young women see themselves in the world, I asked each of them, "What do you look like? Can you describe yourself?" LaShondra answered, readily: "Yeah, I'm beautiful. I look good. I look better than all the rest of them. I always keep myself real nice and clean. Tight clothes and my nails, and all.

When I asked about her family, she replied, "My stepfather is at my house. I din't get along with him *at all*, but um . . . see, my mom needs him. I do understand because he helps her a lot with all her problems. I was tryin' to help her when I caught this case." LaShondra's file had the following notation: "L.'s gfa [grandfather] raped her when she was 11 years old. He served 3 years, County. The gfa raped her mo [mother] also, when she was a little girl. L.'s mo is 32 [years old]. L.'s fa is in prison, SQ [San Quentin, California]. L. is extremely hostile and oppositional towards her mother's husband."

Originally, LaShondra was removed from her family and placed in a group home, supposedly for her own protection. LaShondra's account is typical for young women in group homes and in detention facilities awaiting placements in group homes: Child Protective Services had removed them from their families originally in order to protect them. A report on the New Jersey juvenile legal system found that over half of the youth locked up had not committed any delinquent crime. As mentioned previously, girls often run away from their placements, thus catching cases in the juvenile system, even though the system initiated their placement.[24]

LaShondra had given birth to a healthy daughter two years before I met her, when she was fourteen. The county health department had removed the child from LaShondra's care because of numerous complaints that she was not able to care for her. The county placed the child in a foster family, and the baby had since been adopted by another family. The father of LaShondra's first baby was thirty-two years old.

I met her in detention as she awaited a disposition for a weapons charge. This was how she explained her situation. Her recounting of her story was as disjointed and confusing as her life had been thus far.

> They already took my first baby from me and put her up for adoption. Oohhh how could they do that to me? I wasn't really doin' nothin' wrong with her involved! I mean, she was so little, man, how's she gonna' know the difference I'm out there sellin' my ass or what? 'Lease I'm puttin' food on the table. . . .
>
> My mom is like my sister. I'd do anything for her. Sometimes I pass her on the street, she on her way to the bus to go to St. Martin's to get somethin' to eat. She's not doin' too good right now—she like to smoke the shit, you know [referring to crack cocaine]. So she callt me up and said how somebody was threatening her; so I went to go buy her a little gun. Just a little thing, you know, fo' her to stick up in her bra and shit. But they caught me, said I was buyin' a sawed-off shotgun! Shit, they crazy; I ain't never tried to buy me no shotgun!
>
> I would do anything for my mother! I would cut off my legs for my mother, I swear! She was the only one there for me when I got pregnant and had my baby. She even stayed sober for like eight months 'cause I tolt her she had to be sober to see my baby. I would do anything to reduce her stress. See, she don't know I'm in here now 'cause I don't want her stressin.' When they took my baby, well, she lost her sobriety. We're more like sisters, really.
>
> I'm pregnant now! Oooh I wish I could call my baby's father, but they won't let me in here. He was helping me on the corner, you

know, so they call him my "crime partner." I'm stressin' 'cause I think he be up at County—he's thirty-seven so he wouldn't be in Downey Juvenile!

Damn, I don't know hows I'll ever pull all this together. I want to get my baby back, but I know I can't. The man I got now, he's all right; I mean, he isn't that mean to me and all, but . . . he was my mom's friend, you know? He's known me since I was a little baby!

LaShondra exemplifies what psychologists call a parentified child—someone who takes care of everyone else in the family, doing parenting work, often for her own parents, often for younger siblings. Even from a distance, she tried to take care of her mother (albeit by trying to buy her a small gun). Parentification describes a common and useful survival strategy for many of the young women I met in the system. It is typical of girls in the juvenile system, in need of parenting themselves or even assistance in parenting their own children, to take on some form of care-taking of their mothers and others in their families. As the cover of Nancy Chase's edited volume on the topic describes, "burdened" and parentified children are "those who are compelled to fulfill the role of parent at the expense of their own developmentally appropriate needs and pursuits. With uncanny sensibilities, these children are attuned to their parents' moods, wishes, vulnerabilities, and nuances."[25]

Staying focused and busy meeting everyone else's needs helped avoid or alleviated the pain that the adolescent girls in my sample might have felt if they had slowed down and acknowledged all the ways in which they were being challenged. Here I am not referring to the 15 percent of young women who were pregnant or parenting. Although some young women were literally parentified, here I consider another process, one in which young women are able to disassociate from the hard realities they face. This survival strategy of the unprotected—frantically running around worrying about every one else in their lives, including their moth-ers—can seem preferable to stopping and feeling their own pain and unmet needs. Burdened with their families' problems, they feel needed, effi-cient, and as though they have important tasks to complete. Being the only "parent" in the family relieves young women of experiencing their own vulnerability as lonely, unprotected girls.

LaShondra didn't feel that she had much to work with in her life. Struggling with unhealed childhood wounds, an absent-hearted mother and father, inappropriate attention from adult men, multiple pregnan-cies at young ages, she spent her time taking care of her mother as a way of focusing on anything but her own severe problems. After all, she had already lost her own child to the system.

Attempting to buy a gun brought LaShondra into the juvenile legal system on a weapons charge, considered a serious felony offense. Most likely, she will not receive attention for early-childhood sexual and emotional injuries, family counseling, help with paternity from her so-called boyfriend, or intensive educational training—all approaches that are most likely to begin to put her on a path toward healthy adulthood. LaShondra is going to be processed as a violent offender and will likely receive severe punishment, secure long-term detention, for her misguided, but somehow logical, behavior. That was the last time I saw LaShondra. I gave her a list of community services for young women in her area, and she said, "Thanks for talkin' to me. It was good to talk to you. It was the first time I told my story without crying."

The process of parentification most likely affects disadvantaged families of color differently than other families. Given the disproportionate representation of African American men in prison, the disproportionate number of African American women living in single-headed households with income below the poverty level, in substandard housing, and with lower-paying jobs, daughters in these families will probably become parentified more often than will daughters in affluent families.

In some ways, these wise, young, parentified women are burdened with a beautiful insight: they see the suffering of their mothers, and they want to help. LaShondra echoed what many young women who were in trouble with the law confided to me: that their mother was more like their sister and that they would "do anything" for their mothers, a quality that would be admirable in some contexts but is often tragic in these.

Are Empty Families Better Than No Families?

In sum, I cannot say categorically whether empty families are a better option than no families for court-involved girls. On the one hand, when they know who their families are and have contact with them, they always have the possibility for healing and reconciliation. Maybe, as the young women mature and are able to meet their own needs as adult women, they will be able to forgive their kin and live in their families of origin. On the other hand, when families of origin are locations of abuse and neglect, young women have to break away in order to find and receive the care, love, and security they so rightfully need and deserve.

I witnessed the detrimental effects some families can have when I observed the results that home visits had on court-involved young women. For example, in an adolescent group home for girls who were being adjudicated delinquent, young women would try to earn enough points from good behavior to be granted a weekend home pass. They often left their group home for a family visit with great emotional and spiritual strength, only to return after a few days, late, weary, dispirited, harmed, and in need of restoration. Girls, expected to return by 5:00

p.m. Sundays, would show up on, say, Wednesday morning, after having been reported to the police by staff using the military term AWOL (away without leave). Often, the young women arrived in need of gynecological services such as laboratory work for sexually transmitted infections and pregnancy tests. Although always enlightening, contact with family members who were drinking and drugging, were system-involved themselves, were looking for a fight, or worse, from the young women often were not healing and helpful for them. Young women, already stigmatized by troubles with the court, were particularly vulnerable, and their attempts to find love and consolation at home in their families sometimes led them to further harm and system involvement. The unquestioning ideal of family reunification must take into consideration that original families are not always the best place for children.

The Contemporary Sexualization of Girls: Causes and Effects

Narrative accounts of court-involved girls' lives uncovered three social forces that combined to contribute to high rates of system involvement. I have discussed two: the emotional factor of families' not protecting their girl children or meeting young women's needs and the economic factor of material need. In this section I dissect the cultural factor of an increased sexualization of young women caused by the global, burgeoning, multibillion-dollar youth-sex-beauty industrial complex.

Cases like Portia Barlow's and LaShondra Wolfe's illustrate both how some girls cycle in and out of juvenile corrections and the complicated role that family, whether present or not, plays in their system involvement. Reading hundreds of girls' case files and listening to hours of girls' accounts revealed that early sexual injuries, attempts to escape them, and arrangements to get love and protection often underlie girls' detention histories. Young women deployed various strategies to heal from childhood wounds and thrive as young women.

Despite protests from conservatives and progressives alike (and for quite divergent reasons), girls' awareness has become increasingly sexualized since the mid-1980s: their attention has been drawn to ideas about sex, romantic relationships, and erotic practices in an inordinate fashion and at preteen ages. (I use the terms *sexualization, oversexualization, hypersexualization, and eroticization* interchangeably here.)[26]

The cultural processes of sexualizing girls' awareness take varied forms, including being more or less forcibly immersed in visual images from sexually obsessed media and being allowed to devise sexual solutions to nonsexual problems. A hypersexualization occurs as girls' selves, their lives, and their concerns are inundated with unprecedented gender-stereotypical media images, consumer messages, and a popular youth culture in music videos, teen magazines, cosmetic and drug commercials that essentially drenches them in images of girls and women portrayed mainly as sexual objects. After all, as the rap artist/cover girl Foxy Brown in Illustration 3.1 posits, sex sells. As troubled and vulnerable girls struggle to maintain a focus on concerns such as education, recreation, and family relationships, this cultural force points them toward the single-minded task of becoming attractive to the male heterosexual gaze.[27] The image in Illustration 3.1 of a young, tattooed, African American woman touching herself in a shiny bikini provokes the viewer: What is wrong with being strong? Absolutely nothing, if one is not a child whose complete sense of self-worth and power is derived from the whims of a (adult, male-run) profit-dominated, commercial sexual economy.

By oversexualization, I do not mean that they sell sex or have too much sex. I am referring to teenaged girls who live unprotected by family and other social institutions such as schools. Certain disadvantaged young women are expected to navigate complex sexual and social relations as if they were adult women with a variety of options available to them. The processes of oversexualization of this population of girls in trouble, facing racism and poverty in brutal ways, involve an imbalance between adolescent exploratory sexual activities and other, nonsexual preoccupations. I mean oversexualized in the sense that young women are viewed primarily as sex objects by many male adults in their worlds, view their own place in the world as mostly providing sexual titillation for males, and see sex as their best—or only—resource for problem solving.

Traditionally, girls' sexual and immoral misconduct was linked to their delinquency, and the general popular proscription at the beginning of the twentieth century was that young ladies be chaste in order to be revered. But for contemporary young women new processes are at work. Beginning in the 1980s, with the idea of sexual liberation turned cynically on its head, popular culture increasingly sexualized girls' and women's interests for commercial ends. The new popular mandate was that girls should be sexually interested and available. Yet when they were and did, boys and men were cavalier, inventing sex games and sex parties to get girls to perform oral sex, have sex with each other, or have group sex with men. Girls could not win: they were sexually harmed at home and then disrespected in public.[28] In public culture such as on television and in commercial radio, beginning in the 1980s, girls were increasingly encouraged to flaunt themselves as worthy of male sexual desire. As a result of these cultural changes, a majority of young women in my study were managing a compromised sense of self because their sexual awareness had been impinged on in harmful ways by a media/beauty/pharmaceutical industrial complex that equated images of good-

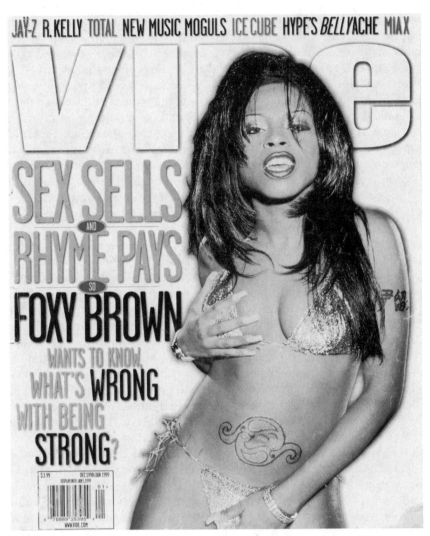

Illustration 3.1. What's wrong with being strong? From the cover of *VIBE* magazine, December 1998/January 1999.

girl femininity with sexiness and overtly eroticized norms (see Illustration 3.2).

Girls' family conflicts, educational problems, as well as utterly routine psychosexual tasks of individuation during puberty and adolescence, are complicated by harmful cultural representations of their female sexuality and gender role expectations. The hip, young, self-confident white girl in the shoe advertisement is portrayed as cool, comfortable, and stylish—displaying cleavage and bare midriff in low-rider, hip-hugging jeans. Even though her halter top says, "I HEART my soul," this is not the image of a playful teenager in a pair of athletic sneakers ready to run around a soccer field. The viewer's attention is drawn instead to her long, blond, slightly unkempt hair and her sultry, sexually provocative

Illustration 3.2. Good girls are sexy girls. From a Skecher's advertisement, late 1990s.

gaze. In Portia's account and those of other young women, I saw this oversexualizing process affect their sense of self and their decision making.

The girls' accounts of their offending behaviors, while often sexualized, followed a morally logical train of events that made sense to the girls at the moment. Given their lack of choices, it was not uncommon to hear comments about parental neglect, sexual abuse, romantic love, and money worries all tied up in one experience:

> How'd I support myself comin' up? Sellin' my ass—that's how! How else you 'spect me to put myself together? Not like a man is gonna help me! My mama always high—my daddy is in jail somewheres. Nobody really payin' much mind anyway. . . . But, shit, I ain't doin' nothin' wrong. 'Least I'm not clubbing people over they head. (Tanishia Gelder, seventeen years old, possession with intent to sell: marijuana)

> My stepbrother molested me. I'll kill that boy if he ever touches me again! My mom was always gone workin' [prostitution], so nobody was there to enroll me in school. I'm quitting [prostitution] now. . . . Oh this [a 2-inch-high dark blue tattoo of her pimp's name inscribed in Gothic lettering on the left side of her neck: "*CHINO'S #1 BOTTOM BITCH.*"]? I signed up to have it removed. (Leticia Gonzales, age fifteen, felony sale of illegal substance: marijuana)

Young women, bombarded with the cultural imperative to be sexy, reproduce the message as if they had thought of it themselves, thus falling into a dialectical, reflexive loop. Their autonomous agentic "I am sexy" attitude makes it difficult to distinguish girls' actual sexual agency and sex-positive attitudes from their oversexualized, media-saturated, survival-sex self-images. Human sexual experience within patriarchy produces a subtle paradox: it is simultaneously freeing and a source of harm. As one scholar framed it, sex can be "a liberating weapon of the powerless and a vehicle of oppression." In this sense, the young women in corrections, who were growing up with few material alternatives, were sexualized from the outside, adopted sexualized images of themselves internally, and then defended these ideas as being simply their own youth culture. The result was a process in which young women facing non-sexual problems—such as trouble at school, trouble with peers, family trouble—devised sexual solutions to them (for example, getting a new boyfriend). The combination of both influences, commodified externally and fetishized internally, resulted in some young women having distorted notions about the role of sex and gender in their adolescence.[29]

While still children, girls in corrections used their youthful appeal to adult male heterosexuality in order to meet their normal childhood needs for food, clothing, shelter, adult guidance, and family love. Such childhood necessities, utterly mundane and crucial, were not being provided to them elsewhere. Traumatized early in childhood, many adultified before their thirteenth birthdays, girls figured out that youth sexiness was a transferable commodity supported by a booming market. In the end, the irony was that the same pundits who deplored the decline in morals among youth owned the advertising companies and corporations that profited from such "immoral" images and voted for the legislators who gained political capital from them.[30]

Sexual Solutions to Nonsexual Problems: Christina Gaffney

Like her father before her, Christina Gaffney was "way into cocaine." The Gaffneys were a no-income working-class family living in the run-down section of a rural region beyond the suburbs in the San Francisco Bay area. Christina's mother was a daytime drinker with a nighttime job, and her father dealt cocaine for money. Christina described her father as a "scary dad." She talked quietly about how he would "get angry and mean" with her sometimes, but stopped short of saying more. I first met her in a probation school, and Christina talked in a small, angry voice about a life of hurt at home and misery in school.

> Oh I don't know, I was like four or six when my babysitter molested me. He made up a game called Ducky Jim. I hated it, but I don't know, I would just freeze. I did this thing I called the "frozing." Like I thought if I froze it would not have happened. . . . I can't explain. . . . He was supposedly a friend of the family; can you believe that? These people are so fucking stupid, I can't believe it. They tried to put me in, like, a ninth-grade math class or something! Hell, I *hate* it here!

Her file had the following comments: "Minor is an affable young lady who is extremely verbal. Although impresses as a young lady who is basically innocent, opposite is believed to be true. Admits to having difficulty controlling her mouth. Extremely streetwise and has learned much from negative experiences."

Christina had long, straight, blond hair and pimply pink skin. The first thing she said as she came through the door to the interview room was, "This place sucks! I hate it here!" She was in detention awaiting a disposition on a truancy warrant; as she put it, "I have bad behavior problems with authority."

Apparently, she faced challenges in other areas of her life as well. Christina's records revealed that she had been pregnant three times: two miscarriages and an abortion, all before her sixteenth birthday. Christina was raped in a bathroom at a bowling alley near her home when she was fifteen years old. When I met her, however, she wanted to talk about cocaine. She said, "I first tried it when I was five years old!" As she grew into her teens, she confided that she "would do anything to get it—even trade head [oral sex] for it. I used to do coke to forget everything that happened to me. But that was a long time ago; I stopped coke two months ago because I got way too far into the game, and I almost got killed from it." Christina said that she grew up "scared of everything—my dad was a major coke dealer!"

I went to meet her on another day at the probation high school she was court-ordered to attend. It was one of the only schools of its kind in an affluent county. The entire school consisted only of two long, dreary halls in a V-shaped configuration and in need of paint, with the school office located where the halls met. The blacktop basketball court, badly in need of repaving, doubled as a parking lot. I had to be careful pulling in and out not to run over a basketball or a youth chasing one. The dismal school site contrasted jarringly with the opulence of the green suburban neighborhood in which it was located.

As I walked up to the hall/school, a teacher was handing out Cup-O-Noodles and bags of Fritos—apparently, lunch. About thirty students, almost all boys, mostly white, were in disorderly groupings, shouting, jostling, and trying to get to the window where the food was being handed out. I noticed little racial or cultural diversity among the adults; they were generally white, and many seemed somewhat depressed and ill-groomed. The men had their shirttails outside their belts and uncombed hair; the women wore sweat pants. The school was a grim mockery of an educational institution. As one boy grabbed a soup out of one of the (few) girls' hands, I heard another young man shout, "Watch out! She's a lesbo and she'll kick your ass!" Much male laughter; much female red-faced shame; no teacher intervention.

But Christina was about to confront a whole new set of problems because, as she explained in a shocked voice, her rapist had shown up in the twelfth-grade class. He taunted her there, and as she put it, "I have all these emotional and drug problems, and now I'm stuck here. If I don't come here every day, I have to go back to lock-up!" Enrolled in the cosmetology class, Christina had already developed another plan: "I'm going to make all these guys fall in love with me and then dump them! I'm going to fuck them all over!"

Christina's problems began at home, in her family, but she planned to deploy a weapon of the weak, a sexualized solution to nonsexual problems. Getting "all these guys" to "fall in love" was the best alternative she could come up with. Harmed at home, forced to choose between a dangerous, depressing school and going back to detention, Christina made the most that she could of her personal resources. Maybe this strategy was not new for young women, but that the adults around her offered no sympathy, intervention, or protection exemplified the contemporary punitive approach toward vulnerable girls in trouble.

Challenging Norms

In the following episode, which I observed in a detention facility, evidence emerged of an eroticized girls' awareness as well as resultant tensions between the perspectives of youth and their self-appointed adult redeemers.

At a girls' group inside a juvenile detention facility, the facilitators—one white woman in her forties and a thirty-something Latina—announced that the day's project would be to make a collage of "images of females in the media" (see Illustration 3.3). Workshop leaders taped a piece of poster board to the chalkboard and passed out various popular magazines such as *Teen People, Essence, VIBE, Seventeen, YM, Time,* and *Ebony*. Immediately the detained minors fell into shouting, "Hey, how come you got the good one, and all I got is this dumb *Time!*" Not allowed to have scissors, girls tore pictures of women and girls from the magazines and, one by one, came to the front of the room to add their contributions to the collage.

L'Teshia Williams, a strong sixteen-year-old African American girl awaiting a hearing on drug possession, came striding up first and planted a photograph of a young African American man modeling men's underwear square in the center of the collage. Slowly, chaotically, and noisily, amid much laughter, fighting, and confusion, girls taped photographs of female celebrities in sequined evening gowns photographed at gala events around the male underwear model in the center of the collage.

When the young women finished designing their artwork, the facilitators asked the group, "What was the original assignment? Why do you think we have the photo of this *man* in the middle like this?" L'Teshia shouted, "Oh he fine! [*sic*] I wanna *do* him! [have sex with him]." As the group leader looked askance at her, she replied, "Hey! You don't got to love to fuck!" The girls broke into laughter, slapping high fives, and shouting out, "Got that right!" The older facilitator frowned and said, "Here, let me put up a picture of a woman to be admired." She taped an image of a middle-aged woman in a suit onto the young women's collage, explaining, "How come you don't have any professional-looking people in your collage? This person is a lawyer. She is Latina, and she defends poor families." Silence came over the group.

The facilitator continued in an authoritative voice, "I don't understand why you all are so obsessed with these celebrities. They all look like 'hoochie mamas' in those slinky little dresses. How can they be role

Illustration 3.3. A collage of images of females in the media, late 1990s. *Credit: Collage created by juvenile female detainees; research conducted with informed consent; used by permission.*

models for you?" The young women, angered and defensive, began protesting, "You are just jealous! You could *never* look that good in a dress!" shouted out one girl. Another young woman chimed in, "You could never even *afford* a dress like that! It probably cost $3,000!" But the facilitator took the last word at this girls' group anyway, intoning, "I wish you all could be more realistic and critical in your understanding of images of women in the media." Glum, muttering, and obviously disgusted with the project, the young women filed out.

Although the plan was good—to articulate a critique of sexist imagery in the media—the delivery simply failed to engage the young women in the desired "critical" conversation. I learned later that peer-led interventions to discuss beauty norms and the sexualization of women in the media are usually much more successful.

The young women in this study continued to challenge the norm of women's chastity from a century ago, proudly sharing their more agentic approach to erotic relationships, which they referred to as being the approach of a "playette." It was sadly ironic that this feminist-seeming, sex-positive rhetoric was deployed by young women so thoroughly objectified by corporate, media, pharmaceutical, and other industry interests. Rarely did I see a realization of many of the possibilities that a woman-centered approach might bring them, including, for example, the freedom not to be sex objects for men.

The experiences that girls from detention reported pointed to a distinction between girls' healthy interests in their own sexuality and their survival-oriented or abuse-triggered preoccupation with male sexual desire. On the one hand, in their conversations, young women in the juvenile system challenged the value of sexual virtue and chastity. Court-involved girls such as L'Teshia wore what used to be considered moral depravity as a badge of ascension into adulthood. It was as if having casual sex were simply one step toward growing up. On the other hand, unhealed wounds from early childhood physical and sexual abuse and unmet survival needs because of neglect awakened girls' attention to male sexual desires sometimes as much as a decade before they might have even thought of sex if they were living safe lives devoid of predators. In other instances, young women in this study spent precious sexual capital strategically to enact escapes—from boredom, from pain, from memories, from emotional hunger, and from physically and psychologically dangerous homes.

Racialized class backgrounds influenced young women's sexual attitudes as well.[31] To get a sense of that influence, I surveyed majority white, first-year college students in an Introduction to Women's Studies class. In addition to asking a variety of questions about their lives, how they spent their time, what they thought of "dating," the "most fun" thing they ever did, the "worst thing" that had ever happened to them, I asked these mostly middle-class youth, "How do you know if/when it is the right time to have sex with somebody?" In the anonymous survey, their answers varied around one predictable theme:

Preferably when I'm married.
Personally, I'm a virgin, but I think that marriage would be ideal,
     but I think love is the best for sex.
Wait until marriage.
Marriage: a monogamous, committed relationship.
When a person is mature enough to handle the responsibilities
     of sex and that person has met someone they really care about.

The differences between the typical rhetoric of these two groups of young women—the girls in detention and the college first-years in a women's studies class—displayed social and class contradictions that young women face growing up today. Ironically, the girls in detention—mostly urban girls of color from lower-income families—reflected a 1970s, liberated women's viewpoint, advocating a kind of free love and sex, more than the mostly white, middle-income college first-years in a women's studies classroom. The once-feminist message, now cunningly repackaged and insidiously commodified beyond recognition, had been fed back to girls who were seen as a market niche. These sexist and racist cultural messages land in the hearts and minds of less-privileged girls differentially because they have neither a strong peer-led alternative youth movement in place nor adults present to provide material and political contexts for critical analyses that might cushion the effects of the media. The messages also arrive in the lives of young women who have few alternatives than sexual solutions to their overwhelming depleted material conditions.

Girls locked up talked about the sexy actresses and models as the beauty ideal. I do not intend here to disparage young women's dreams or taste, to insult their celebrity heroes, or to even indicate disapproval of aspirations to be sexy and beautiful. Instead, I wish to highlight the efforts of the billion-dollar corporate media that direct the aspirations of young women toward a single-minded focus on the achievement of beauty and sexiness (chiefly to please an older heterosexual male gaze). These enterprises could be funneling resources into schools, youth centers, hospitals, and housing, the underfunding of which contributes to young women's being brought into street economies and the juvenile system in the first place.

I sensed a certain desperation to meet nonsexual needs coming through the bravura of the young women in detention. The lack of urgently needed resources distorted the sexual permission that system-involved young women appeared to enjoy. Continually, even though they were seemingly able to access joy and permission to enjoy their young sensuality, their sexual delight was distorted by the urgency of meeting needs that arose because of underfunded schools, unacceptable living conditions, poverty, and being especially vulnerable in their families as their communities struggled to stay afloat.

Early sex is also an area in which girls challenge traditional norms. Seventy percent of the girls I interviewed said that they had had consensual heterosexual intercourse by age fourteen (fully three years before the estimated average age for the general population of U.S. youth), and 47 percent had experienced first consensual sex by age thirteen. Only 9 percent of adolescents in a national survey said that they were thirteen or younger when they first had sexual intercourse.[32] By the time some of the young women in my study met their older boyfriends, they had already had several partners, and most had already been harmed sexually. Table 3.2 shows the ages when girls in this sample reported having had their first consensual sexual experiences.

The age at which children experience their first sex has been gradually lowering in the United States since the 1950s. In one 2003 national report, over 50 percent of young people reported having had some kind of sexual experience by age eighteen.[33] Sexual contact at early ages affects adolescent development in a range of ways. Although most young

Table 3.2
Age of First Consensual Sexual Experience

Age	Number
12 years and under	22
13 years	25
14 years	23
15 years	13
16 years and over	2
No sexual experience yet	16
Total	100

people probably explore and experience their sexuality in consensual ways, we also know that, for some young women, having their awareness become sexualized early in their puberty is not always beneficial.

Furthermore, even though adolescence is a time for increasing sexual knowledge, positive ideas about feelings, bodily sensations, and desire often fall out of the discussions with girls' groups in detention facilities. Adults who work with system-involved girls often focus on sexuality as a danger or a reproduction problem to be solved. For this population, pregnancy, abortion, and parenting are framed not as options but as social problems. Adults who care for girls in detention and on probation do not focus on the experiences of pleasure, flirting, first kisses, and feeling cared for and precious because they do not see the girls as innocent, experimental, or capable of making "healthy choices," which is the way they regard more privileged, white, middle-class, and male teenagers. [34]

At a gender-specific intervention in the form of a girls' discussion group in a temporary juvenile detention facility, twenty-two predominantly African American and Latina girls sat with chairs in a circle in the school library. The facilitator, a white woman in her twenties, explained that the topic for the hour-long session was "healthy relationships." She intoned, "For example, learning how to 'fight fair' is a good thing. By that I mean, make some ground rules with your boyfriend *before* you get angry with each other." The girls started looking around at each other, frowning. "Shit, he jus' go off on me whenever he want to," one girl muttered. The leader, looking a little thrown, continued, explaining why it was important for the young women to learn to "respect themselves" and use birth control. Finally, one young African American detainee interrupted, complaining, "Yeah, yeah, yeah. Everybody *always* tells us, 'Use birth control!' 'Don't have babies!' We know white people don't want us havin' babies! We know all about the patch. But what I wanna know about is, How come the boys always be playin' you? [betraying and tricking through romantic promises to get sex]. Oh, yeah, y'all come in here and tell us all about Norplant and ovaries, but nobody *never* wants to talk about the real stuff, like how it *feels* to get played!" Flustered, the facilitator tried to explain how this was not the case. "Ladies, you need to learn some self-respect and not just let these men talk you into anything. You shouldn't be so overly concerned about men anyway at your age. We're just trying to protect you and the next generation of your children." But the adult facilitator only dug herself deeper into a mess of mixed messages about race, class, violence, and sexuality.

Boyfriends or Boyfoes? Older Men
as Sexual Solutions to Empty Families

When families and school personnel are not available to meet their emotional needs, and a popular culture keeps them focused on one thing, their sexiness, some adolescent girls find nurturing, relief, and adult guidance on the streets of their own neighborhoods.

A great concern among young women who were being adjudicated in the juvenile system and the adults who worked with them was their older boyfriends. The definition of older boyfriend varies across jurisdictions. Usually for young women aged thirteen to seventeen, older boyfriends are defined in statutory rape codes as young men who are either over the age of twenty-one or at least four years older than the young women (who might be able to consent at age sixteen, seventeen, or eighteen, depending on the state statute).[35] Young women know to lie about the age of their boyfriends. When asked in the beginning of an interview if they were "hanging out with anyone," they might talk about having a boyfriend under age eighteen. Often, later in the conversation, they would admit that their friends were in their twenties or older. In all, 46 percent of the young women I interviewed said that they were seeing someone who was over the age of eighteen and at least four years older. Three girls said they were involved with women in their twenties.

L'Teshia Williams typified young women in detention facilities who had missing family members and much sexual experience. She provided an uncannily clear analysis: "My [thirty-seven-year-old] boyfriend helps me a lot. A lot of my decisions to turn towards the street was me, but it was because my family I trusted was my family I was abused by. My man tries to help me out now."

Girls reported that their boyfriends fed them, drove them to school, and provided them with places to get a good night's rest. Largely fending for themselves in adolescence, the young women felt that men who had access to cars, apartments, and food were a positive force in their lives. Consider the following account, related by L'Teshia.

> My daddy was long gone before I was born. When I was growing up, my mom and my aunties mostly took care of me. When I was eleven

years old, they took me to foster care. I had to get away from my family for a while. . . .

See, we was livin' in the cuts. My little brother and me were playin' one day, and he got really sick. He had picked out the little bitty piece of rock crack [cocaine] hidden in the wall outside our door [where her mother had hid her stash for sale]. He went to the hospital and almost died. . . .

I went around, stayin' from my foster mom, to my mom, to my auntie's house. Nobody mostly din't notice us. One day my mom's friend told me to come here, and . . . he started likin' me. He took me to a hotel room and showed me how to do it. He kept me there all weekend until he showed me how to do it right. He's been my boyfriend now for ever since.

I know it's bad, but he is my best friend and I love him so much. He helped me out all the time and always takes me to eat and to get clothes. He don't know I get high—he would be sooo mad! He took me to school every morning and tol' me to "Stay in school!" all the time.

L'Teshia was being adjudicated for drug sales after being picked up on a street corner at 2:00 a.m. Here was an adolescent with grown-up problems. She was lonely, frightened, and needy.

Older men have access to cars, money, and experience that the teenagers in trouble need in order to survive. Girls' boyfriends give them "cash money" to get their hair "hooked up" (braided) and get their acrylic nails done. One young woman told me, "Oh, we just stay with them long enough to get the 'C' [cell phone] off 'em, and then we gone." Men buy them pagers and cell phones, thinking that the girls will then be accessible to them at all times. Young women receive their normal childhood wants, needs, and desires—food, shelter, clothing—as well as beauty products and services and even cell phones (all considered crucial to adolescents). Young women reported that no one else helped them meet their basic needs: not their mothers, fathers, probation officers, or caseworkers—nobody but neighborhood boys including older men.

Hardly anyone would argue that the friend of L'Teshia's mother was a positive candidate to be L'Teshia's paramour; he stood up for her most often and provided her with her basic needs. This was a terrible situation for all concerned, but for L'Teshia, who had emotionally bonded with an adult perpetrator, it was the worst. For the moment, however, she had solved her troubles and had found someone to help take care of her.

As Georgia McCarthy, executive director of a girl-serving agency in Los Angeles explained, "The key to the majority of the girls' problems is the fragmented nurturing and lack of role modeling that they experience.

They sink like stones because they are missing it. The anomalous small percentage of girls who survive their adolescence intact is probably because there was one person who loved them no matter what." However, most adults who were involved in the lives of young women in the system were convinced that older boyfriends were a negative influence. In addition, these relationships were illegal.

In one intriguing study, psychologist Lynn Phillips interviewed both adult women who had "statutorily questionable" relationships when they were teens and adolescent girls currently in relationships with older boyfriends. When talking about their memories of their adolescent involvement with older men, the adult women reminisced that those relationships were debilitating and destructive. In retrospect, they believed that the relationships were not healthy for them. But the young girls currently in relationships with older men had a different viewpoint. The adolescent girls insisted that their relationships with their current lovers were healthy, good for them, and loving. The young women with older boyfriends said they felt more mature than other girls their age. Even though many of the teenagers in the study talked about how controlling, protective, or possessive their older lovers were, they believed that being with a more mature man was good for them.[36] Thus the sexual solutions that the teenagers find seem to serve their purpose at the time, yet they may not hold up in the long run as viable resolutions to the confusions and dilemmas of female adolescence.

Having an older boyfriend was disastrous for many young women in this study, but statutory rape laws were inadequate for sorting out girls' survival strategies. Involvement with older men was possibly life saving at the time for a few. I came to see their involvement with men as a form of sexual harm reduction.[37] Dealing with an older boyfriend could be injurious, but considering the alternative of putting up with ongoing abuse, hunger, or homelessness, dealing with an older man might seem less bad. As a least-harmful compromise strategy, girls' tactics of getting involved with older boys and men in order to meet ordinary needs is neither legal nor healthy, but it might save girls' lives and get them through adolescence.

Conclusion: Adulthood Reconfigured by Sex and Gender

Although a sexualized construction of adulthood may help some young women survive their adolescence, as we heard in the narratives of Portia, LaShondra, L'Teshia, and Christina, it also correlates with subsequent problems. A link between sexuality and delinquency for girls is not new. What is new are prevailing mainstream norms of hypersexualization promoted in advertisements, music videos, and prime-time television shows aimed at young people. Punitive attitudes toward those who transgress have always existed, but, at this time, government and industry appear complicit in contributing to the problems of youth. Unprotected in decaying neighborhoods and with weakened family support, girls adopt demeaning sexualized self-images foisted on them by a marketplace that profits from their degradation.

Troubled girls trouble the ubiquity of mainstream notions of family, healthy sexuality, and adolescent popular culture. As we dig into the troubles of court-involved girls, we see that they are in troubled families. Their families struggle against structural inequities, such as the inadequate provision of health care, the overzealous intrusion of the criminal legal system, and the easy availability of drugs and alcohol. Some young women, left unprotected in these families, deploy their youthful sexiness and get involved with older men as a survival strategy. A profitable billion-dollar mega-industry of popular culture promotes the hypereroticization and subordination of the adolescent girl body for the pleasure of the heterosexual male consumer. Privileged and protected young women, living in families who are able to be actively engaged in furthering their well-being, are able to access a wide range of alternative possibilities in the private sector, such as immersion in after-school activities. In contrast, many of the young women I met in the juvenile legal system were floating in empty families, adrift in a sea of danger and degradation.

By listening to young women who are experiencing the full force of the law, we are able to gain new perspectives on the process of eroticization. From the perspective of the marketing industry, appealing to teenage girls' concerns about budding sexuality provides a profitable market niche. In addition, the wane of the welfare state has reduced not only the material protection provided to families in trouble but even the sense that the state has a responsibility to provide for such families. Poor women, children, and families of color feel the full weight of these forces disproportionately. It would be irresponsible for social science to decouple these cultural developments from their economic and political bases.[38]

As arrests for sexually related delinquency decreased, other categories of arrests for girls rose. A dramatic amount of resistance, rebellion, and rage had developed among girls in trouble. In the next chapter, I explore the role that anger and aggression play in contemporary girls' offenses.

Life

As I walk down the dark corridors of my mind,
drifting through the memories of death and life,
OD's and sickness,
digging in dumpsters and jumping trees,
All I see is pain, forgotten, and wondering,
No true happiness,
no fulfillment of joy.
My past is a blur of darkness and sharp pains,
Convulsions consuming my body,
my stomach in a knot.
My mind racing on useless thoughts of nothing,
My body broke and dry from lack of attention.
My vision in 4 dimensions—seeing people
and hearing voices that exist only in my mind.
From my hiding place in dark corners of the earth,
I watch life pass me by in fast forward,
Leaving me behind.
Peace,

—Chelsea

4

Gender,

Violence,

and Trouble

Seventeen-year-old Claudia Sereno had such a be-
guiling smile that whenever she arrived back in detention, all the counselors would hug her and laugh. When she wasn't in a rage, she was
alert, funny, and smart. Claudia entered the courtroom in an orange
sweatshirt (indicating that she was considered a violent offender); her
bright eyes darted around the rows of seats behind the table where her
public defender waited. Claudia was hoping to see someone she knew
in the spectator area.

Juvenile courts were designed to be less adversarial than adult court.
For example, juvenile court is held without a jury. When one girl found
out there would not be a jury, she said, "Good, 'cause I want a fifteen-
year-old judge and a jury of *my* peers!" The expectation is that the judge,
parents, social workers, prosecutors, and defenders will work together
to discover the "best interests of the child." In juvenile sessions, evidence and witnesses are produced informally. The public is not allowed
to observe juvenile trials because the juvenile court is premised on protecting the identity of the youth offenders and the privacy of the family.

The difference between adult court and juvenile court can be quite
dramatic. I was observing juvenile court one day when, without warning, an adult case was called. The atmosphere in the courtroom trans-
formed in an instant, as if there were an onstage scenery change. People
craned their necks to see what was going on. The judge straightened her
back. The bailiff called out the case in a slightly louder and more self-
important voice, and batteries of defense attorneys and prosecutors

marched in carrying charts and boxes of evidence. A flurry of activity commenced as the jury filed in, and the juvenile defendant was led out shackled in an adult Department of Corrections orange jumpsuit.

Even though Claudia was charged with a violent offense and weapons possession, her public defender had managed to keep her adjudication in the juvenile court. Claudia came through the door from a holding cell adjacent to the courtroom without much ado, wearing her juvenile detention-center sweatshirt and khaki pants, "PROPERTY OF COUNTY JUVENILE" blazoned on the back of both. Her public defender motioned for Claudia to join her, seated at a table facing the judge. Ms. Cheng, the lead attorney at the county public defender's office, argued on Claudia's behalf: "Your Honor, we would like to have some extra time to get the updated psych eval [psychological evaluation] and for us to be able to do a new family investigation before we respond to the petition [enter a plea]. We are going to draw up a different treatment plan, given these new developments in Claudia's case."

Asking for a psychological evaluation meant that Claudia would return to lock-up for as much as thirty more days. Recall Chapter One: Claudia had been admitted into the court system based on a petition claiming she had assaulted a young woman on a street corner late at night. But Claudia had been so emotionally and physically violent at the scene that the police took her to the adolescent psychiatric facility for a cool-down period before bringing her to intake at the detention center. Claudia's entire court hearing took less than five minutes because she was going to be held over until all the necessary reports were completed.

Juvenile courts in the United States handled over 1.5 million delinquency cases in 1999. Ms. Cheng, a public defender in a large California jurisdiction, appeared mostly in front of a Girls' Calendar, a court calendar set aside to hear only cases of girls, part of a unique gender-responsive project introduced in larger counties such as the Cook County system in Illinois. These girls-only court calendars and caseloads were developed in the 1990s to address the unique needs of girls in the juvenile court system.[1]

When a youth came into the system, a probation officer was assigned to conduct a social history of the minor's family. Often it was in the interest of the public defender's offices to cooperate with intake probation units in conducting these preliminary reports, variously termed *family histories, social investigations,* as well as *predisposition reports.* The reports might include an entire history of a juvenile's family, including a social history of her parents, their births, where and when they met. Predisposition reports were often used to provide context and background for the court at sentencing as well.

In the dependency system, some courts utilize guardians ad litem, court-appointed special advocates (CASAs), to testify to facts in the minors' life stories. CASAs are trained as the "judge's eyes and ears." In some cases, judges really need them because a battery of competing interests can be at the defendant's table. For example, it is not uncommon for parents of detained juveniles to be court-ordered to attend parenting classes when their juvenile child is detained. A juvenile judge may order the parents to attend these classes to learn more about adolescence, drug use, socially acceptable punishment and styles of discipline in the family, and even the terms and phases in the juvenile justice system so that the parents can participate in better ways than they have in the raising of their teenagers. These classes can be highly contested arenas where parents and probation officers disagree about how and whether children are "out of control."[2]

Some parents worry that they may be held liable for actions of their minor children. For example, in 1998 in a Detroit school district, when sixty-seven students missed more than a month of school, the parents were threatened with jail time and fines if they did not get their children back into their classrooms. In cases such as these, parents often retain their own counsel. In addition, the court-involved parents of detainees often have their own parole officers to contend with. The one hundred girls in my sample reported that, as far as they knew, 51 percent of their fathers and 38 percent of their mothers had been involved in the adult criminal legal system (arrested, incarcerated in the past, or currently in jail). When a young woman goes to disposition hearings, there thus can be a variety of adults with competing interests at her table: her lawyer, counsel for the parents, social workers, and other caseworkers for parents and children. But, more often, no one but public defenders and state's attorneys show up.[3]

Claudia's aunt arrived in court for her this time. Judge O'Brien, a judge who advocated for girl-specific programs in the probation department, knew Claudia's family history well. This was Claudia's sixth time in a courtroom; she had been in and out of the system since she was fourteen. Her mother had come to her hearings before, but she was not at this one. Besides her aunt and a public defender, Claudia's probation officer sat at the table in the small courtroom. It was unlikely that her aunt would be court-ordered to parenting classes. Claudia was going to age out of the juvenile system soon, and the court was simply grateful that she had an aunt and did not have to be ordered into an out-of-home placement. Claudia was already on probation for stealing from a corner market and for getting into a fight with another girl at El Rio Park. Everyone at the detention center knew Claudia well.

After Claudia was transported from the court back to her unit, I interviewed her half in English and half in Spanish, the preferred communication style of many Spanish-surnamed youth.[4] Claudia had a big, grinning, open face—with a chipped front tooth that made her look charmingly impish and playful. But she was far from her childhood, farther than many of us ever get.

> I love to fight! I cracked my tooth in a fight when a guy hit me with a milk crate! I take my anger out when I'm *triste*.
> *What makes you sad?*
> Well, let's see, uh. I always be fightin' with other girls too. My grandmother died when I was twelve, and I really miss her. My mom is on welfare, strung all out on dope, so I always stayed over with my gramma. *Mi papa* is not in the picture. I'm always mad at my mom too—she kicked me out one night when it was pouring down rain! I din't have nowhere to go so I just went around under the steps in back.

Aggressive behavior has been found to be one of many defensive responses to unmanageable tragedy and family disruption in early childhood.[5] Basically, Claudia was saying that she lost everybody who could ever have protected and cared for her. Her descriptions of aggression were often tied to her feelings of anger and loss in her family. Claudia had a tattoo on her wrist that said "*RIP [rest in peace] My Brother Lil' Rico*." I asked her about her siblings:

> I had my one brother and my older sister, but my cousin shot him last year—right in front of the house out on the street! See my brother, he was OK, man, but he got played by one of his homeys [friends]. *Mira*, I think he owed him some money or some shit. Man, they was into some rough shit, fucked-up shit. . . .
> If somebody irritate me, I get mad. Sometimes I feel stress, uh, disappointed in myself. I get so nervous. I feel nervousness. I get like a rock in my stomach when I don't know what's happening to me. That's why I can jus' go off and beat them people up! Fighting really helps me.

Claudia's descriptions of her feelings echoed other young women's accounts. Youth in my study were rarely provided with locations to simply grieve their losses. Using political or other safe ways to express the real and righteous anger that some young women felt was not modeled for them by adults. In this chapter I provide the narrative accounts of three girls: one assaulted her father; one engaged in physical assault against other girls in her neighborhood; one was involved in a lesbian relationship that became violent (she beat up her girlfriend in a domestic-violence dispute). Their accounts show how cultural prescriptions for girls' compliant subordination operate in direct tension with their righteous rage or with inescapable domestic and community violence.

Punishing Gender Transgression: Girlz 'n the Hood

Dominant gender norms set standards of behavior for girls: that they be heterosexual and monogamous, nurturing and relational, and obedient and (apparently) chaste. Girls' aggression has not been conventionally acceptable for two reasons: because it is aggression and because it is practiced by girls. Mainstream gender directives encompass norms for emotional as well as sexual expression, including expressing anger. Noticing the emotional work that court-involved girls perform in relation to their feelings, their notions of appropriate femininity, and their expressions of aggression makes it possible to answer key questions: What can we learn about gender and aggression by listening to the voices of these girls? And, how do contemporary, disadvantaged young women respond to violent episodes in their lives?[6]

According to the court-involved young women I studied, their aggressive and violent behavior was an inevitable part of living in violent environments. Young women did not necessarily see their physical fights as problematic. Violence, according to their narratives, was an unavoidable outcome of many of their problems. When court personnel did "see gender," girls' violence was primarily characterized as a violation of conventional norms of female expression and behavior. So, not only did the state continue to criminalize girls' sexual behavior, but it subtly widened the net to include criminalizing girls as violent predators as well.

Cultural locations where system-involved young women could express anger and anguish and analyze the sources of such feelings, as well as chances to learn other ways to respond to stressors, were difficult for the girls to come by. Claudia's account highlighted how girls shifted from the low drag of despair, sadness, loss, or hurt to expressing their feelings as an energetic hostility. Young women who were arrested for violent offenses narrated how they came to be comfortable with—and comforted by—expressing anger, aggression, or violence and avoiding sadness and hurt.[7]

A sociology of emotion opens a historic and cultural view of female anger. Experiences are not imprinted psychically in a universal manner, no matter one's gender, race, ethnicity, or socioeconomic position. Nor are the effects of internal processes empirically evident; they must be theorized. Gender, race, and social status affect how we experience our lives, and examining emotional agency shows how these effects occur. By listening to their accounts, we see how girls' decisions are socially derived, how girls make emotional choices, and how girls learn to respond to complex situations in their lives.[8]

Some young women who were locked up talked about their offenses in language reflective of clear-cut defiant intention. Others, however, reported feeling forced into violent situations—Monica Kinney said, "My boyfriend made me do it," and L'Teshia Williams knew she "did it for my dad." Still others used a disassociated, passive voice: Mylen Cruz said, "He got stabbed." Most girls did not frame their behavior as politically rebellious or articulate their actions as feminist-related resistance. Young women did not seem to notice that assaults are considered out-of-the-ordinary behavior for girls; they did not support the idea that their offenses were, in effect, deviant. Many saw fights as inevitable. In some accounts, girls tied their love and sexual relationships into their offending behaviors: "He's not my crime partner—he's my boyfriend." But the interviews with girls locked up confirmed that girls do commit violent offenses. Girls' accounts contradict academic claims that attempt to explain away all girls' violence. Some young women were being represented as violent, and others were being arrested more. However, in addition, girls did recount their armed robberies, assaults, beatings, and stabbing of others, as well as their participation in so-called drive-bys and car-jacks.

From Passive to Passionate: A History of Emotional Norms for Women

An examination of emotional norms extant at the inception of the juvenile court uncovers how girls' and women's assertiveness was captured in the popular imagination and punished in the courts of law at that time. When the juvenile corrections system was founded in 1899, girls were seen as deviant when they were too sexy, given the then-operative norm of a privately sexual wife/mother. In a study of the wards of the juvenile court between 1899 and 1909, 43 percent of girls were brought to court for "incorrigibility" and 31 percent for "immorality." Girls were commonly described as "very wild," going to "dance halls," and "flagrantly immoral."[9] But the presence of girls and women in public began to undermine the logic beneath the notion that men and women occupied separate spheres, a logic that sustained previous gender and sexuality norms. As urban space became crowded and (white, middle-class) women moved from the world of the private and domestic to the more public scene, a certain amount of assertiveness became normalized for all women.[10]

A history of adolescent girls in trouble traces not only their sexual agency but their emotional proscriptions as well. Normative femininity as displayed in the rules for emotional expressions shifted in the twentieth century. In a previous era, a certain amount of emotional acquiescence was expected from middle-class young women. Girls' femininity had traditionally been associated with being loving, caring, and nurturing, and girls lacked permission to express either rage or sexual desire. A century ago, the prevailing gender norm for girls was encompassed in their passivity. As sociologist Talcott Parsons observed: "It seems to be a definite fact that girls are more apt to be relatively docile, to conform in general according to adult expectations, to be 'good,' whereas boys are more apt to be recalcitrant to discipline and defiant of adult authority and expectations. There really is no feminine equivalent of the expression 'bad boy.'"[11] Whereas boys were expected and permitted to be rough and tough, girls were encouraged to be dainty and tender. Studies show that although contemporary norms generally promote self-expression and the healthiness of evenly expressed anger, as recently as the 1950s women were encouraged to suppress angry emotions in the interest of maintaining marriage.

But girls' lives changed in the latter half of the twentieth century. Accounts from the court-involved girls in this study highlight that contemporary offenses for girls transgress emotional norms of a "well-behaved," "well-heeled" femininity. By the beginning of the twenty-first century, girls were expected to be active and assertive but, of course, still feminine—the message we see, for example, in Illustration 4.1. The vigorous, young African American woman running with a ball, braids flying in the wind, is featured in a deodorant advertisement as "one of the guys." Now, middle-class, healthy girls compliant with the status quo are required to be emboldened, passionate, entitled, strong, and assertive. For girls at the margins, however, their aggression transgresses this expectation.

Discomfort with female anger is longstanding. But new norms for emotional agency have become incumbent on girls (see Illustration 4.2).[12] Contemporary media and corporate interests converged in the 2000s to advertise an emotional norm for girls and women that is more passionate than passive. Whereas emotional norms for young women one hundred years ago could be said to have constituted acquiescence, today they are closer to being configured as entitled. Girls walk a fine line as they perform their gender, no matter the era or their social position.[13] For example, advertising directed at girl children often contains overtly violent or sexual imagery as a matter of course. For example in one magazine advertisement for a video game for girls, the image reminds us that fantasy girls like the main player can be "tough," "independent,"—and armed. With her little red top stretched over a well-developed chest, the girl in the drawing is fighting "wicked wolfen" in her "search for a lost brother." We are told she is "adventurous" and "in control." She is also a character in a multi-million-dollar youth entertainment industry,

Illustration 4.1. Sweat like them, but don't smell like them. From a Secret advertisement, late 1990s.

appealing largely to boys, but now featuring advertising campaigns such as these in the hope of attracting girl consumers. In order to do so, the video game industry draws on images that blur orthodox cultural ideas of gender, sexuality, strength, and violence.

In 1984, sociologist Edwin Schur noted that norms and subsequent deviations did the cultural work of controlling female behavior. Table 4.1 lists rules and terms used in contemporary Western dominant cultures to informally constrain certain emotions and behaviors for girls and women. Schur suggested that emotional norms for women included that they neither behave in a cold and calculating manner nor be hysterical or aggressive. These unspoken norms for appropriate emotions for girls and women remain strong. We could add "various wrong emotions" such as rage, fury, anger, aggression, indignation, and hatred. Under "deviance norms," we might add charges of aggravated assault, assault with a deadly weapon, assault and battery, and other violent offenses.

At the turn of the twenty-first century, corporate interests encouraged Western women to want to "have it all"—high-powered, successful careers; children and husbands they care for at home; an active civic and social life; looking young and heterosexually desirable well into their sixties; having a healthy, active sexual life, albeit monogamous, dyadic, heterosexual, and legitimized by church and state. Thus, if the normal (middle-class), modern young woman is on the offensive, "making it in a man's world," assertive, and confident, the new, modern, deviant young woman is nonnormative in more agentic ways: angry, aggressive, and assaultive. Feeble-minded promiscuity has dropped out of our lexicon when we talk about female juvenile offending. Violent gang-girl activity is "in."

Some feminists resisted contending with girls' violence as agentic behavior. Writing about violence is difficult because describing violent scenes borders on participating in their use for titillation or in sensationalizing violence against women. Discussing the violence of girls opens the door for arguments such as "girls are just as violent as boys" or "girls' violence is equal to boys' violence against girls." My research reveals neither to be the case. We know that the rise in arrests of girls is largely a reflection of changes in police activity. Data, both descriptive and statistical, reveal men's violence to be more prevalent and damaging than that perpetrated by girls and women.[14] Here, I wish to focus on the small number of young women who *have* perpetrated violence. I argue that it would be disingenuous not to notice girls' violence, albeit the small amount of it—to minimize it, to valorize it, to gloss over it, or to explain it away as being reflective only of changes in policing or media practices. We need not fear bad news about girls' perpetration of violence. As we begin to document and understand it, we will see that when girls are

Table 4.1
Female Gender Deviance and Norms for Beauty and Emotions

Major Category of Norms	Typical "Offenses and Deviance Labels"
1. Presentations of Self	
a. emotions	too little emotion ("cold," "calculating," "masculine"); or too much emotion ("hysterical"); or various "wrong" emotions (different types of "mental illness").
b. nonverbal communication	"masculine" gestures, postures, use of space, touching, etc.
c. appearance	"plain," "unattractive," "masculine," "overweight," "fat," "old," "drab," "poorly made up"; or "overly made up," "flashy," "cheap."
d. speech and interaction	"unladylike," "bossy," "competitive," "aggressive"; or "timid," "mousy," "nonentity."
2. Marriage/Maternity	
a. marital	"spinster," "old maid"; or "unmarried," "divorcee," "widow"; or "unwed mother"; or "sleeps around."
b. maternity	voluntary childlessness ("selfish"); or "barren"; or abortion ("killer"); or "unwed" mother; or "unmaternal," "unfit mother," etc.
3. Sexuality	
a. behavior	"oversexed," "nymphomaniac," "promiscuous," "loose," "cheap," "whore"; or "cock-teaser," "cold," "frigid."
b. orientation	"butch," "dyke," "queer," etc.
4. Occupational Choice	in a "man's job," "tough," "aggressive," "castrating," "ball-buster," etc.
5. "Deviance Norms"	norm violation "inappropriate" for females (e.g., armed robber, political revolutionary).

Source: Edwin Schur, *Labeling Women Deviant* 1984:53, McGraw-Hill Inc., Reproduced with permission of The McGraw-Hill Companies.

violent, they are indeed "acting like girls"—including as righteously furious young women.

The Gender of Aggression

Traditionally, aggression has been framed as genderless (ironically, meaning male). A considerable literature in psychology, biology, social work, and criminology now focuses on gender and aggression, including a new and growing body of work on girls' aggression and violence. The degree to which aggression is biologically predictable or socially conditioned continues to be measured in epidemiological, medical, criminological, psychological, and other literatures on violence, and much of that work continues to neglect to engage critically with the social and cultural meanings of gender in the study of violence.[15]

The Office of Juvenile Justice and Delinquency Prevention (OJJDP) uses standard Federal Bureau of Investigation definitions. Violent offenses include murder and nonnegligent manslaughter, kidnapping, violent sexual assault, robbery, and aggravated assault. Serious nonviolent offenses include burglary, grand larceny, motor vehicle theft, arson, weapons offenses, and drug trafficking. Juvenile delinquency statistics, studies, and texts generally find that the serious, violent, and chronic offender is male, belongs to a gang, fights with weapons, assaults, car-jacks, and commits arson or robbery. Boys, not girls, sell and buy guns.[16]

"Community violence" and "youth violence" are two phrases criminologists use to frame boys' violence. Community and youth, hence male, violence is differentiated from sexual harassment, domestic violence, rape, child molesting, sexual abuse, and other kinds of violence that, in the main, involve women and girls. Seeking a master narrative that elevates boys' violence to the level of the most crucial social problems of our time, studies of community violence and youth violence contributed greatly to our understanding of the rise in violence in low-income communities in the 1980s and 1990s but did little to deepen our understanding of how different acts of violence are differently gendered, how girls experience violence, and under what conditions young women perpetrate violence.[17]

When aggression is gendered as masculine, it is considered in a variety of modes: it has been argued that sexual abuse makes boys act out; that boys' violence is hormonal, normal, natural, instrumental, more overt than girls, and more prevalent among males because boys have access to guns. Intriguingly, even though psychology has noticed that boys act out after abuse, few criminological theories assert that boys' violent offenses are responses and reactions to early sexual victimization. It would not generally be argued in the gang literature, for example, that the community and youth violence committed by "homeboys, dope fiends, legits, and new jacks" was due to a huge proportion of boys having been repeatedly sexually humiliated and sodomized in early childhood. Such theorizing, besides being incorrect, would simply go against the grain of normative ways of understanding male violence.[18]

Boys' violence has also been linked to hormonal influences. Studies show that boys exhibit high amounts of aggressive behavior because of hormonal flux. Some criminologists argue that violence is genetic, biologically male, or developmentally natural. In this sense, boys' violence is linked to normal masculinity: "boys will be boys." Boys commit more violent crimes than girls do, and boys' violence is more often linked to normal masculinity than is girls' violence ever linked to normal femininity. The sociobiology of male aggression has developed into a large and prosperous subfield in psychology, social work, and criminology and is enjoying a renewal as a cottage industry of training sessions and government-subsidized research projects.[19]

Male violence has also been theorized further as instrumental and is contrasted with girls' relational violence. Many argue that boys' violence is not personal, covert, emotional, or relational but is instead designed to bring about an achievement or material outcome of some kind. Urban theorists and policymakers at OJJDP analyze youth aggression in the context of gangs. Boys, it is argued, are violent because they are required to be violent in gangs. Theories of gang violence build on the notion of the instrumental nature of boys' violence.[20]

Most reports and studies of delinquency and violence in gangs neglect the role that emotions such as anger play as an animator of behavior. Except for Jack Katz's seminal but ahistorical account of how perpetrating crime feels, much of the criminological literature lacks theories of emotion.[21] What could be more emotional and relational than belonging to a gang? It remains a theoretical mystery how girls' aggression is empirically more emotional and relational than boys'. Young men's involvement in gangs is all about relationships, loyalty, and family. For boys' to attack rival gang members (who they are in relationships with) and their own family members (their girlfriends and sisters) is about as relational as it gets. In addition, like boys, many girls claim that they perpetrated aggression against "some old lady" or another complete stranger in order to get victims' purses, gold chains, or other such items. Girls' violence has been theorized as relational because it encompasses strong feelings that need immediate expression, is done in the heat of passion because girls communicate and respond in emotional terms, and mostly hurts those whom girls love. In this sense, the notion that violence is gendered is not new; what is new is that anger, aggression, and violence have begun to be characterized as feminine.[22]

Studies of girls' aggression offer various frames for understanding it. One binary theory of gender and aggression involves the above-mentioned notion of relational aggression—that (mostly girls') behavior is intended to harm relationships through gossip, rumors, facial expressions, and organizing peer rejection. Another dichotomy under which aggression has been studied is through the notion of a gender normative framework. In such research, gender nonnormative aggression for girls is overt, while gender nonnormative aggression for boys is relational. Overt masculine aggression includes physical and verbal aggression; covert female aggression is analyzed in the context of interpersonal relationships, as social or relational aggression. Social aggression includes "actions directed at damaging another's self esteem, social status, or both, and includes behaviors such as facial expressions of disdain, cruel gossiping, and the manipulation of friendship patterns."[23] These dichotomies shed light on the experiences of youth in the juvenile legal system even though samples for those studies did not include children involved in the system.[24]

Relational aggression includes the idea that girls are aggressive toward known victims and seek to disrupt relations through indirect tactics. The theory argues that girls' violence is relational and different from boys because girls respond with violence inside harmful family relationships or with peers at school. Researchers point out that girls attack people known to them: hitting mothers, stepfathers, mother's boyfriends, their own boyfriends/girlfriends, fathers, brothers, caregivers, other girls. Among adult women, an estimated 62 percent of violent offenders (contrasted with only 36 percent of violent men) had a prior relationship with the victim as an intimate, relative, or acquaintance.[25]

In addition to researchers, practitioners and social service providers remarked to me (constantly) that girls were more emotional and relational than boys. Gender-specific training in probation departments around the nation teach curriculum developed by gender specialists and the OJJDP in 2000.[26] In one gender-specific training in a northern California facility, approximately forty adults listened as trainers spent about an hour explaining that girls take a long time to trust adults and other girls because girls need to "be in relationship." As one trainer said, "Some say that girls are harder to deal with, but it is not that. They are just more emotional and have less trust because they are so hurt. It takes a long time to work with girls to get them to trust you. They are always testing you out. But if you keep working with them, eventually they will trust you, and then you can teach them" (Gender-Specific Training for Detention Counselors, Summer 1999).

Adults in the study who worked with the girls in juvenile corrections commonly described girls' violent behavior as a shift in gender roles. They reported that violent girls were "acting like males." As one white, middle-aged probation officer explained, "Claudia thinks she's one of the guys. She's not very ladylike, and that gets her into a lot of trouble. Her first response is to start jumpin' bad [being physically aggressive], but we're working on it!" To a certain extent these comments are insightful—girls were severely sanctioned, formally and informally, when they used masculine survival strategies that involved aggression, the use of weapons, physical assaults, and violence.[27]

However, the situation is more complex, as girls are doing more than just acting like boys—that it is to say, if acting like boys includes masking hurt feelings and sadness with anger, aggression, or violence, as gender norms for males dictate. Contemporary advice for nice girls persists in exhorting them to subvert anger into hurt, depression, or guilt.[28] Psychologist Jean Baker Miller points out that "while our culture constantly evokes anger, it also places constraints on the expression of anger. The constraints for women are different, and more restrictive, than those for men. Women's assigned subordinate position generates anger."[29] Baker Miller goes on to note that cultural concepts of femininity serve to characterize women's expression of anger as pathological. When boys express anger, it is considered a normal part of being a boy, of gender socialization. When girls express anger, it is linked to some pathology.

In such an argument, girls are not allowed a normal anger. Commentators often link girls' anger and aggression to previous victimization, but not that of boys. In one study, boys' were characterized as acting out in response to abuse, whereas girls were found to "act in."[30] Acting in was defined as being depressed, having suicidal ideation, or self-mutilating. This finding illuminates one way in which the norms for expressing anger are gendered. For that matter, findings in that study illuminated one way that gender norms among scholars and practitioners allowed for the anger of girls to be seen (or not seen). Many researchers, across disciplines, now observe that, for girls, entrance to juvenile corrections can emanate from childhood or adolescent trauma that leads to later aggressive or violent outbursts.

Normalizing Aggression

Many in juvenile corrections, youth advocacy, and feminist academia agree and lament that American popular culture seems to be drowning in images of violence, the language of violence, and representations of acts of violence.

Relaxed prohibitions against expressing anger and rage contribute to a widespread, low-level culture of frustration and anger in the twenty-first century United States. In popular discourse, U.S. dominant culture has been constituted since the mid-1980s as litigious, gun crazy, violent, and argumentative—a discourse that girls live in and contribute to as well. One study published by the American Sociological Association begins, "American society is engulfed in a world of violence."[31] Terms such as *slam dance, date rape, road rage,* and *friendly fire* slip into political, social, and media discourse every day. Other violent-tinged phrases, such as *nuke 'em, drive-by,* and *school shootings,* seep into common conversation and have become shorthand for serious public issues. A barrage of violent cultural images is directed at the mainstream populace constantly through television, print advertisements, billboards, and films. In 2002, one self-help phrase was made into a hit Hollywood film, *Anger Management,* a reflection, perhaps, of the fact that lessons in aggression prevention, self-regulation, and emotion control were being made available to preschool children. Boxing and girl-fight films are box office hits (no pun intended). Annoyance and irritation in general are freely expressed on the job, in the supermarket, and even violently, as such expressions become normalized.[32]

The discourse is not merely terminological. A 1997 study by the American Automobile Association found that in more than ten thousand aggressive-driving incidents caused by drivers' anger, at least 218 people were killed and another 12,610 were injured.[33] As depicted in Illustration 4.2, the idea of violence invading families and society has penetrated advertising campaigns for national service organizations. Work is also framed in the news as the site of deadly violence. The U.S. Department of Labor reported that 551 people were victims of homicide on the job in 2004.[34] Violence in the entertainment media has also come to the fore. Scholars focus on the contemporary phenomenon of violence as a form of public entertainment on television, and a debate rages over whether popular censorship would help: "Is it alarmist or merely sensible to ask about what happens to the souls of children nurtured, as in no past society, on images of rape, torture, bombings, and massacres that are channeled into their homes from infancy?"[35] Tragically, for girls and families in this study, the images not only were channeled in but were acted out right in front of their eyes in their living rooms.

Normative expressions of hostility are culturally derived and socially controlled.[36] Anger is a socially shaped form of communication. Its expression, meanings, and responses are socially conditioned as current cultural conditions promote hopelessness about resolving interactions and struggles that give rise to anger. New expressions of so-called masculine gender strategies of resistance—such as when Claudia spoke proudly about "kicking ass"—have emerged into the popular consciousness and girls' behavior. Mugging- and self-defense classes are regularly offered to urban girls at conferences and on all-female college campuses. Kick-boxing classes, offered in health clubs, emerged as a new fad in the 1990s. *Girlfight*, a 2000 film about a girl who is filled with rage and is passionate about boxing, was a beloved favorite whenever we screened it for girls in lock-up. Other films featuring young women boxers got Academy Award nominations.

Court-Involved Girls' Violence

The accounts of young women being adjudicated delinquent reveal the social logic at the epicenter of girls' violent behavior. To understand girls' violence, one must include both a psychosocial framing of adolescence and a critical understanding of connections among

If you asked your child how you act behind the wheel,
would you be embarrassed by the answer?

As a public service, your friends at AAA remind you to drive with courtesy.

Illustration 4.2. AAA campaign against road rage. Used with permission

patriarchy, racism, and poverty. When we broaden the contexts in which we see girls' violent acts occurring to include the realities of the lives of young women, such as their chronic and severe exposure to sexual abuse, sexual harassment, and misogynistic girl hating, we deepen our understanding of their perpetration of violence and can analyze the link between girls' vulnerable social position—unprotected by adult intervention or material advantage—and girls' aggression. Given the moral horizons of gendered opportunities from which urban disadvantaged girls have to "choose," their choices, while not always legal, make social sense.

An archaic theoretical and empirical separation of community violence from family violence, in addition to providing for the meaningless exclusion of girls, blurs our ability to see girls' violence. Defining community violence and domestic violence as exclusive can result in glossing over the situations girls face, witness, experience, and perpetrate in the natural flow of their everyday lives. As many of the studies cited in Chapter Two show, girls who live in poverty and underserved neighborhoods may be in danger of being victimized whether in their apartments or on their way to the store, school, or work. The everyday harshness, anger, fear, and physical abuse, sexual taunting in the street and gendered inequities at home make all violence, including so-called domestic violence, in effect, community violence for girls.

So, for me, the first component in understanding the situations of girls who were adjudicated for violent offenses was broadening traditional definitions of juvenile violence as being only about guns, guys, and gangs to include ways in which anger and aggression were uniquely experienced by girls. The second component was listening closely to violence-involved young women as they revealed that they had been raised amid violence and that witnessing violent acts normalized violence for them, with detrimental consequences.

Episodes of violence did not sort neatly by "type of girl" and barely by type of situation. Among the violent offenders were white suburban girls, working-class white girls, girls of color, girls who regularly got high, and girls who didn't. In interviews with over one hundred court-involved young women, I found that no one "type" of girl was consistently arrested for violent offenses. However, certain socioemotional events and situational locations of unequal power produced patterns that stimulated violence among girls.

Episodes of violent offense cannot be bundled into neat and discrete categories by "type of girl." And the contexts of any offense are not exclusive—usually, several factors are operating at once, as young women's narratives reveal. No one universal explanation fits all circumstances. For example, girls may respond to and with misogyny, homophobia, and self-defense all in one event. The young women adjudicated for violent offenses challenged gender and emotional norms in varied ways. Their offense narratives fell into several, sometimes overlapping categories. They most often described their violence as self-defense; girls, like women, were compelled to crime. They shared evidence of their hurt turned to vengeful rage; framed violence as a function of having been victimized; revealed it as imbibed misogyny; explained their violent offenses as fighting back from harassment or responding to rape, incest, and molestation and as a seeming unavoidable outcome of their normalized everyday violence; felt confused and angry about sexual desire and alternative sexual practices (their own and others); and mistrusted, devalued, and seemingly hated other girls and adult caregivers.[37]

Although many of the narratives were one-sided and often contradictory and confused, the accounts of young women who were being adjudicated for violent offenses included intimate partner violence (Cora), fighting back from direct sexual attack (Mylen); being coerced into a violent incident by an older male friend (Monica); fighting with a family member (often a mother, brother, or father) (Elizabeth); and openly fighting another girl street-style (Claudia), some cases of which are discussed below. Elsewhere, aggression as a response to feeling disrespected has been described as an instrumental and singularly masculine code of street conduct.[38] But many of the accounts of the girls in this study contradicted former theories about gender-coded practices: girls admitted to starting fights because someone looked at them "funny," or in order to get something they wanted, or to fight off feelings of humiliation, rage, hurt, and fear. Sometimes girls were proud of their actions; other times they spoke with regret about their fighting.

Because these experiences could have been, and often are, mediated in more affluent settings by alternatives, support, and privilege, I came to see girls' use of violence as largely the deployment of power by the powerless.[39] Elizabeth Martin's account exemplifies that of other young women who were being adjudicated for seemingly violent offenses that could be seen as the deployment of this weapon of the weak.

Family Violence: Elizabeth Martin

While being driven home from a juvenile facility in northern California, Elizabeth Martin assaulted her father in the car. The bright, blond, sixteen-year-old girl from suburban northern California was now detained again:

> Like, I was in detention in Oakland, and my Dad came to pick me up from there. On the way home, I told my Dad, "Give me the cell phone—I gotta call my boyfriend." So he's all, "No way—you are in big trouble." So all I did was kind of show him this little knife on my key chain, and he goes all ballistic; and when we got home, he calls the police *again*, and now I'm in here for assault with a deadly weapon or brandishing a knife or something like that!

"Like, my dad is *always* criticizing my mom," is how Elizabeth first put it, gradually revealing that ferocious battles took place weekly in the house, usually ending with her father hitting her and her mother. Her detention filed noted that Elizabeth had to be taken to Children's Hospital after her father broke her arm during one of his attacks. She said she preferred living at her boyfriend's house (he was nineteen years old) because, she said ominously, "He really helped me after I tried to kill myself."

Elizabeth's story was one of trouble in her family, most often with her father. It was as if she and her father were in a duel to see who was stronger, who was in charge, who was going to gain power over Elizabeth's life.

> Like, this is all I did. I borrowed my mom's keys—she keeps them hanging behind the back door—and all we did was went to the mall

to do just a little shopping. I knew I shouldn't of have 'cause my Dad had told me I couldn't go, but we had already planned it! I mean, God! . . . So, I'm all, like, hungry and all, and we shoot down Fruitvale to McDonald's 'cause Sherry, she's one of my best friends, she thinks she'll see her man, Todd, there. So, anyway, like, I'm all, "Let's get out of here 'cause I'm gonna get in trouble if I don't get back soon." But, like it's starting to get dark now, so we go back home to my place.

So, like, I get there, and my mom is all bent out of shape; and she and my dad had called the police and said somebody stole the car! I'm all, God! What are you *thinking*? But then they, like, *grab* my *purse* and find my little bit of pot in there, and I'm all, oh shit, I'm in trouble now. They are gonna, like, make a *whole* big deal.

So my fucking father (excuse my French) starts grabbing me and shoving me, and my mom starts yelling, "Jerry, stop it!" and everything just gets totally weird. So, like we all have this big fight, but when the police get there, they take me! They put *me* in the car, and I'm all, "Let me get my shoes!" I can't go with my slippers, and they take me with my slippers! That's why I'm so mad at my dad.

From Elizabeth's testimony and her small file, it was easy to see that she felt she was not being listened to, even as unreasonable as she was being, or cared for, even as she demonstrated disrespect toward her parents. Elizabeth's case is illustrative for several reasons. First, it is unusual for a white, middle-class, suburban young woman to be in detention for aggravated assault. Accounts such as Elizabeth's interrupt the media's stereotypical refrains about African Americans, poverty, and violence. As detailed previously, more girls of color than white girls are in trouble with the law for violent offenses. However, girls of color are disproportionately represented in many phases of the system. The court system in general disproportionately adjudicates the disadvantaged.

Second, Elizabeth's story typifies the situation of many teenage girls who get into what in another era or another setting would be routine family conflicts but now end up with assault charges. Third, Elizabeth's story illustrates the use of police discretion. The law enforcement officer originally detained her for drug possession, but after she "showed" her father a "little knife" in the car on the way home, he returned and arrested her for aggravated assault with a deadly weapon. Clearly, Elizabeth believed she had no way to be heard and cared for in her family, short of her aggressive attempts to get her way.

Family violence was not the only violence that young women in the study experienced. The most painful narratives to hear were accounts of fighting and physical aggression among young women. Misogyny and homophobia expressed in young women's interpersonal relations were not uncommon, and one form was exemplified in Cora's story.

Offenses by Lesbian, Bisexual, Transgender, Queer, and Questioning Youth: Cora Winfield

Cora Winfield declared, "I get drunk and kick my girlfriend's ass just like my dad gets drunk and kicks my mom's!" Raised in a white, East Coast, working-class family by a proud Irish father and U.S.-born mother, this fifteen-year-old's knowledge of her homosexuality was complicated by the homophobia and misogyny in her family of origin.

Expressing a disturbing confusion about her future life choices, Cora talked to me about how she wasn't going to "stay gay." "I ain't gonna be gay my whole life, you know. I probably won't stay gay. I can't take it. Hidin,' pretendin,' gettin' hassled all the time at school or even just hangin' out—I can't take it. I'm always stressin' over where the next fight is gonna go down. I'm sick of being called 'lezzie.' I kick it fine with my homeys. They just treat me like another lil' dude anyways. I don't know about stayin' gay."

Cora shared her rational assessment of the price she believed she would have to pay as she goes through life as a lesbian. Maybe she hoped she could avoid that price by choosing not to be gay. Although it may not be possible for her, she did show a kind of bravado and, ironically, positive thinking by believing she had control over her sexual orientation and her resulting status in society. If Cora had had role models who could show her that it is possible to be a lesbian and have a satisfying, relatively safe life in a supportive and accepting community, she might have lived with less risk of self-destruction.

Cora was lanky and long-legged. Her dirty-blond hair, bobbed straight and tucked behind her ears, fell forward onto her cheeks as she hung her head and talked. She was clearly frightened and depressed, and I found her plan to not be gay her whole life to be a particularly disturbing confession, given the high rate of suicide ideation and attempts among lesbian, bisexual, transgender, queer, and questioning (LBTQ) youth. Experts claim that LBTQ youth are more than three times as likely as other students to report a suicide attempt.[40]

The middle of a chapter about girls and violence is an odd place to locate a discussion about lesbianism. It is not my intention to infer that either discussion has any particular relation to the other, except in cases such as Cora's, where battery by an intimate is concerned. However, it is crucial to attend to the situation of queer girls involved in the court system.

Sexual identity can be a complex developmental process beginning consciously at puberty or before. In the United States since the 1980s,

research shows that a societywide homophobia has provoked a disproportionate number of lesbian teens to drop out of school, run away from
home, be homeless, medicate with street drugs and alcohol, perform
survival sex (trade sex for money, food, or shelter) and prostitution, and
attempt suicide. Those who work with gay and lesbian teen populations
describe drug and alcohol use as deriving from self-hatred, withdrawal,
and anger, and as a way to hide from problems or attempt to fit in with
peers.[41]

Homophobia consists of feelings and expressions of confusion, disgust, anger, hatred, or fear toward people who have sexual, romantic, or
loving longings for other people of the same sex or gender. Descriptions
of the events surrounding these feelings—which girls expressed toward
each other and toward themselves—emerged from the accounts of girls'
troubles and their anger-related offending.

Growing up gay is a challenge for queer and questioning youth in
the general population (not only for children in trouble with the law).
Few data specifically reflect the experiences of this population, and gathering such data is complicated. One of the challenges noticed by adults
in my study who worked with queer youth on the streets and in the
system was that these youth were further harassed after they entered
the legal system. Instead of considering their victimization after they
were forced out of their homes and schools or kicked out of their families, judges charged LBTQ youth who were brought into detention for
drug use and sales, running away, prostitution, and assaults as delinquent offenders.[42]

Girls' misinformation about lesbian and homosexual history, experience, desire, and practice may be related to their striking out in anger
and fear toward each other.[43] The effects of homophobia, both on queer
girls who are victims of violence and on girls who perpetrate violence
because of it, account for a minor, but growing, proportion of aggression
in girls' offending behaviors. As one scholar has noted, "The separation
of a youth's homoerotic passion from the socially sanctioned act of heterosexual dating can generate self-doubt, anger and resentment, and can
ultimately retard or distort the development of interpersonal intimacy
during the adolescent years."[44]

Contemporary adolescence includes a sense of entitlement to explore sexualities. Yet, young women's decisions to explore lesbian desire—or their getting caught exploring it—often results in social exclusion
and marginalization, even though from 1 to 15 percent of the U.S. population is estimated to identify as predominantly gay, lesbian, bisexual,
or questioning. These girls are invisible, often isolated, dealing alone
with social stigma and cultural rejection. Researchers estimate that if,
as some experts say, 10 percent of the population is gay or lesbian, one in

every five families has a gay or lesbian child. Others estimate the homosexual population to be much lower, maybe around 2 to 4 percent.[45]

In an ominous development for young women struggling simultaneously with their sexuality, self-love, and staying out of juvenile corrections, homophobia was on the rise in schools and gay bashing was reportedly widespread in the late 1990s. Ten percent of girls reported "being called lesbian" in a national survey of sexual harassment in schools. In a poll of thousands of the highest-achieving high school students in the United States, almost half admitted prejudice against gays and lesbians. A 2000 study of students in western Massachusetts found that young lesbians and bisexual girls experienced more sexual harassment (72 percent) than did heterosexual girls (63 percent). Specific challenges court-involved girls may face have been noted by human rights groups, such as that homosexual youth may be doubly punished in the system, both for their offense and for their sexual identity.[46]

Gay, lesbian, bisexual, transgender, queer, and questioning (GLBTQ) youth face qualitatively different challenges than straight youth do. Because of misinformation and prejudice, queer youth receive the brunt of social scorn as they develop sexual selves. Sixteen percent of runaways in one study in Los Angeles identified themselves as lesbian, gay, or bisexual. One study of inner-city street youth found that 25 percent reported that they were lesbian, gay, or bisexual. Social service agencies estimate the proportions of homeless youth who identify as gay, lesbian, or bisexual to be as high as 38 percent. Anger, stigma, and self-hatred combine to create immense suffering among this invisible population of youth.[47]

There is no safe cultural space for girls to explore same-sex desire: rarely are girls given open social and cultural permission to explore lesbian sexuality and identity as a normative option. Some LBTQ teenagers—especially young women with more butch (conventionally masculine) demeanor like Cora Winfield—reported that they suffered such vilification at home or in school because of their sexual orientation that they were forced out into the streets. LBTQ youth come to the attention of juvenile authorities and psychiatric facilities in what are believed to be disproportionate numbers through these and other unique processes.[48]

The growing, visible presence of LBTQ youth in correctional facilities had become an area of mounting concern to feminists and youth advocates by the early 2000s. As with the population of lesbian teenagers in the general population, it is not possible to make statistical or demographical claims about LBTQ youth—including youth of color—caught in the net of juvenile corrections. Little data about them—both legal and psychiatric—are collected or available. There is no way to know who they are: finding out would require all LBTQ youth to declare their sexual orientation on official records, and research suggests that doing so would not be safe.[49]

According to 1997 testimony before a Human Rights Commission hearing in San Francisco, GLBTQ youth constitute less than 1 percent of juveniles arrested. One study of the New York juvenile justice system estimated that 4 to 10 percent of the juvenile delinquent population identified as GLBTQ. Another writer estimates that homosexual youth make up about 20 percent of the fifty thousand youths forcibly institutionalized annually. And studies show that the *Diagnostic and Statistical Manual of Mental Disorders–IV* diagnoses of "sexual dysfunction" and "gender identity disorder" have provided pathways for girls to be admitted into adolescent psychiatric wards.[50]

Court personnel are simply not equipped to meet the unique needs of GLBTQ youth. The system is not set up in any way for the comfort of transgender youth: living areas and, increasingly, classrooms, are divided into males and females. Sleeping, showering, and dressing become harrowing locations of harassment for gender-explorative youth and for their frightened and ill-prepared fellow detainees.

Despite the absence of systematic data, anecdotal evidence confirms the reality that lesbianism and bisexuality in the lives of teenage girls are linked to challenges they face in juvenile corrections systems in various ways. In my study, girls talked about their own lesbian sexual identities only after cautiously testing me. Many interviews began by their saying that they had a boyfriend, and only toward the end did they admit to being with other girls. The girls' caution was warranted, given the lack of accurate information and inappropriate behavior I witnessed among the adults in juvenile corrections. Alarmingly, staff who worked with young women and decided their fate in lock-up said, for example, "I don't believe in that life-style" when referring to being required to meet the unique needs of lesbian or bisexual wards.

My sample included an unusually high proportion of girls who confided that their sexual interests were other than heterosexual (nine out of one hundred). I did not assume they were "straight" and was careful to use language that would indicate that I did not assume so. A little more than one-third of participants talked about lesbian relationships, about concerns about other girls being gay, or about family members being gay. Homosexuality in their families was a concern that they brought up. Girls talked about what they thought about other young women who were gay. It was typical to hear girls exploring their ideas about same-sex interest in these ways:

Me and my girl kick it nice and easy when I'm on the outs. It's cool, but my family don't know about it. They think we just friends. My parents would kill me if they ever knew. But I ain't worried—maybe it's just a phase I'm in. (Joanne Billingsly, fifteen years old, assault and battery on school grounds)

I got one friend in here. We always together. We write notes to the same place, and we know the same people. So other girls thinks we gay. But I don't trip—they's a lot of gays up in here but I'm not one. (L'Teshia Williams, sixteen years old, drug sales)

Girls should act her real self—even with makeup, a guy will want her for her real self. Some girls will disrespect themselves and get with a lot of guys. I see boys—all of 'em are dogs until they find the right girl. If a girl is too easy—he'll just do her. I think girls become gay because they don't like guys. They had too much of them. I had a friend; she was pretty—but she never like guys. (LaShondra Wolfe, seventeen years old, weapons possession)

I like guys all right—but I'm attracted to older females. (Claudia Sereno, seventeen years old, assault and weapons possession)

This boy called me a dumb broad for wanting to be a car mechanic, so I kicked his ass. Then I got kicked out of my placement. I'm straight—but you could leave me in a room for a couple hours with Drew Barrymore and a bottle of Hennessey . . . she is sooo cute! (Tank Bremmer, fourteen years old, probation violation)

As these quotes illustrate, the girls approached same-sex relationships in a variety of ways. Other research yields similar accounts. One young woman testified that when she was locked in detention, she was never given a roommate because she was a lesbian and that special showering arrangements were made to prevent her from showering with other girls. Another girl recounted her experience while living in a group home: "I prepared myself to get in a fight when I went downstairs later that night for dinner." This young woman had been driven out of her house by her homophobic mother, but the girls in the group home finally accepted her. Ominous findings from one Human Rights Commission report found that some youth enter the juvenile justice system for hate-related crimes against GLBTQ people.[51]

Battery among lesbian couples was another hidden and growing problem among girls in trouble.[52] Three young women from my study revealed that they had beaten up their girlfriends/lovers.

I was involved with a hooker—she was bisexual. I was always buyin' her things, but we fought a lot. I beat her up off crystal [from being high on methamphetamine], so I caught an ADW [assault with a deadly weapon charge] off that. (Claudia Sereno, seventeen years old, assault and weapons possession)

I beat my girl 'cause she ran away with Miguel. First we left him, but then he started buggin' her. Then we fought. I beat her bad. (Leslie Rollins, fifteen years old, simple assault)

Cora Winfield learned her anger and physical fighting at home and pays for it in public facilities; cases like hers constitute a serious challenge for adults who must figure out how to make the world safe for lesbian teenagers. In Cora's case, for example, discomfort with her own sexuality, turned aggressively outward, resulted in her getting into trouble emotionally and legally. Her fighting stance, the result of having learned violence in the family as well as a plea for attention to her unique needs, made sense to her as she struggled to find meaning in her experiences. Cora talked about her situation, her fears, and her father.

My father is some bigwig in his company, and he thinks he owns the whole damn world! He thinks he can push me and my mom around. If he had any idea about me and my girl, he will kill me. And now he's gonna find out because they're gonna tell him I'm in here on a DV [domestic violence] charge. Like they're gonna tell him I beat up *my girlfriend*—not just some girl. Shit! I am so totally fucked!

I hate this stupid life. I ain't never heard anyone had it so bad as me. I cannot always be like this. This is the worst! I super need me a cold one [beer] just to get through today.

The main thing Cora had going for her at that time was luck—luck to be in a facility where service providers could get her some support. In the hall where she was being held, I passed members of a peer-led queer-youth advocacy project on their way to visit her. Countless other teens go through the agonies of adolescence feeling this hopeless, angry, and sad with no access to community at all. As an adolescent, a young lesbian, and a batterer, Cora faced unique challenges that would require much peer, family, and community support.

Arguably, the eroticization of female adolescent sexuality is promoted by corporate sponsorship (for example, consider the much-discussed wet kiss between an aging Madonna and teen star Britney Spears during prime-time television's annual MTV Awards in 2003). Even so, the state lags in its sensitivity to the notions that lesbian desire is a legitimate experience, that being gay is about more than just sex, that homophobia is devastating especially for young people forming their sense of self, and that elimination of prejudice is essential to fair treatment of LBTQ girls in the juvenile justice system.[53]

Girl-on-Girl Misogyny: Claudia Sereno

Another pattern I found among girls in the system who were expressing intense anger was to say that they hated other girls. Other researchers have observed this development.[54] The degree to which they mistrusted and detested other girls was disturbing. Many young women talked about growing up watching their mothers being devalued and seeing women denigrated in the popular culture in the United States.

> I saw my mom get raped one night when I'm nine [years old]. Our car broke down, and these men came to "help" us." (Sara Leighton, sixteen years old, fighting on school property)

> My dad talks all mean to my mom all the time—she is so stupid, she just takes it! (Cora Winfield, fifteen years old, domestic violence)

Girls absorb misogyny from the larger culture, particularly when they witness women being treated less respectfully and as if they were less important than men. Absorbing misogyny harms young women in two ways: it contributes to so-called girl-on-girl violence, and, as we will see later in the chapter, it prevents them from forming the friendships that could help them thrive, or escape other violence, in their lives. Friendship has been framed as crucial to girls' success in adolescence.[55]

Claudia Sereno's mother and grandmother mostly raised her because her father was "in jail somewheres." Claudia's mother did not work; they all lived with her grandmother until her grandmother died. Claudia quietly explained: "My mom left my *papi* when I was still not born. He hit my mother when she was pregnant with me. He didn't want me to be born. So my mama left him." Claudia said she was in juvenile hall for "goin' crazy on this little bitch from school." "We got into it at the corner of B'way and Feldman. She said she didn't like the way I looked at her! I'm all, wassup wi' that? So we got into it. . . . Anyways, I feel like if I do somethin' it's on me; I get myself into this' and I have to suffer the consequences. Ain't nobody's fault but my own. I'm goin' to be way better when I get out."

Claudia had a history of drug abuse, trauma, and separation from her caregivers: "They took me away from my mama when she was in rehab—I was nine years old. I went with my *abuela* [grandmother], who I love so much cuz my mama—you know, she couldn't take care of us, you know. . . . But I tried to commit suicide when I was thirteen. I took pills. I don't like to talk about it, *tú sabes* [you know]. Sometimes I wake up in the middle of the night and just cry and cry."

Claudia ran away from home for the first time when she was ten years old "because my aunt was beating me." Claudia said she was trying to figure out why she was always fighting with girls at school. "I already got two ADWs on me! Listen, so I thought, um, *mira* . . . I tried to get pregnant with my boyfriend, but he told me, 'Get your life together, and I'll get you pregnant.' I told him, 'If I get my life together, I won't want *your* baby!'" Claudia confessed that she and her twenty-year-old boyfriend liked to get high on speed. She also eventually talked about a crush on a woman she liked. At times at odds with herself, this bright, clever, animated young woman, so full of life, definitely had a tendency to express herself in an assaultive manner. During many of our conversations in drab, institutional interview rooms in detention facilities and psychiatric wards, girls explained that they were "stressed and depressed" and did not know "how to handle their anger." They recounted stories about bloody fights with other girls, using weapons such as knives.

> I got kicked out of school so many times for fighting, whatever. See these scars? This scratch? They from fighting the other girls at school. I have a temper—I fight back. Girls jump me. I get in so many fights because females hate me. I have so many enemies. All my life girls been pickin' on me. Like, *mira,* I saw this girl in a phone booth, and she was lookin' at me funny. I hadda jump her, and I grabbed her gold chain around her neck. I don't like anyone frontin' me like that. (Claudia Sereno, seventeen years old, assault and weapons possession)

> There was a girl at school, and I gossiped about her behind her back. She beat me up. So I got a knife from the school kitchen and stabbed her twice in the back. (DanYelle Robertson, fifteen years old; assault with a deadly weapon: knife)

In their interviews, girls reported feeling plagued by unresolved arguments and fights with other girls and rival groups; they often skipped school because it did not feel safe. In 2003, 25 percent of high school girls surveyed reported having been in a fight at school at least once in the preceding year. Furthermore, girls feeling under siege by other girls at school is not just an inner-city problem. According to one government report, rural students were more likely than their urban and suburban counterparts to report being bullied at school.[56]

In addition to contributing to girl-on-girl violence, girls' misogyny prevented them from forming beneficial friendships with other girls. It is difficult to notice the absence of something, but after talking with young women in the harsh conditions on the units for many hours, I began to think not only about the experiences they did have but about the experiences they were missing. It dawned on me that their lives and accounts were devoid of the solidarity and healing found by forging friendships and drawing on healthy support from other girls and women. As Jatoma Ngiri, a social service provider at Girls First! Academy in Oakland, California, explained: "These girls need to learn to come together and work together. Working together is how they will heal. The girls are so divided and male-identified. When they come together, especially survivors of childhood abuse, they see how they have undermined their own success by staying apart. Working together *is* the healing—healing *is* the coming together."

Friendships to which system-involved young women might potentially turn for help and nurturing are hard to come by. Unlike young women in one study of girls' friendships who quarreled and then worked things out, young women caught up in the courts encounter endless difficulty navigating camaraderie with each other. Indeed, in one ethnography of mainstream girls' friendships, the author did not have to describe even one argument. Other work has notice girl-imbibed misogyny, although the girls were constituted as being mean, not violent.[57]

Psychologists have described friendships among youths as the "most rewarding and satisfying of all human relationships,"[58] a state sadly not evident in the lives of the majority of girls in this sample. Young women spoke about feeling disappointed, threatened, and bored by other girls and adult women. Girls sitting on correctional wards and units often talked about how much they mistrusted other young women: "They talk all about your business behind your back." They repeatedly said that they preferred to hang out with males; they complained that girls will "stab you in the back if you don't watch out," "females are triflin,'" and "I don't communicate a lot with girls because they talk too much and I have to beat them up."[59]

Conclusion

We need not fear noticing the (few) girls who feel angry, aggressive, and then perpetrate violence. Sexual, physical, and emotional abuse and neglect in their childhood and adolescence, in addition to feelings of hopelessness, worthlessness, and depression, contribute to their suppressed rage. In addition, from meeting and listening to the young women in this study, we can understand girls' anger as an agentic expression of femininity—a strong, assertive, human femininity. In the socialization of boys, aggression, toughness, and spirit are clearly delineated. But the role of anger and aggression for girls is less clear, and contextualizing young women's aggression elucidates varied ways that girls' aggression can be understood.

Young women in the study made logical sense of their behaviors as they described their lives and choices. They said repeatedly that they felt they committed violent offenses in order to escape the sexualization, gender oppression, and unbearable feelings that came up when they remembered unhealed trauma. Girls recounted that expressing their fears and rage led them into angry confrontations:

> I think if I would have growed up in a better home, I wouldn't have so much anger, and I probably wouldn't be up in here. Weed helps, but my anger just keep on growin' in me. (Mona Montoya, fourteen, drunk and disorderly conduct)

> I threatened my foster mother with a knife and got sent up in here. I hope I don't go off again. . . . My daddy used to jus' go off on my mom, and he still in [jail] for beating on her. . . . I'm on the three-feet rule now, and that does help, but it's weird. (Rhoda Blumstein, fifteen years old)[60]

> I don't know what comes over me! My anger just comes up and out. I don't know what to do. . . . I hope I don't go off on one of these bitch-ass counselors up in here. (Claudia Sereno, seventeen years old, assault and weapons possession)

Taking their anger and aggression seriously relocates our attention to the structural conditions of their lives—such as growing up amid poverty and sexism—instead of focusing on the individual psychological failure of the girls surviving those conditions. In that context, girls' aggression is seen as a real response to real problems. The girls' accounts in this chapter showed their violence to be an expression of an imbibed misogyny and a way of attempting to fight back—as a power of the powerless. Laying bare the socioemotional roots of girls' aggression equips them with useful analyses for confronting their frustrations in healthy ways in the future. In this sense, court-involved girls perpetrate relational aggression because their aggression is in direct relation to their oppressive contexts.

That girls are expressing themselves violently has been difficult to see and analyze critically. Many adults who worked with the girls simply repeated the same refrains—"girls are harder to handle than boys," "girls are acting like males." Girls were perceived to be more manipulative than boys, emotionally out of control, prone to outbursts, constantly running away from placements, and violent in their responses to authority. However, these descriptions of girls' violent offenses did not place their offending behaviors in any structural or emotional framework—with any kind of social logic—that allowed for a clear intervention strategy.

The court-involved girls I interviewed knew that violent offending was wrong but did not refer to their anger, aggression, or violence as either unusual or masculine. We commit an injustice against those young women in desperate need of emotional, educational, political, and psychological assistance when we do not take a careful, critical look at the contexts of their experiences, their anger, and its expression through violence. In the recognition and validation of girls' anger lies the potential for the realization of gender-specific theory and praxis.

Trapped in This Game

Trapped in this game
unable to seek my way to the light
I'm strugglin' for my name
holdin' me back . . . but I'm goin' win this fight.

They say that you ain't ever goin' be shit
That you is just another nobody in tha world
They tell you that success ain't your way
That your life is 4 ever goin' be in tha dope game.

I may have been caught up
Stuck in the way it was played
But today I've taken anotha look
and began tah change my ways.

Everyday is a different struggle
Every struggle causes a different feeling
but for every feeling that I experience
I gotta keep my head up and keep steering.

I gotta stay strong and keep it real
Always keep in mind that this ain't no joke
My life is a precious given of the one up above
So never take another hit of dope.

—Gabby M.

5

Children,

Gender, and

Corrections

Sitting in my office in early 2004, I received an email forwarded to me by a colleague; it apparently was circulating as a plea on behalf of a detained youth:

> What if I told you that there is a little boy (age 15) who was born female and has acted and been treated as a little boy and lived and gone to school as a little boy since the age of three? Further, what if I told you that HE was caught up in the juvenile justice system and was being warehoused in the female section of the Juvenile Detention Center, complete with bras, panties, and female pronouns? How would he fit into your *Gender Specific Resource Manual*? . . . It appears that the facility and the people working there (I have not been allowed to go talk to them) have no gender skills that allow them to help him to become strong and happy. They cannot even find it in their hearts to use the appropriate pronouns. I found your information at [the Office of Juvenile Justice and Delinquency Prevention at the Department of Justice]. . . . It may be a new concept to some people, but little girls who want to be boys cannot be cured nor do they need to be. They need to be nurtured and loved just exactly like your manual suggests for "regular girls."

A group of legal advocates were in the process of developing model professional standards for the care and treatment of gay, lesbian, bisexual, transgender, queer, and questioning (GLBTQ) youth in juvenile systems, and the message highlighted a challenge they faced: How can the legal system be gender-specific yet not blind to gender orientation? The need to develop contemporary gender interventions to meet the unique needs of all children, including GLBTQ youth, who find themselves in the juvenile court system became increasingly urgent as awareness of the plight of GLBTQ youth in the system became apparent.[1]

The email illustrates a key contradiction: juvenile corrections means different things to different actors in the system. Girls who transgress the law are represented as violating mainstream gender norms for femininity and are labeled assaultive, oppositional, ungovernable, or incorrigible. Girls are constituted as too sexy: out on the streets at night or during school hours, promiscuous, or participating in prostitution. If they are selling drugs, their court files tie in a narrative about a so-called older male. Yet according to young women, their romantic pursuits, erotic experiences, and even their expressions of anger and aggression are reflective largely of the norms of their peers. A young woman does not see herself as promiscuous; she is just having a good time or falling in love or "handlin' her business." She fights when she becomes angry or threatened, when someone is looking at her "funny." She gladly takes "the fall for my homey" because he is her boyfriend.

At times, stakeholders' goals are at cultural cross-purposes in the corrections drama. Dominant, normative moral values are different for different groups: academics and experts who develop theories of race, gender, and sexuality, theories that drive state policies; representatives of the state who are charged with resocializing and punishing aberrant youth; the practitioners who implement the policies when they deliver direct services; and the youth themselves. The challenge and promise of juvenile corrections today include developing ways to simultaneously protect children's civil rights, honor differences among youth, uphold statutes and codes that are sometimes at variance with one another, and inculcate shared social values. This chapter highlights the challenges of simultaneously responding in theory and in practice to the gender, race, and sexuality of youth under state control.

In this chapter, I focus specifically on an appraisal of the development and implementation of one response to the rise in girls' arrests and detentions in the juvenile legal system: gender-responsive policies and programming. After outlining an etiology of gender-specific policies, I present examples from my observations, discuss the strengths of gender-appropriate interventions, highlight where we are mired in cultural myths about gender, and conclude with suggestions for improvements in the conceptualization of the policy and the delivery of programs. Key questions that this chapter answers include: How do gender-appropriate policies in juvenile systems work? How should they work? And what does it mean to be gender-responsive in the current cultural and political climate? Although the chapter focuses particularly on gender-specific projects, I further develop my contention that the term *gender* is relatively meaningless without qualifiers and analyses that consider multiple factors such as race, ethnicity, socioeconomic class, and sexual orientation. Listening to young women adjudicated delinquent and observing them with their caregivers continues to uncover ways that racism and poverty influence girls' choices as much as the lessons they are taught by those seeking to "correct" them.[2]

The Construction and Control of Gender in/by/and the Court

Feminist activism and scholarship in the 1970s produced new theories about gender and crime. Freda Adler's landmark study observed that female offending (at that time, traditionally prostitution and shoplifting) had begun to cross the boundaries into traditional masculine crimes (grand larceny, embezzlement, bank robberies, and violent crimes).[3] Theoretically, a new female assertiveness led women beyond traditional limits. Mainstream scholars prematurely refuted these early, gendered criminological theories, and, as with most feminist analyses of gender and crime, the theoretical thread was marginalized for decades. When the notion of gender as a hierarchical sex/gender system of power and social control gained theoretical prominence, the analytical focus shifted away from characteristics of offenders to institutions of social control. In the early 1980s, research challenged male-based morality theories, positing that girls learn differently and that girls and women operate morally differently from boys and men. By the early 2000s, in the everyday parlance of juvenile corrections, the term *gender* was synonymous with girl.[4]

Over a relatively short time, a considerable body of research on court-involved girls by sociologists, developmental psychologists, and scholars of jurisprudence began to contradict earlier, gender-neutral criminology. This contemporary work includes studying adult women in prison and gang girls and uncovers how patriarchal and postcolonial racialization works differently for girls and women involved in the legal systems than for men, the role that victimization plays in the lives of girls and women who come to the attention of authorities, and how having limited material resources affects girls' and women's choices in particular. The enduring theme throughout this seminal work is that gender matters. This research has been crucial in effecting a sea change in the handling of young and adult women prisoners and moving policy and governmental programs toward what has been termed a *gender-appropriate response.*[5]

Because of an overreliance on incarceration in the United States since the 1980s, arrest and detention rates for girls have increased. Confusion among scholars, practitioners, and advocates about what gender, race, and sexuality meant resulted in the uneven development of legal standards in juvenile justice and contributed, along with increasing detention rates for girls, to three important and related trends. First, a growing, disproportionate representation of a minority population of African American, Latino/Chicano, Native American, and Asian/Pacific Islander children became apparent in the juvenile court system. Second, an influx of girls into the legal system required the delivery of some kind of gender-responsive programming. Third, a slow but increasing necessity for attending to the urgent and unmet needs of GLBTQ youth in the juvenile court system became apparent among (feminist) caregivers.

Disproportionate minority representation (DMR), the disproportionate representation of children of color in the various stages of the juvenile legal system compared with their representation in the general population, has been established as a serious problem in all phases of the juvenile system; it is reflected in comparative rates for arrest, detention, sentencing, and long-term incarceration.[6] Since 1988, the Office of Juvenile Justice and Delinquency Prevention (OJJDP) has issued policy directives to immediately decrease disproportionate minority confinement. The term *minority* referred to nonwhite juveniles, but as we will see, the increasingly visible presence of girls and GLBTQ youth in corrections troubled this construction of the term.

Policy development in the second area, variously known as gender-appropriate, gender-responsive, and gender-specific programming, influences the handling of girls in the system. Gender interventions affect the juvenile system in three areas: in the laws and policies of the system as well as the statutes that govern its institutions; in the training of court personnel and staff; and in the delivery of adequate gender-appropriate projects in youth programming.[7]

Although gender-specific policy has concerned itself largely with the handling of girls, in the third trend, law and community services are responding increasingly to the unique needs of GLBTQ children in the system. Meeting this third challenge, I argue, may ultimately require broadening the approaches developed to address the two other trends (DMR and gender-specific programming). GLBTQ youth include youth of color and girls, and they may, therefore, experience the brunt not only of homophobia but also of racism and sexism. Gender-specific programming should, therefore, reflect behavior that treats GLBTQ people respectfully and humanely. Educating the staff, as well as the peer population of youth, about the needs and rights of GLBTQ youth presents an enormous challenge. However innovative the theory or policy may be, staff members deliver the programs and enforce the protection, thus translating theory into practice. Line staff who work on juvenile living units must have the opportunity to learn what it means, and what it does not mean, to be gender-explorative or nonheterosexual. Staff, along with young people, must be able to articulate and defend the basic legal, civil, and human rights of GLBTQ youth. Staff training is continually cited as an urgent priority by researchers, court personnel, and community advocates.[8]

Thus were gender-responsive policies and programming, while the site of much hope, charged with a great deal of work.

What Is Gender-Responsive Policy, and Why Now?

The alarming rise in arrests and detention of girls beginning in the 1980s spurred concern among government officials, the media, and community-based agencies. OJJDP responded to these trends by funding programs that were gender-responsive to minor female offenders. In the *Juvenile Justice and Delinquency Prevention (JJDP) Act of 1992*, the U.S. Congress linked gender-specific programming to federal funding. The OJJDP issued discretionary grants that specifically included support for programs designed to promote systemic change on behalf of girls involved in the juvenile justice system. The policy was developed by feminist criminologists, gender experts, and juvenile system leaders.[9]

Researchers and juvenile system personnel began to focus intensely on girls in the system, noticing patterns among female juvenile offenders. These efforts led to measuring and theorizing girl-related delinquency. Scholars identified a profile of the female juvenile offender by initiating large-scale survey projects in several states across the nation. These studies discovered that girls' needs are tied to specific and identifiable risk and protective factors to which gender-specific interventions could be addressed.

Researchers interviewed and observed probation officers and intake workers and examined case files as well in order to determine workers' unique gendered perceptions of court-involved girls and women. Criminal justice experts questioned whether justice for girls could be provided given the current ideology in the juvenile legal system. Ethnography in secure facilities revealed that gendered punishments were taking place. Girls and women were being reframed as violent and severely mentally challenged when they deployed tactics of agentic resistance to oppression. Even though the majority of girls and women in the criminal legal system had been victims of sexual and violent crimes, victimization and its after-effects were being injudiciously characterized as risk factors for future offending, instead of as constituting a serious health need. Critical analysis revealed the danger of degendering violence by insinuating that girls are just as violent as boys. Researchers argued that the increase in arrests for girls for violent offenses was best explained by a change in police attitudes and that explanations for girls' violence could not be disassociated from the structural and cultural worlds in which girls live. This body of scholarship presented an overwhelming case for focusing on gender-appropriate solutions to female offending.[10]

Gender-appropriate policy was grounded in this seminal research. The *JJDP Act of 1992* called for developing and adopting policies "to prohibit gender bias in placement and treatment and establishing programs to ensure that female youth have access to the full range of health and mental health services, treatment for physical or sexual assault and abuse, self defense instruction, education in parenting, education in general, and other training and vocational services" (*JJDP Act of 1992*). By 2005, gender-specific programming had become part of the official rhetoric of the U.S. Department of Justice. One description that OJJDP offers for these programs reads: "[They are programs] that are designed to meet the unique needs of young delinquent and at-risk females, that value the female perspective, that celebrate and honor the female experience, that respect and take into account female development, and that empower young women to reach their full potential."[11]

Proponents argued that gender interventions were a crucial component in healing girls and diverting them from juvenile corrections. Sponsored by a wide range of organizations around the nation, gender-responsive programs were successful in redirecting girls away from further involvement in juvenile offenses, according to some agency directors.[12] As one advocate from the "new girls' movement" wrote, "Girls, particularly those from communities of color and low-income communities, require more than problem prevention to claim their voice and become community leaders. Programs working with girls must develop new approaches that address girls' needs for support and connections, view girls as assets, help them come to voice, and offer space for critical thinking."[13]

Strengths in Gender-Specific Policy

In a large, well-maintained psychiatric facility for girls aged thirteen to seventeen, young women in the classroom were hard at work. In this girl-only treatment center, each girl, on admission, received a therapeutic treatment plan and met with a social worker who made sure she was getting all the help and support she needed; a psychologist who administered individual therapy, if necessary; a psychiatrist who prescribed and supervised a medication regime; a teacher who set up an individual learning plan; a nurse practitioner; and a mentor. These adult treatment teams met weekly and paid focused attention to each young woman. This facility was known nationwide for its high success rate with female adolescents with histories of habitual serious offending. "We take anybody, and we never have a placement failure," the director confidently explained. The classroom was busy with artwork and assignments; slogans such as "ONLY YOU CAN STOP YOU!" plastered the walls. Images of women from throughout history adorned the room, and brightly colored bulletin boards displayed schoolwork, rules, and goals for all to see. One teacher and only nine girls were in the entire classroom.

Today's lesson was "What Is Diversity?" Girls were asked to read over a short essay and answer questions in a workbook. They could work in groups or alone. Two Latina-looking girls sat to the left of me, secretly holding hands under the table. An African American girl sat near the front and, after a while, began to nervously shift in her seat and sigh loudly. Quiet talking was going on in the back of the room among a group of three girls who were working together. These young women were maybe fifteen or sixteen years old. All of a sudden, the girl in the front erupted into a tirade: "I can't do this! I don't know what the fuck all this means! I need to get out of here! I hate it here!" Immediately, the teacher and one other girl moved to sit next to her. The teacher knelt down close to her and put her hand on the frustrated young woman's back, saying soothingly, "I'm going to go over all of this very carefully with you. Let's start at the top and go slow." The other girl said to her quietly, in a big-sister tone, "Teneshia, work your program, girl. You remember what your Learning Experience Goal was? Now's a good chance to work it. I know you can do it, girl!" The other girls in the room visibly stiffened at Teneshia's outburst. One young woman looked upset and frightened but stayed glued to her seat. Everybody seemed anxious and then relieved as the teacher and the other student worked to soothe and diffuse Teneshia's frustration. In girl-only spaces such as these, young women work together, teach each other, and give each other the support they need and deserve.

Even though this was an adolescent psychiatric facility, many gender-relevant programs I observed in correctional facilities delivered the theory and policy that gender responsiveness was supposed to provide to young women. As scholars from a variety of disciplines increasingly became aware of girls' unique needs for specialized attention, research revealed that, even in highly structured environments, young women thrive when they are encouraged to help each other. With girls forming approximately one-fifth of detention populations, female-specific or girl-only spaces are important because they allow girls' unique needs to be identified.

Although by the time the OJJDP programs were initiated the monolithic category *girl* was being contested by scholars and practitioners in general, research did show that girls flourished in girl-only classrooms and other settings. So, gender-specific programming facilitated those kinds of spaces.[14]

The immense promise of gender-specific projects is reflected in the clarity and thoroughness of the curricula for initiating the policy and programs that were created by community consultants and the OJJDP on the basis of a decade of hard-earned experience in the field. Easy to follow, with handouts and modules, one well-organized guide is contained in three huge binders that offer guidelines for policy makers, ways to "train the trainers," as well as suggestions for how to design the programs themselves.[15]

A positive aspect of gender-specific projects is that they are most often motivated by good intentions. Good will is generated when community and governmental actors come together to brainstorm and develop interventions to benefit girls. The veritable cottage industry of conferences, training sessions, and evaluations generates national collegiality, allowing governmental bureaucrats and academic researchers to give talks and presentations about their new specialty. Coalitions at the local and national level are easily funded: Who could be against girls? These collaborations provide locations where otherwise warring factions (such as community advocates and probation officials) can come together to focus on a common problem: the care and treatment of young women in juvenile justice.[16]

Gender-specific programs also provide a benefit because of the tendency to hire and retain female personnel, thus boosting the employment of women in correctional facilities. As more women employees have contact with young women in lock-up or courtroom situations, the mentoring of girls by adult women increases. And because the majority of girls in my sample, for example, were sexually or physically harmed by men, working with women sometimes provides girls with relief, consolation, and healing.

Finally, a largely unarticulated benefit that gender-appropriate responses provide is promotion of the perspective that gender is crucial for understanding children's life pathways. After all, every aspect of adolescence is imbued with the implications of gender: youth development; physical and mental health care; understanding sexualities; mentoring; relating to family and neighbors; education; and work—all are experienced through prisms of gender. Noticing gender in the adolescents in juvenile justice opens the door for increased understanding of the social forces that create and maintain the system itself, as well as children's involvement in it.

Deficits in Gender-Specific Practices

Even though the plight of girls in the juvenile legal system has increasingly come to the attention of leaders, progress in the development and implementation of gender-appropriate policy is sporadic at best and is resisted by many, as was hinted at in the beginning of this chapter and as can be detected in the comments in this section by adults in the system.

Although the theory may have been sophisticated and well-intended, gender-responsive programs are, at times, rife with contradictions in their delivery and suffer from much resistance by staff and girls. For me, spending time in some correctional facilities with several years of experience as girl-focused sites felt like being in a pre-gender-consciousness time warp.

The first day I ventured out to do fieldwork in 1996, I traveled the hall in a facility in northern California and saw announcements of my site-based research displayed on bulletin boards at every turn—employees knew they were being observed. This particular facility was touted as one of the innovative sites that focused on girls, so I was excited to begin. I ran into two probation officers standing in the hall involved in a candid conversation. They were big guys, one white, the other African American, in shirts and ties, still carrying their briefcases, obviously just arriving at their offices on this Monday morning: "Holy smoke, man, I checked my message machine and there were like five messages from her, 'Officer Johnston, could you *pleeease* call me? [in a high-pitched squeaky tone, imitating a small, whiney child]. I don't even know what I'm in here fo' and where my baby at. You are my only hope!' [laughing] Man, you *know* I didn't call her back. She's leavin' a message on my phone every hour! What a hassle! And I haven't even arrived to my office yet!" Very quickly I got the picture: not only were girls in trouble with the law but some law officials saw girls as trouble.

This experience was not an isolated one; other research confirms this finding.[17] My observations of and interviews with law enforcement, court personnel, social workers, and other service providers brought to light some of the tensions between the conceptualization and the delivery of gender-specific programs. Comments and interactions in training sessions and interviews with practitioners of gender-specific programming revealed their struggles with the concepts, as well as their controversial assumptions about the meanings of femininity and girls' sexuality.

In practice, girls are constituted as being difficult: hard to work with, requiring much time and attention. This framing is subtly reinforced in the policy literature as well as in the design of the programs. For example, policy makers believe that "most girls need to talk things through:

to verbally process events, experiences, and feelings."[18] Not surprisingly, the following typical descriptions of young women provided by adults working in the system fall into this framework. The quotes highlight areas where the conceptualization of the policy is lost by the time it is delivered in the everyday work in the field and illustrate how, even after receiving gender-specific training, some resistant line staff retain a pre-gender-appropriate mind-set.

> You have to get to know them and get them to trust you because girls are more relational than boys. . . . It takes a *long* time to work with a girl. (middle-aged, white, working-class woman, program coordinator)

> "Girls are complicated. . . . I don't like to work with them so much. They always come on to me [sexually], and I just get tired of it. I don't know how to handle them. Even their *mothers* come on to me! I need a female partner to help me deal with them. (thirty-something, working-class Chicano, probation officer)

In this context, working with girls means different things to different people. For example, in general, in my study, psychologists were (relatively) highly paid to spend the time necessary to work with complicated patients, while counselors/guards working eight-hour turns in a juvenile facility just wanted to get through the shift. The notion that girls required special energy went against the work habits of nine-to-five, salaried civil servants and the expectations of shift workers. Asking more from them than just the brief amount of time and energy it takes to work with boys made workers feel "put upon." So, when asked to compare girls with boys, detention and probation personnel regularly found girls less good than or not as good as boys.

> Girls are more emotional than boys. . . . Everything is a big ol' drama trauma with them! Tha's why we handle 'em a little differently. (middle-aged, African American, middle-class woman, guard)

> Girls are just harder to work with. . . . The boys will follow the rules; they are quieter. The girls never listen; they just tangle with you on everything. (young, white, working-class woman, guard)

These quotes indicate deep embeddedness in the mind-set of male corrections.[19] Gender-appropriate policy seeks to unpack this way of thinking: boys' experiences should not constitute the standard by which we assess girls' experiences; gender does not work in parallel ways. These commentators were actually noticing the effects of sexism, not differences in the nature of youth.

Racial discourse about girls is another area where analyses are missing. To say that there is a lack of critical discussion about race and racism would be an understatement—this point cannot be overemphasized. As one (black) youth activist (and formerly incarcerated girl) said, "How can you even *talk* about girls in lock-up if you don't talk about race?" It is not insignificant that most line staff in detention facilities are men and women of color, while most of the gender-specific project deliverers are white women. Most of the criminologists who develop general policies are white men, although white women tend to specialize in the area of gender-responsive policy. Many comments by personnel in my study who were supposed to be involved with gender-specific policy and programs carried racial undertones, revealing a poor understanding of the history and sociology of race relations in the United States:

> These girls act too rude and too loud; . . . they need to learn manners and better grooming. (forty-something, African American, middle-class woman, probation officer)

> You know their mothers really don't raise them right. . . . Their *mothers* come to court in tube tops and short shorts. (middle-aged, white, working-class woman, social worker)

> Well, you see, it's in their culture to act like this. There is more crime in black neighborhoods because blacks commit more of the crimes. (young, working-class Latino, police officer)

> Schools and juvenile probation inherited family problems that go all the way back to slavery. (middle-aged, white, middle-class woman, probation officer)

This kind of commentary was difficult to address directly because it was not offered openly. Some comments were made to me, a white woman, in confidential interviews after I assured participants they would be protected by confidentiality. African American and Latina adult participants told me things like "I bet there's a white sheet in her closet" when referring to white supervisors. When white juvenile court personnel identified problems with race in their interviews with me, the discourse was coded, often being about upbringing or neighborhoods ("Their mothers don't raise them right," "They come from bad neighborhoods"). Unaddressed racial tension has been theorized as an impediment in other institutions, and I found it was a barrier in the delivery of gender-specific services for girls as well.[20]

Another gap between policy and practice is the persistent framing of girls' sexuality as a constant danger. Although the policy promises to value the female perspective, in the field assumptions that, for example, all girls' sexuality is a problem and all girls are heterosexual abound.

Young women are assumed to be—and therefore are seen only when they are—promiscuous and overinterested in boys, sex, and having babies.[21] I witnessed girls in secure facilities shepherded into therapy-like meetings focused on topics such as getting out of prostitution, an activity in which a tiny minority of young women (barely) acknowledged participating. Out of touch with standards that contemporary youth considered normative, many of the middle-aged, middle-class adults who delivered gender programming bombarded girls in lock-up with humiliating harangues.

Typical comments throughout longer interviews and interactions with personnel revealed subtle pathologizing of and moralizing about girls' sexuality:

> They are obsessed with boys.

> Girls are always saying, 'I'm bored,' but how can they have a good mentality? All they think about is hair, nails, their man, and babies!

> Girls are so emotional that they do end up "relating" to each other [implying sexual relations].

Comments such as these, made by adults who designed as well as delivered gender-specific programs, revealed the urgent need to continue to refine the theories, monitor the trainers, and reconceptualize project delivery.

Even court representatives who were opposed to gender-specific interventions struggled with the paradox of how to adjudicate contemporary young women without stigmatizing and labeling them. The district attorney from a mid-sized department, a retirement-aged, African American, middle-class man, revealed his dilemma: "You feminists come in here and tell me, 'Don't charge them with prostitution! It just labels them forever!' But what am I supposed to do? OK, we pick them up on the stroll at 3:00 . . . in the morning. We can charge them with loitering or curfew, but then how do we get them the [health and psychological] services they desperately need? . . . We cannot even identify who is who in the system anymore!"[22] He continued, "And you know what? Some of these girls are out here acting like males now, with knives and fights and all. . . . You got to shake out their hair, and you will find razor blades in there!" Although this court official was openly resistant to gender-responsive interventions, he accurately described a dilemma often debated among youth workers: advocates do not want girls labeled as prostitutes, but, at the same time, they need to know which girls need sexual- and health-related gender-specific services.

In another controversial policy arena, gender-specific proponents consider it crucial to protect girls from boys. Unfortunately, this approach shores up the false assumption that all girls are heterosexual. For example, the training module on safety suggests to juvenile justice personnel that "rerouting girls so they do not have to walk by the boys' facilities may reduce . . . excessive primping. . . . [Girls] will feel emotionally safer if [their] spaces are free from the demands for attention from adolescent males."[23] Although these kinds of directives appear, at first glance, benign and even helpful, the underlying message about girls' beauty habits, girls' safety with boys, and their sexual attraction to adolescent males does the cultural work of constructing heterosexuality and femininity as the norm. Boys may be dangerous for all girls, but not all girls engage in "excessive primping" for boys. Furthermore, the solution of rerouting girls instead of challenging boys' behavior contributes to the problem in the first place.

Another key goal of gender-responsive specialists is to teach girls about their relational aggression. As discussed in depth in Chapter Four, girls' aggression has come to concern scholars and practitioners. Gender-specific service providers are taught that understanding relational aggression is crucial to understanding female behavior. The concept of relational aggression includes the notion that girls express their anger in a polite way rather than through vandalism or violence. The basic premise is that girls may not feel safe to express disagreement openly, so "they resort to methods that are oblique." Examples of relational aggression by girls include "backstabbing, spreading lies, using information to gain power, and lashing out." Trainers who deliver gender-responsive programming are taught that girls may be "manipulative."[24]

In some delivery settings, relational aggression is oversimplified as being in direct and equal opposition to boys' instrumental aggression. Being in gangs and being violent are posited as ways that boys gain honor, protect their reputations, and inspire respect. One problem with this gendered framing of girls' aggression as relational is that it ignores the fact that many young women are being adjudicated delinquent for aggressive and assaultive offenses on the streets, in schools, and in the community. There is nothing oblique about aggravated assault. By demoting righteous rage to being a cause of merely relational violence, gender-specific programs are possibly missing opportunities to move away from excoriation and correction of individual girls' attitudes and choices and toward exploration of systemic gendered inequalities. Gender-specific policy and programming could provide much-needed sites where stereotypes of girls' aggression as either dangerously out of control or slightly innocuous can be challenged.

Many of the employees I interviewed who devote their working lives to caring for and rehabilitating young people were excited about gender-specific programs. Others, clearly, were not, saying they thought them a "waste of time": "The real problem is all these young males runnin' around harming society" was a typical comment I heard in private from personnel who resisted gender-responsive innovations. In confidential interviews, often only after I assured them that their identity would be kept private, juvenile legal personnel revealed their, at best, ambivalence about and, at worst, their complete opposition to the basic concepts of gender intervention. In interviews, many employees could not offer a definition of gender much beyond "feminine ways," "whether you are ladylike," and other similarly vapid concepts. A large part of the problem is the silencing of public discussion about gender, much like the marked lack of open discussion about race in the workplace. Ironically, fearing accusations of being sexist, racist, or old-fashioned, people who work with youth end up participating in outdated, patronizing, and racialized practices.

In sum, I believe that gender-specific policy for girls in the corrections system can be improved by reconceptualizing the "difficulty" of working with girls; opening up a discussion about race and racism; noticing that all girls are not heterosexual and that all girls' sexuality is not a problem (in other words, noticing that all girls do not seek to adopt white, middle-class norms regarding beauty, love, speech, or lifestyle); countering stereotypes about girls' aggression; and, finally, promoting discussion about gender issues in order to raise awareness about the necessity for gender-specific programs for system-involved girls.

Sex, Violence, and Other Gender Myths

Central but unarticulated tasks of gender-specific projects are to help young women understand what gender is and, ultimately, for them to begin to articulate what gender means to them. But how are these tasks to be accomplished? In sociology, sex and gender are distinct in theoretical discussion. The term *sex* refers to biological, physiological differences between boys and men and girls and women, although these binary categories are contended among scholars. Some of the biological or physiological characteristics utilized to differentiate among sexes are mammary glands and breasts, uteruses, ovaries, vaginas, testicles, penises, as well as what are sometimes called secondary sexual characteristics, such as amount of facial hair, pitch of voice, size of Adam's apple.[25]

Gender, however, indicates the socially constructed practices, behaviors, attitudes, representations, and portrayals of masculinity and femininity. Contemporary sociologists of gender have moved away from binary dualities and see gender as fluid, multiple, and intersecting with race, class, and sexualities. (*Black's Law Dictionary* does not even attempt a definition: my edition goes from "Gdn," the abbreviation for guardian, right to "genealogy.")[26] The sociology of gender gives us the possibility of combining ideas about race, class, and sexualities in new and useful ways when analyzing these forces in the lives of girls in trouble with the law. Drawing on such a sociology of gender will allow young women to meet the challenges they face growing up poor in a profit-driven, consumerist economy; nonwhite in a racialized society; female in a patriarchy; and lesbian or queer in a homophobic world.

Through hands-on experience and long hours of careful observation, I have become convinced that gender-specific programs need to be re-tooled and the people who teach in them need to be retrained. In my research, I read gender-specific policies and observed gender-specific programs that promoted the teaching of outdated, static framings of gender, ignored the existence of transgender youth altogether, and encouraged girls to conform to archaic feminine identities that are not a part of their reality, let alone, I would argue, in their best interests. These bright detainees learned early on not that their values were meaningful and worthy of pursuit but that they needed to align their conduct with norms that were not relevant to their visions and challenges.

Outmoded framings of gender are derived from what I call "gender myths." The reality that can be observed or charted in arrest statistics or put to other kinds of detailed empirical scrutiny belies the fables being told about girls. One myth, for example, frames boys as primarily independent, physical, and violent and girls as relational, emotional, and sexy. This kind of binary thinking causes theoretical impoverishment. Instead of having a rich continuum to draw from, we have a notion of gender that is simplified and bifurcated beyond recognition. Such simplification stunts both the development of more sophisticated responses to all juveniles' misconduct in the public-policy and legal arenas and the subsequent revitalization of policies and laws.

Various disparities between theory and actuality became apparent to me after I spent time observing programs, as well as attending professional training conferences in a variety of fields of juvenile justice. Here I present three examples of inaccuracy in understanding gendered juvenile justice outcomes.

Gender Myth Number 1. Girls get into trouble mostly for prostitution. A media panic launched in the 1990s, ostensibly about sexual trafficking, reflects a popular myth about underage prostitution. In 2000, Congress passed the *Victims of Trafficking and Violence Protection Act* at a time when actual arrests for female juvenile prostitution were at their lowest since the 1980s. The bill claimed that "approximately 50,000 women and children are trafficked into the United States each year."

Building on the general sexual hysteria of the Clinton years, a 2004 *New York Times Magazine* exposé—featuring on the cover a young girl in knee socks—touted that "tens of thousands of women and girls" are forced into prostitution in the cities and towns of the United States.[27] However, in 2004 only 1,300 arrests of young women were for prostitution, out of a total of over 660,000 arrests of girls for all reasons (see Tables 1.1 and 1.3).

Not that young women who are trafficked victims would—or should—be getting arrested for prostitution, but where are all the tens of thousands of sexually commerced girls? We know that police are more likely to categorize young girls than women as victims and refer girls to other authorities, such as social services. In addition, law enforcement tactics sometimes blur boundaries between prostituted and trafficked girls. But, even so, if all the clients can find these girls, why can't the police? If tens of thousands of children are being trafficked, it is likely that when young women are caught participating in the sex trade, we would find that they had been sold into sex slavery. Instead, at the moment, relatively few young women are adjudicated in the juvenile legal system for sexual misconduct.[28]

Another aspect of this gender myth is to assume that girls but no boys participate in sexual commerce. Although only 34 percent of all juvenile arrests for prostitution in 2004 were of boys, between 1990 and 2000, from 44 percent to 52 percent—more than half—of all juvenile arrests for prostitution were of boys. A 2004 report from the National Incidence Based Reporting System found that in over 60 percent of the juvenile prostitution incidents known to the police, the sex providers were boys. Additional research needs to investigate sexual trafficking, juvenile prostitution, and gender because current data challenge outmoded ways of thinking about gender and sexuality.[29]

This myth is further eroded by the complex role that race and racism play in sexualizing girls' offenses. The representation of the black female as hypersexual has been documented since the colonial era. A history of sexual politics reveals that African American women's sexual embodiment has been labeled as deviant and threatening by privileged groups (whites, males, child savers) throughout American history. Girls of color being processed in juvenile corrections continue to be seen through a similar lens. Even though data prove differently, court personnel persist in suspecting African American girls of being prostitutes, and often minority girls' sexuality in particular is focused on when court personnel assess adolescence, values, and morals.[30]

Gender Myth Number 2. When girls are violent, they are acting like boys. Assaults, battery, and unlawful possession and use of weapons are widely considered by the media and by juvenile corrections to be male offenses. When girls get caught up in the system for violent offenses, often they are framed by court officials as "acting like males." However, rarely discussed in meaningful ways in the media and among juvenile corrections officials are the facts that aggravated assaults rank higher as a reason for arrests of girls than of boys and arrests for simple assaults rank equally for girls and for boys (see Table 1.3). The social construction of girls as violent and of violent girls as masculine could be explored with young women in gender-responsive programming.

A corollary of this myth, that "boys are violent" and "girls are sexy," also precludes our seeing the realities in the cases of court-involved girls, who are victims of an a priori discourse that theorizes their experiences without sufficient evidence. Of all young women under eighteen in the entire United States in 2004, approximately thirteen hundred were arrested for prostitution, while slightly more than fourteen thousand were arrested for aggravated assault (see Tables 1.1 and 1.3). That "boys are violent" and "girls are sexy" is another gender myth that can be dispelled—not perpetuated—in gender-responsive programs.

Gender Myth Number 3. There are no gay youth in the juvenile system. The last area where mystification rises to an almost absurd level is being debunked by the growing awareness of GLBTQ youth in the juvenile legal system. With the increase in the visibility of GLBTQ youth, an opportunity arises to pro-actively educate staff and youth about the unique strengths and possibilities that GLBTQ youth can draw on to speed their healthy rejuvenation and to provide just outcomes. When I spoke to court personnel about learning about this topic, I was repeatedly told, "Oh, I don't believe in that kind of a lifestyle. I refuse to support that kind of activity." Even when I countered that discussion groups are held with girls about prostitution when no one "supports that lifestyle," it was clear that, as elsewhere in American society at the turn of the twenty-first century, some practitioners and personnel feared being educated about this topic. Gender-specific policy has much to offer in exploring the myths and realities of nonheterosexual and nonnormatively gendered youth. The myth that "boys will be boys" is challenged daily by GLBTQ youth who refuse to be silent, pathologized, and invisible. Breaking down the myths that GLBTQ youth do not hail from poor, urban communities of color, do not exist in juvenile facilities, and have no legal, civil, or human rights to recognition and care is surely a fruitful direction for gender intervention in juvenile justice.

The above comment by a detention counselor that girls are so emotional that they "relate" to each other emphasizes the growing concern about the invisibility of GLBTQ youth in juvenile corrections and, when they were visible, their mistreatment. Although we do not know the exact number of GLBTQ youth in the system, we do know that court personnel are not equipped to meet the unique needs of GLBTQ youth. It makes sense to develop mandatory, gender-appropriate interventions that include training and policy implementation for the protection of GLBTQ youth in the juvenile system.

Conclusion: It's Gender-Specific, But Is It Feminist?

Gender-responsive projects will not be redemptive if they reproduce racialized, archaic ideals of femininity and patriarchal expectations for love and romance. Gender-specific projects should be places where gender is operationalized in order to demystify the inequality that brings many young women to the attention of authorities in the first place: unequal access to education, health care, safe housing, living wages for their families, and more. Gender-responsive programming must meet young women where they are developmentally, intellectually, and politically. Our projects should give them assistance in confronting the challenges that race, sexuality, and class pose for them as they grow up in the United States today. Gender-responsive policies should support the teaching of critical-thinking skills. For example, girls need to see that the criminalization of their gender strategies for survival in their families, schools, and communities is not a personal psychological problem that they face all alone. They need to understand that, by talking with each other and with caring adults, they can develop successful strategies and take advantage of alternative choices for their lives.

My interviews with juvenile justice officials and my observations of gender interventions revealed a reliance on anachronistic and relatively unsophisticated notions of masculinity and femininity. Gender-appropriate programs should not consist simply of talking to young women about relationships and birth control. The meaning, enactment, expression, and expectations of ideals of femininity and masculinity vary in and across African, Puerto Rican, Mexican, Korean, Vietnamese, Japanese, and Chinese American families and communities. We have much to learn also from GLBTQ youth and adults who challenge normative understandings of gender in society every day. These experiences and ideas can serve to restructure gendered discussions.

I return to the biological girl who is a boy—the transgender young person about whom an email was circulating. What should the system do? Gender-specific projects should start not by ascertaining how wrong or right someone's femininity or masculinity is but by helping young people and their families see how children's strategies are derived from the urge for self-preservation and the search for love and care. Gender responsiveness must work less toward bringing youth into alignment with old-fashioned norms and more toward empowering them to challenge stereotypes and develop healthy tools for communicating their feelings and ideas. Gender-specific programs are doors through which improvement in the system and its mission may be advanced. The good news is that there are girl-only spaces where this work can continue.

In developing policy and designing interventions, we should consider whether they essentialize gender; reinforce outdated and constricting dualities; miss the opportunity to challenge harmful stereotypes; ignore race, ethnicity, and/or class; are heteronormative; ignore gender as a system of power; ignore gender as a system of communication about love, romance, beauty, sex, and the body; or fail to address girls' experiences of violence. A policy that is responsive to the concerns of young women in trouble with the law should reach beyond an analysis of gender. The notion of gender alone is insufficient for addressing girls' multiple, complex needs and challenges. Gender-appropriate services will be enhanced as they are improved to include nuanced notions of gender. Without incorporating a contextualization of girls' lives that challenges the status quo, gender-specific policy may simply reinforce the sexual and racial oppression that contributes to the entry of young women into the correctional system in the first place.

Empowering Women

Empowering women is a special task,
It takes understanding, love, patience and a certain kind of "rap"
When reaching out to your sistas, be aware of the important issues
Women remember to be good to yourselves
You only get one temple, one mind, one body, one health
Together, we all can make a stand, unite, build, create and share
Encourage your neighbor to get involved,
If we help each other, We help us all!

—Ebony Evans

Poem delivered at a poetry slam/fundraiser for the Young Women's Empowerment Project, Chicago, June 12, 2004.

6

Conclusion

Pathways, Policies,
Programs, and
Politics

I conclude this study about contemporary girls in trouble by describing two moments of conflict among girls that took place in completely different settings. Recounting these events provides a foundation for seeing how expressions of anger and violence are mediated by location, socioeconomic status, and the quality of adult intervention. Contextual comparisons allow us to observe that girls' troubles are not as much about violence, sexuality, or gender as they are about the ways that those forces are constituted for them in their lives. After presenting and discussing both scenes, I share recommendations made by the young women in this study for changes in the juvenile corrections system. I turn next to one of the chief debates among advocates for youth: Do we empower them or protect them? If the general call is to empower, exactly what is the power we wish to instill? When the hue and cry is raised for the protection of children, I query, protect them from what? I then present three areas for policy review and three arenas where fruitful policy discussions about girls' experiences in juvenile systems are taking place. I next highlight seven programs I observed where girls were engaged in redirecting their lives. I conclude with eight modest recommendations. I focus on these particular policies, programs, and recommendations, out of many, to highlight the possibilities for continuing the important work carried out by youth advocates since the inception of the juvenile court.

A Tale of Two Fights: The Varied Contexts of Girls' Conflict

What difference does context make to girls' expressions of aggression? To answer this question, I describe here two conflicts involving girls. The first fight took place in a detention facility and the second in a model magnet high school, known as a beacon in its district. The "type of girl" didn't vary by institutional setting, in that young women in each location shared a variety of demographics: some were poor, some were raised in distressed urban environments, some were girls of color, some were from single-mother families, some were survivors of childhood trauma, and some were lesbian or bisexual. However, the specific context in which the girls were going to school did vary.

Scene 1. A "Condition"

Deep in the bowels of the secure, cement juvenile facility, the schoolrooms were lit by fluorescent lights and whatever daylight came through dirty windows with gray metal grates covering them. From the outside, the new detention center looked like a junior college—built of bricks and glass with wide cement paths intersecting green lawns. As I walked across the grounds, the smell of fresh-cut grass and the distant lull of the water sprinklers contrasted with the gruff commands shouted by a counselor directing a *movement*, the term for moving groups of detained populations.

As discussed in Chapter One, each county or jurisdiction in the United States governs its juvenile corrections system according to state laws. This particular facility operated military-style. Transporting juveniles from building to building required them to march in formation, in rows of five, those in each successive row with their left arms on the left shoulders of those in the row in front of them. As each row filed into the dormitory bunks, detainees sat on the edges of their beds, legs dangling, hands at their sides, facing front, completely motionless and totally silent until all were in place. During indoor movements, detainees were instructed to walk with their arms crossed across their chests and their hands tucked under their armpits, facing front, no talking. Their t-shirts had to be tucked into their elastic-waist, khaki trousers. The color of detainees' t-shirts designated their unit and sometimes their offense. Here, maximum-risk units wore orange; girls' units wore green. In this particular institution, all day, every day, every movement—to the showers, to meals, to school, to the outdoor physical program, to visiting—was conducted in the same way: all in silence except for the barking of the counselors, everyone dressed alike and moving very slowly. That was what being locked up was like.

As students filed into the classroom I observed, they plopped down into chair-desks, scrunching as low down into their seats as possible. Girls started variously chatting, pounding beats on their desktops, calling out to each other, squirming, singing to themselves, or talking, some in English, some in Spanish. Some sat straight up and looked ahead quietly. Some stared curiously at me and expectantly at the teacher at the head of the room. There were twenty-four girls in the classroom, a teacher, and a teacher's aide. The air was stale; windows with chicken-wire in the glass were sealed shut. The classroom walls were completely bare, painted an industrial, colorless beige: no posters, no completed assignments tacked up on bulletin boards. All around the room, initials, faint, age-old, had been scratched at desk level into the cement, through the paint, along with scrawled messages decipherable only by teenagers from the same neighborhoods. No chalk, no erasers, no paper, books, or pencils. When I looked carefully, I noticed that even door and window handles had been removed. Desks were bolted to the floor.

Instruction started with the teacher shouting, "Talking is dead!" Immediate, complete, motionless silence ensued. The teacher's aide passed out one sheet of a Xeroxed worksheet and one stubby pencil to each girl, counting each pencil as she went. The "discussion" began around a video, "The Wonders of the Amazon," a documentary about wildlife in a certain section of Brazil. One of the girls called out, "Oh, hey, we seen that last week!" From across the room, someone else answered, "Oh, no we didn't, bitch!" "Who you callin' bitch?" Within seconds general uproar ensued, girls jumping up and shouting, throwing shoes at each other, and taking swings. Some girls immediately dropped to the floor and crouched in a kind of fetal position with their arms covering their heads. At first, the teacher tried to intervene verbally; meanwhile, the teacher's aide made it to the door and shouted for counselors to "call a condition!"[1]

Two counselors entered immediately and began physically disengaging girls and siphoning off all juveniles not involved into the hallway outside the classroom, ordering them to continue to take the "duck and cover" position. Girls in the hallway immediately hit the floor, face down, with their arms covering their heads. Apparently, detainees were instructed to assume this position to indicate their submission and to protect themselves during outbreaks of physical chaos.

As the condition progressed, the locked door to the unit burst open and nine counselors stormed into the classroom, each taking a girl down to the floor; some had to double-team wildly flailing, screaming teenagers. Girls were yelling things like, "I'm gonna kick your ass when I get out of here!" With fingernails digging and teeth sinking into flesh, saliva and blood flying around the room, the girls were yelling and fighting with all their energy. Ranging from burly men of color in their twenties to frail-looking white women in their fifties, the detention-facility employees moved in a fast, large show of force to dispel the free-for-all fight. Over the loudspeaker throughout the facility, you could hear a frantic, purposeful announcement, "Code Red in G–5! Code Red in G–5!"

Then one counselor took out a small item that looked like a ciga-rette lighter and pepper-sprayed the face of one shouting, fighting, angry, "out-of-control" minor who wouldn't/couldn't stop punching, kicking, and flailing. I could hear her screams and crying long after, as they show-ered her down on the other side of the unit. The whole event lasted a maximum of four minutes. All the girls were put in their rooms, the euphemism for cells in juvenile halls, for a locked-down cooling-off pe-riod. Some girls continued to bang and shout on their doors, and they received even more room time.

The next day three of the girls involved explained that tension be-tween two groups of girls had been simmering for awhile. Apparently, one of the young women had some trouble with the cousin of another young woman. Each girl had a group of friends from her neighborhood. All three girls minimized the event: "Aw, that ain't nothin.' These girls just be actin' crazy up in here." "Shit, I'ma kick her ass when I get outta here. That bitch be dissin' me all the time. Ain't no thing gettin' room time offa that." One girl pointed out something else: "Do you realize that . . . the only time they ever talk to us is after we fight? We all get lots of visits from counselors, and they bosses, and the PO [probation officer] finally comes around, and people like you, and God knows who else! They come take us out the room and say, 'Now, hey, what's goin' on with you?' That's the only ever time they ask us anything—only if we fight!"

Here, as in many of the institutions in my study, when girls were involved in conflict and aggression, they received detailed scrutiny. This kind of free-for-all was typical in some facilities on both girls' and boys' units, especially in the more punishment-driven settings. However, the concerns raised when there were conditions on the girls' units were quali-tatively different from those raised by boys' confrontations. Almost al-ways, the reason offered for boys' battles was "gangs," but girls' combat needed to be explored and explained, as if staff were mystified by girls' aggression.

Scene 2. Model High School

The second incident took place in a bilingual (Spanish-English) public school in a city in the Rocky Mountain region. Although it was in a run-down neighborhood with classrooms in shabby-looking trailers, it was well regarded as a model school. To the loud sounds of traffic and construction outside, students shuffled in, boys and girls, jostling and talking to each other. One girl sat on her friend's lap and gave her a sisterly hug, saying "'Sup, girlfriend?" Another boy leaned in close to a girl and was whispering something to her as she laughed. Students seemed openly relaxed and physically comfortable with each other. All students carried big, overstuffed, canvas backpacks/book bags and were essentially wearing the same outfit, regardless of gender: oversized shirts with sports, Ben Davis, or Nike logos; large, baggy jeans; big, puffy, designer-label basketball shoes (Nike for African Americans and Fila for Latino/as).

In the twelfth-grade class, about half the students spoke English as a first language; the rest spoke Spanish, Tagalog, or Hmong at home. All were bilingual in English and Spanish. Today's lesson featured a guest speaker who talked about her work as a mental health counselor in a Spanish-speaking neighborhood clinic. The speaker began her talk, and we were soon spellbound. Originally from Venezuela, she had a lilting Spanish accent and was delightfully animated. She asked the class questions that they could easily answer and thus led a participatory discussion rather than giving an hour-long lecture. When asked what colleges they planned to attend, they all immediately began shouting out, "Boulder!" "Madison!" "State!" "Yale!" One boy said, "Howard!" and another said, "I'm goin' to UNLV on a basketball scholarship!" as some of the other boys grunted and high-fived each other.

But about thirty-five minutes into her presentation, students became restless, and as the teacher later framed it, "a little rambunctious." One girl looked over at another girl and said, threateningly, "What you lookin' at?" The other girl looked back defiantly and said, "Nothin'! What's your problem?" The teacher immediately moved to intervene. "What's going on? Let's talk this out." A tiny mediation ensued. The first girl explained that she thought the other girl was looking at her funny and "didn't like anyone up in her business." The other young woman listened quietly as the first girl said her piece, waiting until she finished speaking. "I wasn't looking at you in any kind of way. I'm sorry if you thought I was. But I do know what Divina said about me to you in first period, and I don't appreciate it at all!" "Well, I'm not Divina so don't be botherin' with me!" After a few more sentences and interactions, both girls backed down and quietly said they were sorry to each other. The teacher finished by inviting the guest to continue talking for a few minutes, and, by the time class was over, all were clapping and cheering for the speaker.

Analysis: The Difference Context Makes

By contrasting the grim, punitive setting in which many "conditions" occur with a classroom equipped to handle conflict, we can bring girls' fighting into relief. In supportive settings, where girls feel they have enough resources, time, energy, and safety to express emotions, they handily worked through their fears and anger in healthful, pro-girl ways. The classroom in the magnet high school reflected a philosophy that valued communication, respect, and hope. In contrast, the punitive philosophy in the juvenile facility reflected a fundamental mistrust of children. Maintaining order and control was the central task; obedience to authority the method used to guide juveniles. Within such a philosophy, individual honor and dignity are difficult for youth to develop. The guiding notion of the punishment-and-correction paradigm is to provide the bare minimum—food, supplies, gear—for detainees. Evening programming included proselytizing religious groups, who visited weekly. Ideas about gender were outdated: girls' violence was explained by their emotional hysteria; boys' violence was, well, "boys will be boys."

The events in the classroom at the model high school reflected decades of work by advocates, scholars, and educators who insisted that by thickening the cultures of care in the lives of youth, children could learn to thrive in their environments. That these students were in a classroom and not in a detention facility mattered and influenced the nonviolent outcome. Bilingual classrooms honor multiple cultures. Small classroom size allows young people latitude, both in their academic work and in their social and psychological development. Being able to slow down and talk things out in a safe setting afforded the two young women the opportunity to see how to resolve the threat presented by annoyance, anger, fear, and distrust. Less polarized expectations about gendered behavior allow young people to interact in an atmosphere of acceptance.

What do we learn from seeing the expression of anger and aggression in different settings? Girls' behavioral choices and emotional expressions are socially constituted, depending on the moral horizons available to them. What was "rambunctious" in one group could be fatal in another. When adults intervened appropriately, frustration and anger were diffused and did not turn into brutality. As I explained previously, the young women involved in both these displays of frustration, anger, and aggression were demographically similar in many ways. However, the differences in their situations, contexts, options, and alternatives determined the quality of adult intervention and guidance in their lives as well as the quality of emotional literacy and sophistication they had each mastered. Factors such as these reveal the social logic of young women's choices, more than personality type, racial or cultural heritage, family background, or socioeconomic status.

What Is in the "Best Interests of the Child"? The Girls Speak

The juvenile court was founded on the doctrine of the best interests of the child. Use of this doctrine differentiated the care of the juvenile court from the justice of the adult court, a punitive setting that focused on protecting the community from criminals. The assumption in the juvenile division was that the court would intervene as a kind and just parent to determine how the child could best be rehabilitated.[2]

Let's listen to young women's thoughts about what is in their best interest. Young women, simply by the fact that they are young, do not necessarily always know what is best for them; they may not know about adult laws, health care, or safety concerns. That is why, in the best of worlds, adults intervene to guide and care for the vulnerable. However, as we have seen throughout this book, many of the adults in the lives of girls in trouble did not act in their best interests, and, in many instances, the girls, wise beyond their years, knew exactly what they had to do in order to survive. In that spirit, I asked young women what they required in order to get out of trouble. So, for example, LeYona Jackson, who was "takin' the fall for my homey," sitting in detention on a disposition for drug sales, which she had most likely been involved with solely because of her boyfriend, knew clearly what her problems were and, rationally, how to solve them. "I need to go to church! Church! Take me home! I need to make a relationship with my mom, my sister, and my brother. I should spend time with my family, not be all out on the streets with my man! When I get out, I want to write a story about my life. I want to tell all these young teens what it's really like!"

LeYona's comments were typical. Many young women knew to look to the community to assist them and understood as well the benefits of creative outlets for identifying and communicating their ideas. The young women responded readily to the question: "What do you think you need?"

> If I could move in with my dad in Arizona, if my mom were to accidentally die, or if I were to become an actress. (Leslie Rollins, fifteen years old, simple assault)

> I need to change my character. I need someone to tell my problems to. I need someone I can trust. (LaShondra Wolfe, seventeen years old, weapons possession)

Interestingly, being listened to was the resource they requested most often. Adults reported it as one of their most effective tools for working with troubled girls. At a citywide Girl's Conference in Chicago in 2002, the item that young women said they needed most was for adults to "listen to us." However, throughout my observations in juvenile facilities, I rarely witnessed adults listening to young women. I observed adults lecturing, correcting, warning, admonishing, and teasing girls, but it was uncommon to witness a child simply getting to talk her heart out to a concerned adult listener.

"Empty-family girls" like Claudia Sereno and Carina Menendez also had ideas about what they needed:

> I know I don't want to go to no group homes! I like to go on my own—or maybe a good foster home where they really pay attention

to you! If my mother goes straight—I can clean up. (Claudia Sereno, seventeen, aggravated battery)

I would like very much to get away from my *papi.* I know that sounds bad, but I wish we could have our own house. He could come visit us! (Carina Menendez, fifteen, armed robbery)

I'm not going back with old friends when I get out of here. I don't want to do no drink or smoke drugs anymore! But I will smoke cigarettes. . . . I'm gonna get my car again too. (L'Teshia Williams, sixteen, drug possession)

Many girls asked for help understanding and expressing their feelings. Surprising to me, many asked for counseling. Carina said, "I need me some type of help that gets your priority straight. I need the kind of help to get you ready to get out—counseling. I want to learn how to control my temper."

When working with, observing, and interviewing young women, I noticed how beneficial it was for them to write and to use other creative skills to facilitate their self-expression. Youth advocates know that young people, and especially this population of wounded, unhealed, adultified, stifled young people, yearn to express their fears, thoughts, dreams, ideas, and hopes through art, music, theater, and other creative outlets. Illustration 6.1 is a letter and a drawing that one young woman made to give to a friend in a different unit. Many young women enjoyed writing poetry, writing letters of advice to other young women, as well as viewing feature films and documentaries about young women like themselves and discussing them. Resources such as these abound for facilitating socioemotional development and fostering healthy interactions among young women trapped in the juvenile system.

Many young women identified and articulated quite detailed plans for what they needed in order to thrive. If they are portrayed at all, girls in trouble are often seen in the news media, films, studies, and fiction as reactive, overemotional, out of control, or needy, silenced, and lost. But there are many sides to the young women traversing the juvenile corrections system, and I observed advocates nurturing and encouraging girls' self-knowing sides by beginning to listen to them and allowing them to express themselves.[3]

Protection versus Empowerment

Among experts in the handling of girls in corrections—scholars, practitioners, and advocates—a debate is in progress over what exactly they wish to accomplish. Is the aim to protect young women from

Illustration 6.1. A poem and drawing for a friend in lock-up. *Credit: Anonymous detainee; research collected with informed consent; used by permission.*

adulthood (i.e., predators, sexuality, and labor), or, ultimately, to empower them with a knowledge of history and the ability to maneuver in and critique a complicated world? Should the state punish girls for acting like males, or should it direct girls toward mainstream feminine ideals, "for their own good"? The protection-versus-empowerment dynamic shows up in public discourses around everything from whether girls need to be protected from knowing about sexual options and reproductive rights to whether it is a good idea to teach girls martial arts and self-defense (especially girls locked up for violent offenses).[4]

This debate needs to be explicitly gendered and needs as well to incorporate analyses of socioeconomic status and racial and ethnic heritage. After all, the cultural debates over what morality U.S. voters in the 2004 election were supporting, the portrayal of gender norms in Islam, the "war" against Western values, the "threat" of gay marriage—all these discussions are discourses about the proper role of women in society. This proper role is what must be articulated, explored, and challenged by adults and girls in the gender interventions in juvenile corrections. Both the state and the families seek the best outcomes for their daughters; defining the best outcome is what is at stake.

The gendered construction of adulthood provides another arena where tensions between protectionism and empowerment emerge. Children (read: girls) cannot give sexual consent before the age of eighteen in many states, yet we remand children (read: boys) as young as twelve years old to adult courtrooms for violent crimes. In an odd sense, girls are protected from their adult decisions, while boys are seen as cunning and capable, no matter that they haven't entered their teenage years. The trend to slowly lower the age at which children can be adjudicated as adults, when placed next to the gradual increase in the age of sexual consent, lays this paradox bare.

Sending juveniles to adult court has, at its center, the logic that lowering the age of culpability will capture and punish more criminals (meaning boys—and, not coincidentally, boys of color). Paradoxically, the legal age of majority has, at its heart, the social logic that the state must raise the age of consent to sexual intercourse in order to protect girls. By comparing the language of the laws as well as the statistical outcomes of these two trends, we see that more and more boys are legally constructed as cold-hearted killers, while girls are constituted as innocent victims of bad men; thus these trends engender tensions between ideas of empowerment and protection in childhood. The rationale for disallowing children to consent to certain acts contradicts the logic of assigning them culpability for other acts. This discussion raises a formidable legal question: Which children can we treat like adults? In general, we tend to protect society from boys, protect girls from society, and truly empower and protect neither.[5]

Crucial to understanding the empowerment paradigm and the notion of the power of the powerless is identifying the power(s) that the powerful have that advocates would like to empower young women with. When we listen to and observe girls who have been adjudicated delinquent, we can understand power as the ability to access material and symbolic resources. Structural factors such as safe homes and communities; well-equipped schools; sane, sober, and solvent parents/guardians; and superb health care were overwhelmingly absent from these girls' lives. Through gender interventions, girls in the system are gradually gaining access to symbolic resources such as pride in culture, race, class, and gender; knowledge of the history of worldwide struggles against racism, sexism, poverty, and homophobia; joy found through books, art, music, sports, creativity, and the pursuit of happiness; and confidence in one's ability to negotiate with adults about vital issues.

Table 6.1

The Cost of Detention versus the Cost of College

State	Cost for one year to maintain a youth in detention	Cost for one year of room, board, and tuition at a university	Difference
California	$ 38,200	$30,000	+$ 8,200
Colorado	$ 44,749	$24,037	+$ 20,712
Illinois	$ 80,365	$10,020	+$ 70,345
Missouri	$ 51,420	$14,964	+$ 36,456
New York	$130,670	$21,095	+$109,575

Source: For New York: Correctional Association of New York at www.correctional association.org and State University of New York at www.suny.edu. For Illinois: Illinois Department of Corrections at www.idoc.state.il.us and Illinois State University at www.comptroller.ilstu.edu. For California: Resources for Youth (2000), 15: one year in the California Youth Authority versus one year at Stanford University. For Colorado: Colorado Division of Youth Corrections at www.cdhs.state.co.us and Colorado State University at www.sfs.colostate.edu. For Missouri: Missouri Department of Social Services, Division of Youth Services, *Annual Report 2003,* and Central Missouri State University at www.cmsu.edu.

Public Policy: Putting Theory into Action

The juvenile justice system appears to have inherited the problems that failed social, political, and economic public policies regarding family, health, education, and social welfare could not solve. Since the mid-1970s, as funding for public schools declined and children dropped out, juvenile corrections has been expanding. With public housing in disrepair and increasingly unlivable, poor children end up in the backs of police cars on their way to juvenile halls. Curfew laws, designed to make the streets safe at night, merely increase the number of children who come to the attention of juvenile authorities. It is as if we bring our nonresponsive and unruly children to the doors of the juvenile legal system and say, "Here. Fix them."

But the juvenile court system has nowhere near the resources, nor the will, to do such a thing. As a matter of fact, it costs more to maintain a child locked up for a year than to put her through a year of college. Table 6.1 displays comparisons for costs in five states: California, Colorado, Illinois, Missouri, and New York. As the table shows, for example, it costs California taxpayers $8,200 more per year to maintain a young person as a ward of the court in the California Youth Authority than it does for room, board, and tuition at Stanford University (a private university). For the other states, I chose the out-of-state costs. My point here is obvious: it would be a wiser investment to put teenagers through college than to warehouse them in detention facilities, an experience they will surely have more trouble recovering from than college. In addition to arguing for policies that shunt youth out of the legal system, this section focuses on selected policies in the juvenile system that yield empowering results for female offenders.

Areas for Policy Review

As detailed in Chapter Five, an uneven evolution of legal standards and public policy in juvenile justice contributed to three important, alarming, and not unrelated trends. The first was the development of disproportionate minority representation (DMR) in the juvenile court system. The second was concern over the adequate delivery of gender-responsive programming for the influx of girls into the legal system. The third trend regarded the increasing need for attending to the unique and unmet needs of gay, lesbian, bisexual, transgender, queer, and questioning (GLBTQ) youth in the juvenile court system. Here I highlight some policies and attempts at implementation that address these grave developments as well as present the United Nations *Convention on the Rights of the Child* as a model for public policy regarding children and adolescents, including those in the juvenile justice system.

Disproportionate Minority Representation. The presence of DMR indicates that the percentage of children of color in the various stages of the juvenile legal system is disproportionate to their proportions in the general population. How does disproportionate minority representation affect girls? Girls of color fare worse than white girls at every stage of the juvenile system. Compared with their counterparts in the general population, their proportions are higher at arrest, at detention, at court hearings, and in residential placement. For example, minority girls account for 53 percent of all girls in residential placement nationally. According to a sample of 154 girls in a study profiling female delinquents committed to the Illinois Department of Corrections, 45 percent of the young women were African American. Anecdotal evidence supports these claims. Enter girls' detention units across the nation, and, of the thirty to sixty girls you see, up to 100 percent may be girls of color. The stigma associated with having had contact with the police and being processed in the system is immeasurable, and it adds to the already heavy burden of labels some young women of color carry through adolescence.[6]

Working to disband DMR provides an opportunity for policy analysts and advocates to coalesce and to update social definitions of gender, race, and anti-incarceration advocacy. For example, organizations that do anti-prison work, organizations that advocate for girls, and organizations that do antiracism work could come together over the notion of dismantling DMR. Such groups, which have varied approaches but similar visions, could develop a solid plan to end DMR in the juvenile court system.

In the discourses around problems such as DMR I see the strength of building initiatives that speak to more than gender issues. How ironic that I conclude a book about girls and gender by saying that gender, alone, is simply not a strong enough instrument to analyze the set of challenges that combine in the lives of troubled girls. The data support my contention that a flattened and archaic theoretical analysis of gender that is insufficiently intertwined with an understanding of other social forces such as racism, heteronormativity, and poverty will fall short of its redemptive value as a tool for social analysis and change.

Gender-Specific Zero-Tolerance Policies. A second policy area that affects girls is gender-specific programming. In Chapter Five, I detailed the definition, etiology, and prevalence of these programs; here I present a brief discussion of one aspect of such programming that may prove fruitful: zero tolerance for violence against girls.

Zero tolerance is the term for public school policies that allow students who violate school rules or break the law to be expelled or suspended quickly. This policy could be broadened to include zero tolerance for homophobia and violence against girls. Such a policy holds promise if it is peer-enforced and gender-responsive in meaningful and just ways. Currently, zero tolerance is a punishment-oriented and blaming endeavor; progressives consider it a failed policy. The most serious critique of zero tolerance is its intolerance of children; specifically it has often been deployed as a way to punish boys of color at school. If it were deployed differently, as zero tolerance for harm against girls, as well as against the trampling of the constitutional rights of lesbian, bisexual, and transgender girls, zero-tolerance violators would, for example, be required to complete empowerment seminars that cover the history of civil and human rights struggles.[7]

Lesbian, Bisexual, Transgender, Queer, and Questioning Girls and the Model Standards Project. The third area of growing concern for youth and advocates, as well as to confused staff and administrators, is the presence of GLBTQ youth in juvenile corrections and the need to respect their human rights. Except on rare occasions, as of the time of this research, neither court personnel nor university experts, in the main, were equipped to address the unique needs of lesbian, bisexual, transgender, queer, and questioning (LBTQ) girls. This predicament is described in Chapter Four; here I want to address an initiative designed to address these concerns.

Although gender-specific intervention has been directed largely at

the handling of girls, policy edicts, legal solutions, and community services must begin to respond to the unique needs of GLBTQ children in
the system. Ironically, meeting this challenge will ultimately mean re-
vising the solutions that gender responsiveness previously offered. Generally, for example, gender-specific programs do not address the unique
needs of transgender youth. Gender in gender-specific programs usually
refers to reified masculine or feminine behavior and does not rely on an
understanding of such behavior as a fluid continuum. A dire need is the
education of staff as well as the youths' peers around what it means to
be a GLBTQ person and how people should comport themselves in a
humanistic way around GLBTQ people.

To address this concern specifically, the Model Standards Project
has been developed. The project was launched in 2000 as a collaborative
national effort with over forty legal, social, and educational organizations represented; it is headed by two agencies based in San Francisco:
the National Center for Lesbian Rights and Legal Services for Children.
The Model Standards Project's purpose includes the development of model
professional standards for the care and protection of GLBTQ youth in
juvenile court systems (both dependency and delinquency).[8] For example,
the Draft Principles include declarations such as:

1. Public systems must embrace diversity of all kinds, respect
   the inherent dignity and worth of each person, and create
   environments in which all young people are treated fairly and
   with respect.
2. Child welfare and juvenile justice agencies are responsible
   for ensuring that all services to youth in state custody are
   inclusive, sensitive, and responsive to the needs of individual
   youth.

As of this writing, the Annie E. Casey Foundation and the Child Welfare
League of America were working together to publish the Model Standards.

The United Nations *Convention on the Rights of the Child.* *The Convention on the Rights of the Child*, a document that was issued after
years of discussion at United Nations meetings around the world in the
1970s, is one of the most powerful public-policy documents in the area
of child and adolescent well-being. The *Convention* specifically guaran-
tees the right of each child to dignity, protection, and care. The *Convention* sets as an international standard that a child is any person under the
age of eighteen years and is deserving of unique and special refuge from
adult caprice. It thus provides a solid basis for continued demands to
desist in adjudicating children in adult criminal courts.

In addition, according to this historic document, "The child has the right to protection from discrimination of any kind, irrespective of the child's or his or her parent's or legal guardian's race, colour, sex, language, religion, political or other opinion, national, ethnic, or social origin, property, disability, birth or other status." On the basis of these guidelines, the disproportionate minority representation of children of color in the juvenile system is a violation of the right of children to fair and just treatment under international law.

This agreement also affords children in the justice system other protections:

> A child in conflict with the law has the right to treatment which promotes the child's sense of dignity and worth, takes the child's age into account, and aims at his or her reintegration into society. The child is entitled to basic guarantees as well as legal or other assistance for his or her defence.
>
> The child has the right to have his or her privacy fully respected at all stages of the [legal] proceedings. The child has the right to the establishment of a minimum age below which children shall be presumed not to have the capacity to infringe the penal law.

The *Convention* also protects children from the state's imposition of adult punishment, including capital punishment of people who committed their crimes when they were children.

In the United States, the landmark Supreme Court decision in *Roper v. Simmons*, making it unconstitutional to execute people who committed their crimes when they were minors, lends support to the demand for the U.S. government to sign the *Convention*. The unanimous international appeal at the 2002 World Congress of the Child was for the United States to adopt and enforce the provisions of the *Convention*. It sets international standards that advocates for children can petition from the state and that serve as a map of new pathways to policy reform.

Arenas for Policy Discussions

In devising new policies in the areas described above and in other areas, policy makers need to work with and consult each other in order to avoid duplication of efforts. I describe here a few promising efforts in this direction.

The Top of the Pyramid Roundtable. The Children and Family Justice Center of the Northwestern University School of Law invited several groups of Chicago-based community activists; juvenile court and probation officials; school, health, and legal experts; academics; and service providers to the Top of the Pyramid (TOP) Girls Roundtable in

February 2003. This meeting was designed to begin a community dialogue about services and programs for girls in the juvenile justice system who were in highest peril of "slipping through the cracks"—school had failed them, dependency services had failed them, families had failed them. The invitation articulated the problem:

> Although much has been written about girls in the past seven years, there seems to be little progress in the how or what to do about girls who are at the "top of the pyramid"—those girls who are on probation, have been sent to the Juvenile Temporary Detention Center, may have been sent to out-of-state placement or Department of Corrections. They are returned to the community or place where the situation for them has not changed—the gangs are still there, the drugs and alcohol are still there, family problems are still there, and schooling has been interrupted and may not be welcoming. These girls are at high risk for re-offense, for early pregnancy, for substance abuse, for dropping out of school, and for homelessness.
>
> We need to develop a collective vision to move forward in creating an infrastructure of community based services to embrace these girls in a meaningful way without the barriers. By focusing on girls at the "top of the pyramid"—about 200 girls per year—we can determine what should be in place and who would work best with this population and assume that if services are defined and funded long term, the services will be in place for the prevention, early intervention, and meaningful intervention for all girls.

Approximately thirty people have convened several times since that first meeting. Factions that rarely even speak to each other, such as community advocates and juvenile prosecutors, have come face to face to work out some of their seemingly opposing agendas. At the April 2003 meeting the following goals were identified:

1. Determine and assess existing community services and programs for TOP girls.
2. Determine a strategy for creating an infrastructure of comprehensive community-based services for TOP girls.
3. Develop a plan for implementing strategies over next year and beyond.
4. Identify [a] core group willing to continue working actively on the strategy/implementation plan.
5. Identify others willing to be involved in other ways.
6. Link with local/national programs and initiatives impacting TOP girls.

The work of this initiative will continue, but I offer it here as a model of how policy can be hammered out among government officials, academics, and legal scholars, as well as community advocates.

The Chicago Girls Coalition. Another organization that translates theoretically driven policy into action is the Chicago Girls Coalition. Across the nation in the 1990s, girls' coalitions formed in Seattle, San Francisco, and Boston, and one was instituted in Chicago in 2001. As of this writing, the Coalition is housed in the Girl Scouts of America office and comprises a loose-knit group of approximately fifty girl-serving agencies. The Coalition meets four times a year to share resources, participate in training sessions, hold conferences, and engage in various other activities such as generating an announcement listserv. It functions mostly as a resource provider in the Chicago metropolitan area, as a place where organizations and individuals "committed to enhancing the lives of girls" can "expand resources and strengthen support."[9]

Best Practices

The good news to the ending of a story of so much tragedy and hopelessness is that solutions to the problems described in this book are available. There are abundant sources of creative ideas for invigorating downcast youth. The lack of leadership and national will and the struggle to find time and energy and money inhibit us. While Halliburton banked billions in a war against Iraq, American youth languished in dungeons. Urban gardening projects, after-school peer counseling, life-skills classes that teach minors how to acquire identification cards and operate bank accounts, teen philanthropy projects, ecological exploration and clean-up programs, ethnic studies for teens, "teaching gentleness" and other violence-prevention curricula, street kids' theater projects—these are examples of the successful programs I visited for young people, who told me they were "psyched" (thrilled) to be able to work in them.

I highlight here several programs, just a few of the thousands of projects being instituted in neighborhoods around the world on behalf of young women. I selected these programs on the basis of several criteria. They were for girls. They were conscious of being gender-responsive. The girl participants were enthusiastic about them. And, not least of all, they were close to where I was living or working at the time of the fieldwork. Accessibility was a criterion because if you were to head out your door, around your neighborhood, or down the street from where you work, you would or should discover youth advocacy, albeit underfunded and short-staffed. Where there are girls, there should be girl-serving organizations and activities.

The Center for Young Women's Development (CYWD), San Francisco

CYWD's mission includes providing "gender specific, peer based opportunities for high-risk, low- and no-income young women to build healthier lives and healthier communities." This is a modest initiative for a community-based organization, but this one is different: CYWD, operating a million-dollar budget, is completely girl-run and is currently headed by a former court-involved young woman, Marlene Sanchez. This nationally known, award-winning program, run by teenage girls who have lived in the street economy, originated as the effort of then-doctoral student Rachel Pfeffer. First opened as the Street Survival Project out of a storefront in downtown San Francisco in 1993, CYWD continues to thrive.[10] CYWD is one of the few agencies in the nation that is run by youth, serves girls who are court-involved, and pays stipends to all workers/participants.

The Center runs several programs for young women who struggle with adult problems. Many of the participants live on their own, facing interpersonal violence as they fight charges in the juvenile justice system. Programs include the Girls' Detention Advocacy Project, the Sisters Rising Project (an employment component), and the Nelly Velasco Project for young, queer women of color.[11]

CYWD is unique in that the young women train new employees and then age out of the project. As the staff members reach their early twenties, they move on and leave openings for younger women to come in and get off the streets. As of this writing, there were funded slots for seventeen young women. Their work takes them onto the streets at night for outreach work, into schoolrooms to work with other youths, onto the detention units where girls are housed in lock-up, and all the way to the White House, where they went in 1998 to meet with President Bill Clinton and receive an award. With sufficient effort, centers such as these could open across the nation, offering refuge and revitalization to young women trapped in the street economy.

The Girls Services Unit, San Francisco

One of the first probation services units to focus solely on girls, this San Francisco City and County Probation Department program is funded primarily through California's Juvenile Justice and Crime Prevention Act and the United Way of the Bay Area. In 1999, under the leadership of Community Programs director and long-time youth advocate Cheyenne Bell, the San Francisco Juvenile Probation Department and the San Francisco District Attorney's Office created the position of coordinator of girls' services/victim advocate for girls in detention. In 2001, this partnership was expanded to fund community-based organizations offering direct services to girls in detention. In 2002, the Juvenile Probation Department and the United Way of the Bay Area established the Girls Justice Initiative, an innovative program that links case management and services offered to girls in detention to community-based agencies in the San Francisco Bay area. The goal of the Initiative is to increase the quality and quantity of gender-specific prevention and intervention services for girls on probation and, by doing so, to decrease their incarceration, out-of-home placement, and recidivism.

Despite being located in the drab and dreary setting of a detention facility and juvenile court, the Initiative office is a hub of joy and activity, with young women working hard and girls coming and going. Some of the services that the unit oversees are gender-specific programming for girls in lock-up, detention-based case management, an after-care program for girls leaving detention, and a mentoring program that links girls in detention who are not receiving family visits with culturally appropriate and caring college interns who visit them on a weekly basis. Through the leadership of Gena Castro and Julie Posadas-Guzman, co-founders and directors of the Girls Justice Initiative, each year the program also trains probation officers and an estimated fifty community-based agencies on best practices for working with girls in the juvenile justice system.

Because a large percentage of the girls detained in San Francisco's juvenile hall are not from San Francisco, many of the girls return to their city or county of origin without being linked to appropriate services that would increase their resiliency (and therefore decrease their recidivism rates). A main goal of the Girls Justice Initiative, therefore, is to create a network of gender-specific services and training sessions in surrounding Bay Area cities and counties.

Beyondmedia Education, Chicago

Beyondmedia Education (www.beyondmedia.org) is another example of a program working to achieve social justice for women and girls. A collaborative community organization, it uses media arts to give voice to members of some of the most marginalized groups, including women and girls in prison, young women, queer youth, and girls with disabilities.

GIRLS! ACTION! MEDIA!, a core program of Beyondmedia, provides low-income girls free access to media arts through hands-on workshops with trained artists; these workshops result in professional-quality videos and other media that bring the girls' issues to public audiences. Workshops offer safe spaces for girls and young women to explore their lives and develop as leaders and activists while learning important media-arts, technology, and public-speaking skills.

As seen at the Austin Gay & Lesbian Film Festival, Chicago Youth Media Festival (winner!), Independent Film & Video Chicago (1st place!), ImageOut: the Rochester Lesbian & Gay Film And Video Festival, Inside Out: Toronto Lesbian & Gay Film and Video Festival, Los Angeles Latino International Film Festival, Seattle Lesbian & Gay Film Festival, MIX Mexico: the 9th Sexual Diversity Film & Video Festival, Mexico City, New Fest: The 16th New York Lesbian & Gay Film Festival, San Francisco International Lesbian & Gay Film Festival, Vancouver Queer Film + Video Festival, and Women in the Director's Chair International Film and Video Festival!

Almost
A Fish Eaten by a Shark
A video by Zaida Sanabia and Beyondmedia

Zaida is making a video about forming a Gay-Straight Alliance at her school. She wants to include a teacher's homophobic comment, but the principal wants to shut her down. Zaida incorporates the voices of her gay and lesbian peers and compelling statistics to paint a sobering picture of school and family life for LGBTQ youth.

An excellent discussion starter and educational tool for school and organizational settings.

Running Time: 17 minutes

ORDER FORM: A Fish (Almost) Eaten by a Shark

Prices: Individuals $30 plus $5 s/h
        Institutions $100 plus $15 s/h

Beyondmedia Education

Name: _____

Organization / Affiliation : _____

Address: _____

Phone: _____   Email: _____

Options: VHS___ DVD___   English___ Spanish___

Send check, money order, purchase order to:
Beyondmedia Education
7013 N. Glenwood
Chicago, IL 60626
phone 773.973.2280
fax 773.973.3367
beyond@beyondmedia.org
Or buy online on our website!

Illustration 6.2. Flyer for a video about the filmmaker's efforts to start a gay-straight alliance at her high school. *Credit: Conceived and created by Beyondmedia Education, 2003.*

One of the goals of GIRLS! ACTION! MEDIA! is making Chicago high schools safe for queer youth. A key activity is screening a video that Beyondmedia made with a seventeen-year-old filmmaker, Zaida Sanabia, about her efforts to document a gay-straight alliance in her high school. *A Fish (Almost) Eaten by a Shark* chronicles the struggles of Zaida as she makes her video. In the midst of filming the club's activities, Zaida is told to hand over some of the footage to the school principal or be banned from the school. According to the promotional material, the video incorporates the voices of gay and lesbian youth and compelling statistics to paint a sobering picture of school and family life for GLBTQ youth (see Illustration 6.2).

On a tree-lined, cobblestone street right on the El tracks in the heart of the funky, mixed hippie/urban Rogers Park neighborhood of north-side Chicago, Beyondmedia's storefront studio/office is a welcoming and exciting agency to visit. Silk-screened revolutionary posters exhort those entering to respect women, honor youth, and act against injustice. A long table invites you to sit down and work.

Zaida, a graceful and shy young woman, first became involved with Beyondmedia as a workshop participant in 2001. She was later hired as an intern and is now on staff. She began explaining her experiences doing this work in a quiet and strong voice: "I always get nervous 'cuz you never know what's going to come. [In the high school setting] there is more connecting; they're youth, and I'm a youth. But sometimes I feel like they look up to me, like I'm more than them. I don't like that so much because, in general, all our issues are the same issues." (On an evaluation form an audience member wrote, "Zaida Sanabia is a lot stronger than I.") At this point, Salome Chasnoff, Beyondmedia's executive director, interrupted our interview to exclaim excitedly, "Zaida! 'A Fish' was just accepted by the Vancouver Film Festival!" The staff was enthusiastic on hearing this news. Zaida continued by talking about being Latina: "The main thing about being a Latina is being a woman. In the tradition, they say a girl can't do this or a girl can't do that. Girls must. . . . stay home, help cook and clean. It is still going on in our Latino families, but maybe not as much as before."

Through the creative work of making films and other media, in centers such as Beyondmedia, young women are able to talk about all aspects of being a girl: being Latina or African American, being a lesbian, living in a poor neighborhood. In order to get at the causes of girls getting into trouble, we must find ways to make their lives in their communities better. Beyondmedia is doing this important and life-saving work with young women, right in the communities from which some of them were sent into corrections.

Young Women's Empowerment Project (YWEP), Chicago

YWEP is a north-side Chicago initiative that incorporates a broad definition of zero tolerance for sexism, racism, and homophobia while working to challenge stereotypes about young women and their struggles to navigate adolescence (www.youarepriceless.org). YWEP is an example of a project that incorporates the rare advocacy option of "harm reduction" (see Chapter Three). YWEP receives funding from a variety of women's and progressive foundations. All its projects are free to young women aged thirteen to twenty-four.

YWEP was founded in 2000 in Chicago as a physical and emotional gathering place for young women who are affected by street economies and the sex trade. YWEP's particularly loving website, "you are priceless," reads:

> our mission is to offer safe, respectful, free of judgment spaces for girls and young women impacted by the sex trade and street economies to recognize and develop their goals, dreams, and desires— this work is personal to us, it is about our lives.
>
> what is the "sex trade and street economies"?
>
> we use this term to mean all the different ways that girls and young women (and others too) trade sex for money, gifts, drugs or survival needs, including exotic dancing, escorting, lingerie modeling, phone sex, dungeon, adult internet sites, movies and more. sometimes other people can arrange it. it can be a part of surviving on the street or in your neighborhood. it can be your decision based on the options you have. we are always learning more ways and would like to hear about your experiences and how you describe it.[12]

Because the street economy is pervasive and, usually, harmful to girls, it is surprising that there is not a formal name for the experiences of millions of girls around the world, including many of the young women in this book, who grow up in this billion-dollar industry, which thrives, basically, because of male heterosexual lust and greed. The term "sexual trafficking of girls" does not reflect how young women talk about their sexual survival strategies.

The young women organized a Pancake and Poetry Benefit in the summer of 2004 to raise money for and awareness about their project. In contrast to the girls whose accounts we read throughout this book, the girls at the benefit were running around amid a flurry of activity, laughter, fun, and hard work. The old neighborhood church that the benefit was held in is a beautiful brick and wood structure that almost shimmered with the excitement and tension of the young women who were nervously preparing the pancakes and their poems. Each table was decorated with glitter, and a large, hand-printed sign gave the rules for the poetry slam, such as, "No boo-ing." The love and sense of fun emanating from the adults in attendance was palpable; there was so much encouragement for the young women to tell the truth about their lives.

The moderator for the event was a slim, dark-haired young woman who was obviously enjoying herself and her great sense of humor. One by one, she invited young people to come up to the mic and share a poem, a piece of artwork, or a smile. The topics on the young people's minds that day ranged from eating in a restaurant and being treated rudely for being openly gay, to dancing naked for boyfriends and friends of boyfriends, to entreaties for sistahs to take good care of themselves. Every single person who spoke or shared was applauded and encouraged; no adults needed to "correct" the young women or admonish them for drinking or drugging. One could see how, as the youth advocate quoted in Chapter Four put it, "working together *is* the healing." Through community organizing, challenging stereotypes together, and finding creative ways to express themselves, young women were making the difficult and totally possible climb toward safety and good health. It was hard to leave the event; everyone lingered because it was so much fun. It raised money for the young women's projects as well as an immeasurable amount of love and support and hope for all.

Rogers Park Young Women's Action Team (YWAT), Chicago

YWAT is sponsored by the Friends of Battered Women and Their Children, a domestic violence agency located in Chicago's north side. As part of a YWAT project, a group of fourteen young women, aged fourteen to eighteen, conducted a survey of girls who regularly traversed Howard Street, a busy, small-business-filled avenue in a slightly rundown, delightfully old, and vibrant neighborhood full of apartment buildings for single young people and families of color in north side Chicago. The streets of Rogers Park, where the YWAT is located, feel good—lots of laughter and chatter on warm summer nights—unless you are a young woman walking alone. Then the streets can become a treacherous gauntlet that instills embarrassment, painful self-consciousness, and suppressed fear and anger. The young women answering the survey said that times must have changed from when people greeted each other in the street with a "What's happenin'?" or "How you doin,' sistah?" The girls reported that young men called out to them mercilessly, teasing them, discussing their bodies, and using disrespectful language in loud voices. The young women said they also felt frightened by the boys' advances and comments.

Based on the survey findings regarding violence and harassment, the girls launched an anti-street-harassment campaign, R-E-S-P-E-C-T—Let Me Tell You What It Means to Me, in June 2004. After they published their report, they decided to organize a street-sign campaign. They designed flyers for businesses and residents to post in their windows (see Illustration 6.3).[13] Several Chicago aldermen and a state representative attended the launching of the campaign. Later that day, young women in groups of three and four went around the neighborhood, laughing and carrying the signs, asking residents and businesspeople to participate. The campaign was a victory and an example of how young women can engage directly in their environments and address their concerns in self-empowering ways. This effort was not in and of itself enough to change the course of sexism and racism. Nonetheless, the campaign was a concrete way to include political leaders and community members in a rejoinder to the hypersexualization and eroticization of young women's bodies and lives.

Girl Talk, Chicago

Girl Talk, a community-based organization, provides girl-focused programs for young women in the Cook County Juvenile Temporary Detention Center (www.girltalkchicago.org). One of the first projects of its kind in the nation, it is supported by donations and foundation grants. It was begun in 1993 by four community organizations that support it. Girl Talk operates four programs. One, called Girl Talk, consists of a weekly program in which young women come together from various units in lock-up for a two-hour, girl-only session. In an atmosphere of respect, they voice their concerns and opinions, work on a creative project, or simply receive attention and care. The environment is relatively safe

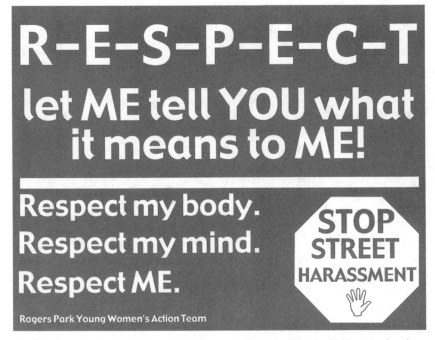

Illustration 6.3. Flyer for an anti-street-harassment campaign. *Credit: Conceived and created by the young women in the Rogers Park Young Women's Action Team.*

compared with day-to-day life on the units. Girl Talk is the only space where girl advocacy occurs in the detention center.

The second program that Girl Talk operates is a Friday-night session, Girls Leadership Group, in which young women in lock-up work together on projects such as theater and talent shows and enjoy the consistent presence and loving commitment of community girl advocates. The third program Girl Talk initiated is the Talk Out project, which is run by formerly incarcerated girls who carry on the work they began when in lock-up.

On a cold winter night in 2004, Girl Talk held its first fundraiser/art show in the community at a funky arts center and café in Bucktown, an artsy, west-side Chicago neighborhood. Throughout the studio hung poems and artwork by the girls, accompanied by posters with stark statistics telling the grim story of girls in the juvenile system. Four groups of artwork and poems had been mounted into four collages that were about to be displayed on Chicago Transit Authority buses and trains. The room was abuzz with energy and excitement as the young women began their program. Formerly incarcerated girls came forward one by one to tell their stories and to recite poems that they had written for the occasion. The gallery café was packed, and all were focused on the deep messages that the young women were conveying. Most energizing was the spirit of the young women, who rarely received this kind of attention and who were clearly basking in the love and support from all the people listening to them.

A fourth program at Girl Talk is the Campaign for Incarcerated Girls' Bill of Health Rights. It started in July 2003, when the Health and Medicine Policy Research Group (HMPRG) of Chicago, an independent, not-for-profit policy-research center, held a conference entitled "Healing Girls in the Juvenile Justice System: The Challenge to our Community." HMPRG brought together an impressive array of adolescent health practitioners, advocates, experts (including Chicago local the Reverend Jesse Jackson), and a panel of formerly incarcerated girls organized by Girl Talk to focus on the health care crisis of court-involved young women.

As a follow-up to the conference proceedings, HMPRG worked with the Talk Out group to develop the Incarcerated Girls' Bill of Health Rights (see Text Box 6.1).[14] Approximately fifty young women who were on probation or had been in the Cook County Juvenile Temporary Detention (JTDC) facility began by discussing what health meant to them, how they defined health, and ways that incarceration affected their health. Girls on the three different housing units at JTDC developed lists of their "top 10" health care concerns. Formerly incarcerated girls in the Talk Out group developed their lists relating to their experiences in detention and then reviewed all the girls' input to compile the final list.

A **right** is defined as something that all people deserve, simply because they are human beings. This bill of rights was created by young women who are or have been incarcerated in Cook County's Juvenile Temporary Detention Center. **These are rights that all young women deserve, regardless of their involvement with the juvenile justice system.**

1. **Family Contact.** We believe girls should be able to see their children more than once a week and without a judge's special permission. Girls should be allowed to see their immediate family members regardless of age.

2. **Accurate Information.** We believe girls should have access to information about their health records and their court case details.

3. **Personal Privacy and Confidentiality.** We believe girls have a right to privacy that includes their personal information as well as their bodies and personal space.

4. **Food, Water, and Exercise.** We believe girls should have access to nutritious food, sufficient water, and daily exercise.

5. **Proper Hygiene.** We believe girls should have more time to bathe, quality bathing products, as well as clean clothes and towels more often.

6. **Adequate & Respectful Mental Health Care.** We believe girls should have access to counseling services for their mental health.

7. **Another Chance.** We believe girls have the right not to be treated as criminals upon their release from detention and to be connected with community resources prior to release.

8. **Medical care.** We believe girls have a right to receive medical attention and medicine when they are ill.

9. **Gender-specific care.** We believe young women struggle with issues that are specifically related to their experience as girls, and deserve support in doing so from people who understand those issues.

10. **Freedom from Discrimination and Verbal & Physical Abuse.** We believe girls have a right to be respected by both staff and peers.

Text Box 6.1. Bill of Health Rights for Incarcerated Girls. Through a partnership between the Health and Medicine Policy Research Group, Chicago, and Girl Talk, this document was created in 2005 by girls both in and recently released from detention.

They unveiled the Bill and brought it to Lobby Day in the state capital in the spring of 2005; they have plans to use it in their work with the Cook County JTDC. Such is the power of empowered girls.

The Missouri Department of Youth Services, St. Louis

The Missouri Department of Youth Services (DYS) earned its reputation as a leader with its humane child protective system.[15] Here, in the heartland of the nation, the DYS's 2001 statement of core beliefs and philosophy concerning individual needs and rights reads like a tender missive to a beloved child:

> We all need each other.
> We all need to master basic living skills before we can move on to higher levels of self-actualization.
> We all have physical, emotional, mental, and spiritual needs including:
> Attention, Belonging, Safety, Structure, Discipline, Recognition, Acceptance.
> We all have the right to receive unconditional love and care.
> We all have the right to our different perceptions.
> We are all special and unique.
> We are all a combination of our present and our past.
> We all must experiment, try new behaviors, succeed, and fail as change occurs.
> All behavior has a purpose.
> We all want to do well and succeed.
> All of our significant battles are waged within ourselves.
> We believe there are no bad families and that kids and families must be viewed in the context of their gender, culture, and environment.

Missouri conducted an experiment in 1983, when it discontinued its use of large facilities. The state now houses children in groups of twenty to forty and is thus able to provide much more personal, local, and concerted care of the youth in its custody than it previously had been. DYS leaders explained that they built the political will to change their system by working in liaison with the community, police chiefs, legislators, and judges. Advocates created a bipartisan advisory board in order to develop new approaches to working with youth in trouble with the law. The DYS could make these changes for a variety of reasons. Because it had the backing of the government and the law, as well as community leaders, it was able to do away with large, secure buildings warehousing hundreds of teenagers and move toward smaller facilities with more humanistic plans.

In 2004 DYS had approximately two hundred girls in the long-term correctional system, and I met about twenty of them when I joined a tour of the facilities one rainy day. The young women were eager to talk about their experiences, especially over a soda pop and pizza lunch. I was accustomed to entering secure units and facing walls and bars and locked doors. I was not prepared to sit in circles with the detainees, laughing and talking with them in an accepting and nonthreatening atmosphere.

The entire facility was set in a rural county. It utilized the ranch/cottage system and thus consisted of individual cabinlike dormitories, with main halls for dining and school. Girls lived in spruced up rooms, decorated in the traditional (preteen) way—photographs of music stars (rappers) torn from magazines and taped to the walls, stuffed animals on the beds. But the physical plant itself was not what was amazing, it was the youth. Girls walked about in groups, by themselves, with boys, in a free and open manner. Fresh-faced and eager to converse and laugh, the girls talked easily about their time there and gave us a tour of the grounds. Compared with the spare, military-style dungeons elsewhere, the facilities in the Missouri system deserve focused attention because advocates will surely learn from the good work there about changing large, bureaucratic, and archaic public youth systems.

Conclusion: Moving beyond Gender

We cannot begin to interpret or prevent girls' sexual misconduct or perpetration of violence without first noticing their existence. We must move past the punishment of gender transgressions and move toward gender healing. Only after we grapple with hidden meanings, underlying causes, and cultural myths can we hope to move toward intervening and diverting girls from juvenile corrections. For intervention, prevention, or treatment programs to work, they must deal with the realities, meanings, and effects of troubled girls' experiences. After all, although the young women in this study passed through the juvenile justice system for varying reasons, the real story was where they began: with their needs unmet because of neglect and abuse. Until this issue is addressed socially, we cannot solve it legally. The punitive direction in which the system was headed by the early 2000s does us all more harm than good.

On the basis of observing and interviewing youth and adult participants in projects that were girl- and gender-focused, as well as conferring with experts and advocates and synthesizing their recommendations, I offer the following suggestions for directions in which we should move.

1. Immediately address the DMR crisis with a specific focus on girls of color. Develop and implement training and curricula for gender-specific programming that addresses race and racism specifically and analytically at every phase and in every discussion.

2. Immediately address the problem of the lack of adequate services for GLBTQ youth in the juvenile system with a specific focus on youth of color. Develop and implement training and curricula for gender-specific programming that addresses diverse sexualities specifically and analytically at every phase and in every discussion.

3. Appoint youth to sit on boards of directors, task forces, and police, probation, and court commissions so that their experience and wisdom are considered by the judicial and executive branches of our state correctional systems. Young women of color should be included in federal, state, county, and local top-level meetings where funding for and administrative decisions about young people's lives are made. Assist in the organization of peer-led initiatives and training for youth in order to stay informed about their changing needs.

4. Create safe places that are co-ed so that gender-explorative youth will not be forced to identify as either male or female. In the same way that we do not require bi-racial children to choose one race definitively, we must begin to move away from binary limits on gender and move toward fluid understandings of the performativity and experience of gender, especially among children. Consider the implications of having bi-gendered or multigendered children in every setting.

5. Assign every employee who works with children the task of protecting the basic human and civil rights of every child. Set professional standards for staff and trainers by, for example, establishing gender, sexuality, and race "security clearances" they have to pass before they can advance in their careers.

6. Develop and implement training and curricula that grapple with the performativity of masculinities. Begin boy-based, gender-specific discussion groups focused on relational aggression, safety, healthy relationships, and other topics that girls are taught. Implement programs that notice that boys have gender, that masculinity is malleable and variant.

7. Provide immediate emergency federal funding for the housing, health care, and education of disadvantaged youth of color, on demand, wherever they are located. Declare a national disaster in the sectors of the federal government responsible for

meeting the needs of disadvantaged children of color and immediately implement emergency operations to address the crisis of children in juvenile corrections. After all, the government of the United States is responsible for having created a crisis among youth by failing to provide adequate housing, education, health care, and employment for families.

8. Join the movement away from the secure, punitive warehousing of young people. Fund and open community-based alternatives including substance-dependence programs, especially for children.

In this book I have gathered the narratives of young women who were struggling to survive in failed juvenile corrections systems, as well as the accounts of adults who worked with them. I have outlined the concerns of young women who were in trouble with the law and have provided a sociological context for understanding their beliefs, attitudes, and behavior.

In Chapter One, I explained how girls get arrested and what being locked up is like, and I introduced the study participants. Chapter Two considered the overwhelming quantity and vicious quality of the physical, sexual, and emotional assault and neglect that the young women in the juvenile system reported experiencing before they came to the attention of authorities. I urged us to broaden the definition of community violence so that it captures the unique experiences of girls; in particular, it should include rape, domestic violence, sexual harassment, homophobic and misogynistic attacks, molestation, and incest. I explained that although these experiences have in the past been considered the private problems of girls and women, as both male and female populations rise in the juvenile and criminal justice systems, these experiences have created a public crisis.

In Chapter Three, I noted that gender, sexuality, and emotional norms have changed for young women since the inception of the juvenile-court system in the late nineteenth century. Contemporary mainstream girls experience a considerable amount of pressure to be passionate rather than passive. Popular media culture shapes and controls girls' needs, desires, expectations, choices, and behaviors in ways never before experienced. These changing gender norms, rising consumerism, and a lack of helpful material and symbolic resources for young women who come from disadvantaged communities contributed to young women developing what I came to call sexualized solutions to nonsexual problems. Girls in trouble with the law recounted voluminous experiences being sexualized, such as having sexual relations at very early ages and having romantic and sexual relationships with people much older than they were.

These and other sexual experiences are linked in particular ways to girls' stories of court involvement.

Chapter Four detailed the gender of aggression and discussed its implications for contemporary girls in the juvenile court system. I brought into view the girls' fears and hatred toward each other. In my interviews with girls in detention, emotional responses to being objectified and gay-bashed came to the fore as factors in anger-related experiences. Girls being adjudicated delinquent for violent offenses revealed that they were responding to harassment, coercion, and sexual abuse. In order to understand contemporary girls' violent offenses, we have to look at several pieces of the puzzle. Police attitudes and the gendered discretion of court personnel influence the rise in arrests and detention of girls for violent offenses. Reconfiguring family fights as aggravated assault has resulted in a spike of arrests of girls for violent offenses. Another aspect of girls' experiences with aggression lies in the history of gender norms for emotional expression. Locating girls' aggression in its political and social contexts equips us to provide gender interventions. The problems of court-involved young women will not be solved without addressing the crisis in emotional literacy they experience and without nurturing the emotional agency they do have. In this chapter, in addition to dispelling the myth that girls are more violent than boys or even more violent than ever, I wanted readers to notice the social logic beneath the violence that girls do perpetrate. Given the moral horizons of the gendered opportunities from which urban, disadvantaged girls make their so-called selections, their life choices, while not always legal, make social sense.

In Chapter Five, I outlined one response to the increase of young women in the system: gender-specific policy and programming for girls. Through ethnography and interviews, we learned what gender-responsive programming is, how it works, and how it can be improved. It is not that "gender is not enough," but that considering gender without race, class, sexuality, ability—that is, in more nuanced ways—will not produce meaningful interventions. Chapter Five provided empirical evidence that gender is productive and mediating; gender was constructed by the girls I studied, and gender norms controlled them. In other words, girls' gender identities are produced as they represent them and as they are judged by adults in the system. But young women's gender subjectivity cannot be separated from their racial heritage, their ethnicity, their history, their sexual orientation, or their class position. Their expressions of gender—their strategies for enacting their femininity and masculinity—varied by context. Gender and race were seen to be neither the essence of them nor a pure construction. The girls were not either black or girls. That is why the empowerment/protection debate is so complex and so crucial. The social problems of racism, sexism, and heterosexism merge in girls' experiences in juvenile corrections. The solutions must come from merged places as well. Gender-specific interventions should be places where gender stereotypes are dismantled and advocacy for girls happens.

We must work to ensure that local officials and the juvenile corrections system stop several negative practices such as harboring sexists and tolerating homophobes; increasing the number of beds in correctional institutions and building more juvenile detention facilities than schools; allowing community violence to prevail in poor neighborhoods; permitting racialized stereotypes to flourish among staff who work with young people; failing to eradicate the disproportionate representation of children of color in the juvenile court system; perpetuating sexist stereotypes of girls and women as sexual objects; and exploiting children's helplessness by prioritizing spending on other national concerns (such as the military) rather than on children's health and educational needs.

Even so, the community can do more than it does. We can provide locations where cultural myths about race, ethnicity, femininity, and masculinity are challenged. Gender-responsive programming should mean that staff, community advocates, and youth think critically about the stereotyping of urban youth and how that prejudice limits their access to opportunities based on gender, class, race, ethnicity, and sexualities. Gender-responsive projects should be locations where resistance to gender stereotyping is modeled. If we do not teach young women about the history of racism and sexism or offer them job skills and increased opportunities, but simply teach them about healthy relationships and parenting skills, then the gender-specific programs we have designed as interventions may reinforce the gender inequities that contributed to the abuse and violence that bring girls into the system in the first place. Children who are in trouble with the law will be truly rehabilitated when we encourage them to come together in peer-led interventions in which they can dismantle girl hating and other gender myths. Girls deserve nothing less.

Notes

Introduction

1. For examples of gender-neutral studies that focus on boys or men, see Anderson 1999; Bourgois 1995; Cohen 1955; Irwin 1970; Katz 1988; Sanchez-Jankowski 1991. See also Hirschi 1969; Sutherland 1939.
2. For detailed histories of varied framings of girls' delinquency, refer to Alexander 1995; Beisel 1997; Davis 1929; Freedman 1981; Konopka 1966; Kunzel 1993; Tappan 1947; Tice 1998.
3. Here I stand on the shoulders of giants, and it would be impossible to list all the scholars who have made crucial contributions to this effort. Seminal work by Meda Chesney-Lind (Chesney-Lind and Shelden, 1992) opened a door in criminology for scholars to focus on delinquent girls and revealed that it was girls' survival strategies that were being criminalized. Educator Lyn Mikel Brown documents the politics of anger and fighting in schoolgirls' lives (1998, 2003). Studies attending to the sexuality of adolescent girls have brought a feminist agenda to that sociology (Irvine 1994; Phillips 2000; Thompson 1995; Tolman 2002). Jody Miller's distinguished work on girl gangs (2001) and Adrienne Wing and Christine Willis's work on girls of color in trouble (1997) set the standard for theorizing about the experiences of girls living in danger. See also Artz 1998; Belknap and Holsinger 1998; Bloom et al. 2002; Campbell 1984; Chesney-Lind and Belknap 2004; Davis 1999; Giordano, Cernkovich, and Lowery 2004; Lamb 2001; Mann 1984; Miranda 2003; Richie 1996; Steffensmeier and Allan 1996; Walkerdine, Lucey, and Melody 2001; Way 1998.
4. For an example of how girls' qualitative experiences are chiefly excluded from criminology texts, see any introductory text in criminology—e.g., Siegel 2005. The pathologies of adolescent girls are outlined in Pollak and Friedman 1969. Richardson, Taylor, and Whittier 2003 and other introductory texts in women's studies demonstrate that qualitative explorations of girls who are punished for transgressing the law are rarely included. Stephens 1995 is an example of an anthropology reader on childhood without mention of children in trouble with the law. Devine 1996 focuses on school violence as a problem about guns and guys. I point this omission out simply to document that dozens of anthologies of essays foundational in the study of childhood and adolescence have omitted entirely the topic of girls' conflicts with delinquency, incarceration, and the law. See also Eder 1997; Elkind 1998; Fass and Mason 2000; West and Petrik 1992. For critical exceptions see Austin and Willard 1998; Griffin 1993; Males 1999.

1 *New Troubles for Girls*

1. All names, descriptions, locations, details of cases, exact situations, charges, job titles, and many other identifying features have been omitted or altered to protect project participants' anonymity and confidentiality. All descriptions of events and interactions and all quotes come directly from interviews or observations of study participants.

2. Sources for data in this paragraph are Keller 2002; Snyder 2005; Snyder and Sickmund 1999; Stahl 2003.

3. Although we know that these data are flawed for making claims about precise case counts (see note for table 1.1), my intention here is to use government statistics to begin a discussion of the impact and meanings of these trends. For thorough discussions of caveats when reporting and interpreting figures from the FBI data sets, see, for example, Snyder 2005. The FBI defines aggravated assaults as unlawful attacks by one person on another for the purpose of inflicting severe bodily injury or death. This type of assault is usually accomplished by the use of a weapon. Simple assaults are not of an aggravated nature and do not result in serious injury to the victim.

4. U.S. Census Bureau, *Census 2000 Summary File 1*, Table P14, http://www.census.gov (accessed October 30, 2005); Snyder, Puzzanchera, and Kang 2005 (accessed October 30, 2005).

5. Stahl, Finnegan, and Kang 2003.

6. Office of Juvenile Justice and Delinquency Prevention 2001.

7. See discussion in Britton 2003 regarding the historical meanings of these discursive labels.

8. San Francisco Juvenile Probation Department, Mission Statement, 1999.

9. See also *Girl Trouble*, a 2004 documentary film by Lexi Leban and Lidia Szajko, featuring accounts of three young women in the juvenile system. One of the young women in the film would not go to the emergency room at the hospital because a warrant had been issued for her arrest and she surmised (correctly) that the county hospital and the juvenile legal system worked in concert (http://www.girltrouble.org).

10. Schaffner 2005; Snyder 2003.

11. Sociologist Joan Acker developed the idea of gendered organizations (1990). For detailed analyses of the genderedness of the criminal and juvenile legal system, see Bond-Maupin, Maupin, and Leisenring 2002; Bloom 2003; Britton 2003; Gaarder, Rodriguez, and Zatz 2004; McCorkel 2003.

12. Snyder and Sickmund 1999.

13. For a fuller discussion, see Girls Inc. and the Office of Juvenile Justice and Delinquency Prevention 1996.

14. See also Adams, Gulotta, and Clancy 1985; Schaffner 1999a. Statement about girls as victims of violence from Acoca and Dedel 1998.

15. O'Hare and Mather 2003; O'Hare and Mather define severely distressed neighborhoods as "census tracts having three out of four characteristics: high poverty rate; high percentage of female-headed households; high percentage of high school dropouts; or high percentage of working-age males unattached to the labor force" (4). Sickmund, Sladky, and Kang 2004 (accessed October 31, 2005); Snyder and Sickmund 2006; see also Girls Inc. and the Office of Juvenile Justice and Delinquency Prevention 1996.

16. For statistics regarding juveniles in corrections, see http://www.ojjdp.ncjrs.org (accessed June 16, 2005).

17. California Board of Corrections, Facility Construction Projects, http:// www.bdcorr.ca.gov (accessed June 22, 2005). The census count for all eight centers in Illinois was 1,404 youth total, 105 girls, as of June 15, 2005; personal communication, Bruce Olson, Illinois Department of Corrections, June 16, 2005.
18. See the documentary *Orphan Trains, 1854–1929* 2000.
19. For other examples of improvised terminology based on fieldwork, see Hochschild 1989 (gender strategies) and Richie 1996 (gender entrapment).
20. Police use the term *females* to describe girls and women; regressive hip-hop/ rap videos describe young women as females; and the girls themselves use the term, having adopted it from arguably misogynistic popular culture.
21. Beauvoir 1952, 58.
22. See Schaffner 2005.
23. Black 1991, 600.
24. United Nations 1989.
25. "5150" was the California health code indicating psychological impairment. Beat police officers and other legal officials in this study sometimes used it as a verb to mean "to evaluate psychologically as a danger to self or others."
26. Pajer et al. 2001, 297.
27. For the history of gender expectations and kinship norms, see Freedman 1981 and Smith-Rosenberg 1985. For the history of delinquency, see Mennel 1973. For the history of female delinquency, sexuality, and the law, see Adams 1997; Alexander 1995; Devlin 1997; Odem 1995; Schlossman 1977; Smart and Smart 1978; Tappan 1947. See also Pollak and Friedman 1969; Gordon 1988.
28. Sources for this paragraph are Addams 1909; Agustin 2005; Breckinridge and Abbott 1917; Naffine 1987; Chesney-Lind and Shelden 1992; Glueck and Glueck 1934; Poulin 1996; Pollock 1999.
29. Pisciotta 1982.
30. Odem and Schlossman 1991; Conway and Bogdan 1977.
31. Such behavior, although perhaps more accepted, is still highly contested by the public and will likely structure political arguments over religion, sexuality, and the state well into the twenty-first century. See discussions in Bernstein 2001; Bernstein and Reimann 2001; Jakobsen and Pellegrini 2004; Luker 1984, 1996; O'Connell Davidson 2005; Wilcox 1999; Woodhead 1997. Contradictions erupted in 2005 in the popular media through the obsession with girl-on-girl kisses, "wardrobe malfunctions," gay marriage, and celebrity sex trials. See also LaFerla 2003.
32. Henry J. Kaiser Family Foundation 2003, 14.
33. Alan Guttmacher Institute 1994; Henry J. Kaiser Family Foundation 2003; Cooper, Delmonico, and Burg 2001; Ryan, Manlove, and Franzetta 2003. See also Bernstein 2001.
34. "Who will make knowledge, and how?" is a quote from DeVault 1999, 1.
35. Some criminological-methodology texts (for example, Maxfield and Babbie 2005) mention only in passing the disclosure of trauma. Wells and Rankin apparently discovered, in 1995, that the National Crime Victimization Survey may miss important declarations regarding girls' victimization. Pope, Lovell, and Brandl 2001 typifies many textbooks that lack engagement with the challenges that research among girls and women might present. There are many fine exceptions, including Campbell 2001; DeVault 1999; Fine 1992; Mohanty 2003; Naples 2003; Miller 2001; O'Connell Davidson and Layder 1998; Reinharz 1992; Smith 1987; Tolman and Brydon-Miller 2001; Wolf 1997.

36. Brydon-Miller 2001, 86.
37. See Burke 1950; Sykes and Matza 1957.
38. See Girls Inc., and the Office of Juvenile Justice and Delinquency Prevention 1996. In 1997, girls constituted 22 percent of the population in private placements, compared with 13 percent of the population in public residential facilities (Snyder and Sickmund 1999). See also Gilligan, Lyons, and Hammer 1989; Pipher 1994.
39. I used SPSS to analyze one hundred interviews conducted with the same instrument, coded for demographics, as well as prevalence of experiences, comments, and events. Although all the young women I came into contact with contributed to the study, I used an N=100 for the overall formal data reporting. (The first eight interviews served as a pilot. Forty-eight young women who participated were interviewed informally or with different interview schedules, or were in focus-group settings, or were not court-involved.) Although approximately one in five of all interviews (eighteen out of one hundred) were conducted totally or partially in Spanish, slightly less than half (eighteen out of forty-one) of interviews with Latinas were conducted in Spanish. The tables, unless otherwise noted, are based on this sample of one hundred.
40. Snyder and Sickmund 1999; Schaffner 2005.
41. Hsia, Bridges, and McHale 2004.
42. Ibid.
43. See, for example, Baca Zinn and Dill 1994; Hurtado 2003; Leadbeater and Way 1996.
44. See Fine 1992; Fine and Sandstrom 1988; Grover 2004; Hurtado 2003.
45. In the late 1990s, before the advent of text messaging, young women used languages they made up—entire alphabets and code phrases—to leave each other detailed messages by "blowing up" each others' pagers. They did this by entering the numbers and symbols on the telephone pad that stood for or created letters (for example, "77" is "M") onto each other's pagers.
46. For further discussion of processes of inner emotional work and their relation to gender strategies, see Briggs 1991; Chodorow 1995. Quote from "Those Jeans," by Ginuwine, 2003. For a discussion of mainstream culture and the hypersexualization of girls, see Walkerdine 1998.

2 *Injury, Gender, and Trouble*

1. A considerable body of multidisciplinary research is devoted to documenting and understanding the sexual exploitation and traumatic injury of girl children. For claims made in this paragraph, see Charles Stewart Mott Foundation 1994; Costin, Karger, and Stoesz 1996; Eisenstein 1988; Elliott and Morse 1989; Finkelhor 1994; Gilgun 1986; Harway and Liss 1999; Herman 1992; Jacobs 1993; Ketterlinus et al. 1992; Lamb 2001; Phelps 1979; Pynoos and Eth 1985; Rich 1978; Sharpe 1976; Thompson 1995; Tolman 2002; Tolman and Higgins 1996; van der Kolk 1987; Widom and Kuhns 1996. See also Brumberg 1997; Eder 1997.
2. See Levine 2003; Rogers Park Young Women's Action Team 2003; Veysey 2003.
3. Abma et al. 1997; Estes and Weiner 2001; Finkelhor 1994; Finkelhor and Baron 1986; Finkelhor and Ormrod 2001; Finkelhor and Jones 2004; Jonson-Reid and Barth 2000; Kilpatrick et al. 2003; Moore, Nord, and Perterson 1989;

Runtz and Briere 1986; Snyder 2000; Stock et al. 1997; Widom 1989; Wordes and Nunez 2002.

4. Schur 1997, 80.
5. Greenfield 1997.
6. Owen and Bloom 1997; Acoca and Dedel 1998; Acoca and Austin 1996.
7. Acoca and Dedel 1998; Acoca and Austin 1996; Briere and Elliott 1994; Herman 1992; Holden, Geffner, and Jouriles 1998; Powers and Jaklitsch 1989; Rogers 1999. Scholars posit that the courts' focus on girls' transgressions rather than on their victimization results in the criminalization of abused girls (Simkins and Katz 2002).
8. Apter 1990; Bernardez 1991; Duncan et al. 1998; Holsinger and Holsinger 2005; Powers and Jaklitsch 1989.
9. Luster and Small 1997, 204.
10. Biglan et al. 1995; Gilgun 1986; Haynie 2003; Herrera and McCloskey 2003; Kataoka et al. 2001; Kelly, Thornberry, and Smith 1997; Luster and Small 1997; Madriz 1997; Silverman et al. 2001; Smith 1997; Stewart, Dennison, and Waterson 2002.
11. Deisher and Rogers 1991, 500. See also Goldman 1987; Herman 1992; Runtz and Briere 1986; and works cited in note 10 (this chapter).
12. Gilgun 1986; Silverman, Reinharz, and Giaconia 1996; Golding 1999; Smith, Thornberry, and Ireland 2004; Stannard 1971.
13. Runtz and Briere 1986.
14. Belknap and Holsinger 1998; Browne and Finkelhor 1986; Herman 1992; Janus et al. 1987; Orenstein 1994; Pfeffer 1997; Powers and Jaklitsch 1989; Schaffner 1999a; Steffensmeier and Allan 1998; Wolfe and Tucker 1998.
15. Herman 1992, 104.
16. American Association of University Women 1992, 83.
17. See Gilligan, Lyons, and Hammer 1989; Pipher 1994; Proweller 1998.
18. See also accounts in American Association of University Women 2001; Rogers Park Young Women's Action Team 2003; Wolfe and Tucker 1998. Artz (1998), in a study of violence and girls in a Canadian school, found a statistically significant difference between violent schoolgirls' assessment that the "unequal treatment of women" was very serious and the milder assessment of "non hitting" girls and all boys. See also Stein 2001.
19. Black 1991.
20. Nan Stein, quoted in Wellesley Centers for Women 1998.
21. American Association of American Women 2001, 2.
22. American Association of University Women 2001; Wolfe and Tucker 1998; Wyatt 2001.
23. Rogers Park Young Women's Action Team 2003; Center for Women Policy Studies 2001.
24. Devoe et al. 2004, iv. Donohue, Schiraldi, and Ziedenberg (1998) and Brooks, Schiraldi, and Ziedenberg (2000) describe the commotion over school violence as hype, arguing that the sensationalized accounts of the anomaly of gun violence in schools in the 1990s was falsely causing a moral panic and was incorrectly constituted as a general trend. Devine's important ethnography about violence in schools neglected to mention sexual or gendered assault (1996). See also Wordes and Nunez 2002.
25. Cited in Wyatt 2001.
26. Although in this section I focus on girls' fighting back against sexual exploitation by boys, gender in girls' fighting matters. In a surprising finding from a

study drawing on in-depth interviews with 110 students (40 girls and 70 boys), girls were offenders in all incidents in which knives were used, a finding researchers had not hypothesized (Lockwood 1997), and girls had similar rates of involvement in school fights as boys. Although boys fought mostly with other boys, girls were involved in as many fights with boys as they were with girls. The study was controversial: the schools selected had high rates of violence.

27. Stein 2001, 144.
28. Hermann 1992; van der Kolk 1987.
29. Kumpfer 1993, 1994.
30. See also findings regarding the effects of family, community, and youth violence in Garbarino et al. 1992; Holden, Geffner, and Jouriles 1998; Jenkins and Bell 1997; Mohr 1997; Osofsky 1998; Zimring 1998.
31. Osofsky 1998, 97.
32. *California Government Code,* sec. 13965 (2000). See also Siegfried, Ko, and Kelley 2004.
33. Bell 1995; Dougherty 1998; Friedrich-Cofer and Huston 1986; Huesmann et al. 2003; John Murray 1997; Osofsky 1997; Singer et al. 1995.
34. A good deal of research across disciplines has been conducted connecting the effects of abuse with later troubling behaviors. See Cauffman 2004; Cauffman et al. 1998; Hennessey et al. 2004; Holden, Geffner, and Jouriles 1998; Obeidallah and Earls 1999; Stein et al. 1997; Steiner, Garcia, and Matthews 1997; Teplin et al. 2002; Wood et al. 2002; van der Kolk and Greenberg 1987. For research supporting the victim-to-offender theory of girls' aggression, as well as considering that sequence within patriarchy, see, for example, Belknap and Holsinger 1998; Bernardez 1988; Brown, Chesney-Lind, and Stein 2004; Campbell 1994; Chesney-Lind and Belknap 2004; Herman 1981, 1992; Herrera and McCloskey 2001; Jacobs 1993; Tucker and Wolfe 1997; Wolfe and Tucker 1998.
35. Pastor, McCormick, and Fine 1996, 15. See also Furstenberg et al. 1999, a study that details ways that parents in disadvantaged communities and troubled urban environments have managed to provide loving and safe homes for their children.

3 *Empty Families, Sexuality, and Trouble*

1. West Group 2003, 994.
2. Thomas first used the idea of girls' sexual capital in his 1923 work, *The Unadjusted Girl.*
3. San Francisco Task Force on Prostitution 1996; O'Leary and Howard 2001; Federal Bureau of Investigation, *Crime in the United States,* Table 40, http://www.fbi.gov (accessed October 29, 2005).
4. Child Trends DataBank, http://www.childtrends.org (accessed November 5, 2005).
5. Sykes and Matza 1957; Thomas 1923. For a critical discussion of the sexualized images of African American girls and women, see Collins 2004; hooks 1992; Walkerdine 1998; Walkerdine, Lucey, and Melody 2001.
6. See discussions in Crenshaw 1995; Kaplan 1997; Kelley 1996; Pough 2004; Rose 1994; *VIBE* 2001. See also *Respect Me, Don't Media Me,* the report of a research project by the young women of Sisters Empowering Sisters (2003).
7. Examples in the United States: Girls Inc.; *Ms.* Foundation for Women Girls

Initiative; new initiatives by the Girl Scouts of America; the girls' coalitions in Seattle, San Francisco, Boston, and Chicago; and the many groups around the world that are demanding the well-being of the girl child (UNICEF, the United Nations Working Group on Girls).

8. See Chapter One for a brief history of girls' delinquency as sexual delinquency; see also Agustin 2005; Soderlund 2005; Thomas 1923; Rosen 1982.
9. Pipher 1994.
10. Lareau 2003; Schaffner 1997. See also Kumpfer and Tait 2000.
11. Sickmund, Sladky, and Kang 2004 (accessed June 20, 2005).
12. Federal Interagency Forum on Child and Family Statistics 2005; Umberson and Chen 1994. See also Simkins and Katz 2002.
13. Ross and Mirowsky 2001, 258.
14. Hayward et al. 2000.
15. U.S. Department of Health and Human Services 2003.
16. Child Trends DataBank, http://www.childtrends.org (accessed November 5, 2005); Federal Interagency Forum on Child and Family Statistics 2005.
17. Gonzales et al. 2000; National Center for Education Statistics 2004 (accessed December 16, 2004).
18. Federal Interagency Forum on Child and Family Statistics 2005; Jencks and Mayer 1990; Lerner and Galambos 1998; Owen and Bloom 1998; U.S. Census Bureau 2003. See also James and Prout 1997.
19. "San Francisco Foster Care Fact Sheet" 1996; National Foster Parent Association 2004; Roberts 2002.
20. Patillo, Weiman, and Western 2004, 9.
21. Beatty 1997; Covington 2003; O'Brien 2001; Patillo, Weiman, and Western 2004; Richie 2002; Sudbury 2005.
22. See also Lauer and Chesney-Lind 2002; Scott and Black 1999; Stack 1997.
23. Dietrich 1984; Gutierrez 1999; Kaufman 2005; Olders 1989.
24. Ryan 2004.
25. Chase 1999.
26. See Walkerdine 1998; Walkerdine, Lucey, and Melody 2001. See also Sisters Empowering Sisters 2003.
27. These notions are documented, explored, and debated elsewhere; for example, see Morgan 2000; Rose 2003. Here I wish to bring the conversation into the realm of the worlds of girls in trouble with the law.
28. See, for example, Denizet-Lewis 2004.
29. See Featherstone 1999; Giddens 1992; Snitow, Stansell, and Thompson 1983; Vance 1984.
30. Schlosser 1997; *Economist* 1998.
31. For studies of sexuality and differences by race and class, see Collins 2004; Hurtado 2003. For discussions of contemporary adolescent sexuality, see Lamb 2001; Levesque 2000; Levine 2002; Martin 1996; Nathanson 1991; Phillips 2000; Ponton 2000; Thompson 1995; Tolman 2002.
32. Alan Guttmacher Institute 1994; Henry J. Kaiser Family Foundation 2003.
33. Henry J. Kaiser Family Foundation 2003.
34. For exceptions, see discussions in works cited in note 31 (this chapter).
35. See Black 1991. Statutory rape codes may also vary by gender and orientation; see Schaffner 2005.
36. Phillips 1999.
37. Harm reduction evolved as a drug treatment strategy in situations where total sobriety was not a prerequisite for receiving services or participating in

a particular program (see Futterman, Lorente, and Silverman 2005; Rosenberg and Phillips 2003). Harm reduction is a compromise developed through community advocacy because so many young people were "failing" their drug treatment programs. For example, if a young person revealed that she was trying to end heroin dependence and that she was "just" using marijuana, the health care provider might support her plan to use a less harmful substance. The controversial San Francisco Needle Exchange Program was an example of a communitywide harm reduction project. Having an older boyfriend can be a harm reduction strategy if, for example, a young woman becomes involved with him in order to facilitate leaving a sexual abuse situation at home.

38. For detailed critiques, see Bernstein 2001; Lancaster and di Leonardo 1997.

4 Gender, Violence, and Trouble

1. Stahl 2003. For an overview of gender-responsive programming, see Greene, Peters, and Associates 2001, and Chapter Five.
2. In 2004, San Francisco City and County Juvenile Court began investigating the idea of developing a CASA system for their delinquency court (personal communication, Julie Posadas-Guzman, coordinator, Girls Services, July 19, 2004). See also Schaffner 1997.
3. Meredith 1999.
4. I interviewed forty-one girls who self-identified as Hispanic, Latina, Mexican, and other Spanish-speaking nationalities. Some of them preferred to speak in Spanish; others were not fluent in either Spanish or English and spoke *mitad mitad* (half and half). See also Flores-Gonzalez 2002; Olmedo 2004; Perez McCluskey 2002.
5. See, for example, van der Kolk 1987.
6. I purposefully conflate the terms *aggression, anger, conflict,* and *violence* here to distinguish the set of emotion and action that brings attention from authorities to girls' sexual practices. Entire treatises have been written on distinguishing just these experiences alone, but it is outside the scope of this project to do that and is not essential to the argument I make. See, for example, Alder and Worral 2004; Lerner 1985; Moretti, Odgers, and Jackson 2004; Schur 1984.
7. See also Baker Miller 1985; McKay, Rogers, and McKay 1989.
8. For seminal works regarding the politics of feelings and gender, see Bernardez 1991; Campbell 1994; Hochschild 1975; Baker Miller 1985. For an analysis of girls' aggression in particular, see Underwood 2003. Also see Brown, Chesney-Lind, and Stein 2004; Lesage 1985.
9. Breckinridge and Abbott 1917.
10. See D'Emilio and Freedman 1988; for comprehensive overviews of studies of shifting gender norms and debates about these shifts generally, see Butler 2004; Ferree, Lorber, and Hess 1999; Richardson, Taylor, and Whittier 2003.
11. Parsons 1942, 605.
12. Cancian and Gordon 1988; Hymowitz and Weissman 1978.
13. See West and Zimmerman 1987. For analyses of gender formation, see Thorne 1993.
14. For discussions of the complications with representations of violence in the social sciences, see Harvey and Gow 1994; Kleinman, Das, and Lock 1997; Moore 1994. For analyses of girls' violence, see Brown, Chesney-Lind, and

Stein 2004; Chesney-Lind 2004; Chesney-Lind and Belknap 2004; Putallaz and Bierman 2004. See also Baskin, Sommers, and Fagan 1993; Moskowitz et al. 2001. For an overview of men's violence, see Archer 1994.

15. For examples of engaged scholarship examining and critiquing representations of girls in conflict, see Alder and Worral 2004; Artz 1998; Brown 2003; Brown, Chesney-Lind, and Stein 2004; Campbell 1984; Chesney-Lind and Belknap 2004; Goodwin 2002; Lamb 2001; Moretti, Odgers, and Jackson 2004; Putallaz and Bierman 2004; Simmons 2002; Underwood 2003. For examples of criminological work on boys and violence, see Loeber 1996; Farrington 1996.

16. See Snyder 2005 for definitions. See also Hagedorn 1997; Tonry and Moore 1998; Delancey Street Foundation 1997; and Sickmund, Snyder, and Poe-Yamagata 1997 for accounts of typical youth (male) violence. As the numbers and proportions of girls' arrests for aggravated assault, motor-vehicle theft, weapons offenses, and drug trafficking rose, we saw the dismaying creation of SHO (serious and habitual offenders) units for girls. For example, the majority of young women in long-term lock-down in Warrenville Correctional Facility in downstate Illinois in 2005 were serving sentences for auto theft (personal communication, Warden Jeffery Bargar, June 23, 2005).

17. For discussions of community and youth violence, see Gilligan 1996; McCord 1997; Pinderhughes 1997; Shoemaker 1996; Snyder 1998; Tonry and Moore 1998; Zimring 1998. For sociological critiques of gender and violence, see Braithwaite and Daly 1994; Connell 1987; Archer 1994.

18. See, for example, a study of teenage girls' "quiet disturbance" (Harris, Blum, and Resnick 1991). See also Elliott, Hagen, and McCord 1997; Garbarino et al. 1992; Hagedorn 1994, 1997; Klein, Maxson, and Miller 1995; Shelden, Tracy, and Brown 2001. Quote from Hagedorn 1994, 197.

19. The literature on the sociobiology of male aggression spans many disciplines. For biosocial criminological analyses, see Farrington 1996; Loeber 1996; Rowe 1996. For a sociological contextualization of masculinity and crimes, see Newburn and Stanko 1994. On gendered violence, see Archer 1994; Coie and Dodge 1998; O'Toole and Schiffman 1997. For a sense of the scope of training for youth advocates working with violent youth, see any issue of *Youth Today*.

20. Campbell 1994; Covington 1998; Crick and Grotpeter 1995; Esbensen 2000. For considerations of male violence as normal, instrumental, almost valiant, or simply as gender-neutral, see Anderson 1999; Bourgois 1995; Hagedorn 1997; Katz 1988, Sanchez-Jankowski 1991.

21. Katz 1988.

22. Even our best and most comprehensive texts neglect to include chapters on anger or other such feelings as a factor in gang violence; see, for example, Klein, Maxson, and Miller 1995. See also Crick et al. 2001; Katz 1988; Rosenthal, Lewis, and Cohen 1996; and note 24 (this chapter).

23. Galen and Underwood 1997, 589.

24. For binary theories of gender and aggression, see Coie and Dodge 1997; Conway 2005; Crick 1997; Crick and Bigbee 1998; Leschied et al. 2001; Underwood 2003.

25. Greenfield and Snell 1999.

26. Bloom et al. 2002; Bloom, Owen, and Covington 2003; Morgan and Peters 2000; Steineger and Peters 2000.

27. See Poulin 1996; Scripps Howard 1996. In polls, Americans persist in seeing

women as emotional and men as aggressive, even though pressure exists in mainstream popular culture to view men and women equally (Newport 2001). Some criminologists now argue that boys and girls are, unfortunately, acting more like adults (see Schaffner 2005).

28. See Baker Miller 1985; Lerner 1985; McKay, Rogers, and McKay 1989.
29. Baker Miller 1985, 1.
30. Dougherty 1998.
31. Levine and Rosich 1996. See also Garbarino et al. 1992; Garbarino and Kostelny 1997; Leiberman 1981; Tannen 1998.
32. Carvajal 1999. See *Girlfight, Million Dollar Baby, Set It Off.*
33. American Automobile Association 1997, 1999.
34. U.S. Department of Labor 2005, accessed November 5, 2005.
35. Bok 1998, 3. Watch, for example, any segment of popular daytime television shows, such as *The Jerry Springer Show,* to observe the cultural turn toward a ubiquitous normalization of violence in everyday life.
36. For works that argue from varying disciplinary perspectives for the cultural derivation and social control of expressions of hostility, see, for example, Briggs 1979; Campbell 1994; Scheler 1994.
37. See Acoca 1998; Belknap and Holsinger 1998; Campbell 1984; Miller 2001; Richie 1996; Tucker and Wolfe 1997.
38. Anderson 1997, 1999.
39. Brown, Chesney-Lind, and Stein 2004; Havel 1978; Scott 1985.
40. Fergusson, Horwood, and Beautrais 1999; Human Rights Watch 2001.
41. Braverman and Strasburger 1993; Fleisher and Fillman 1995; Human Rights Watch 2001; Kruks 1991; Pfeffer 1997; Remafedi and Blum 1986; Yates et al. 1991.
42. See Dang 1997.
43. See Pastor, McCormick, and Fine 1996; Way 1996.
44. Savin-Williams 2001, 307.
45. For research cited in this paragraph, see Braverman and Strasburger 1993; Curtin 2002; Fontaine and Hammond 1996; Human Rights Watch 2001; Jordan 2000; Michael et al. 1994; Remafedi and Blum 1986; Rubin 1990; Zemsky 1991.
46. American Association of University Women 2001; *Bay Area Reporter* 1998; Brooke 1998; D'Augelli and Dark 1995; Fineran 2001; Kurwa 1998; Ness 1998; Sullivan 1998; Yates et al. 1988.
47. Busen and Beech 1998; Human Rights Watch 2001; Owens 1998.
48. Curtin 2002; Fineran 2001; Scholinski 1997.
49. Curtin 2002; Wyatt 2001.
50. American Psychiatric Association 1994; Dang 1997; Feinstein et al. 2001; Herdt 1989; Hunter 1990; Kennedy 1991; Owens 1998; Scholinski 1997.
51. Dang 1997; *Foster Care Youth United* 1994.
52. Lobel 1986; Scherzer 1998.
53. See D'Augelli 1998; Blumenfeld and Raymond 1988; Fontaine and Hammond 1996; Kruks 1991; Remafedi and Blum 1986; Savin-Williams 2001; Sedgwick 1993.
54. Thompson 1994; Brown 2003; Acoca and Dedel 1998.
55. This topic is dear to feminist scholars who study adolescent girls. See Brown 1998, 2003; Feldman and Elliott 1990; Johnson, Roberts, and Worell 1999; Leadbeater and Way 1996; Pipher 1994.
56. Centers for Disease Control and Prevention 2004; Devoe et al. 2004. Given

the media furor over school shootings in the 1990s, violence on school property was framed (and contested) as a serious, growing social problem; see Devine 1996; Gibbs 2001; Kantrowitz and Wingert 1999; Brooks, Schiraldi, and Ziedenberg 2000.

57. See studies of girls' friendships by Brown, Way, and Duff 1999; Griffiths 1995; Hey 1997. For discussions of girls' fighting and meanness toward each other, see Brown 2003; Lamb 2001; Simmons 2002.

58. Savin-Williams and Berndt 1990, 277.

59. When the young women in my study did talk about relationships and feelings, I noticed a lack of "emotional literacy," the ability to articulate emotions with the competence necessary to communicate and thus achieve intimacy in friendship (see Steiner 1997). They used a tightly circumscribed vocabulary for distinguishing their feelings by name—for instance, "angry," "afraid," "hurt," "sad." Girls mostly said things like "I just go off," "I'm stressin,'" "My anger just come up." See Savin-Williams and Berndt 1990.

60. Rhoda was being treated in a secure adolescent psychiatric facility for an aggressive conduct disorder, changed from a probation disposition to a psychological diagnosis. In psychiatric wards, a three-feet rule (or variations) required that no person get closer than a yard to a certain resident. This rule was prescribed and implemented as a protection for both perpetrators and victims.

5 *Children, Gender, and Corrections*

1. For more information regarding the Model Standards Project, refer to the websites of the National Center for Lesbian Rights, http://www.nclrights.org, and Legal Services for Children, http://www.lsc-sf.org. For a critique of gender-specific services see also Goodkind 2005.

2. A considerable body of gender theory develops notions of intersectionality; for example, see Anzaldua 1987; Bhavnani 2001; Crenshaw 1995; Collins 1992.

3. Adler 1975.

4. See Adler 1975; Gilligan 1982; MacKinnon 1989; Rubin 1975; Simon 1975. See also Curran 1984; James and Thornton 1980.

5. See, for examples, Acoca 1999; Belknap 1996; Bloom, Owen, and Covington 2003; Dohrn 2004; Giordano 1999; Haney 1996; Hahn-Rafter 1995; Holsinger 2000; Messerschmidt 1997; Miller 2001; Richie 1996. See also Chapter One, specifically the sections on the gendered nature of juvenile justice and the history of the legal system for girls.

6. For example, Snyder and Sickmund (1999) found that African American youth constitute 15 percent of the population but 26 percent of all juvenile arrests, 30 percent of delinquency referrals to juvenile court, 45 percent of juveniles detained in delinquency cases, 40 percent of juveniles in secure detention facilities, and 46 percent of juveniles transferred to adult criminal court after judicial hearings. In one year in Cook County, Illinois, 99 percent of all juveniles transferred to adult criminal court were African Americans (Kooy 2002). See Office of Juvenile Justice and Delinquency Prevention 1999; Hsia, Bridges, and McHale 2004.

7. See Bloom, Owen, and Covington 2003; Morgan and Peters 2000; Owen and Bloom 1998.

8. For studies noting the centrality of workers' perspectives on handling incarcerated populations, see Bond-Maupin, Maupin, and Leisenring 2002; Bloom

et al. 2002; Britton 2003; Gaarder, Rodriguez, and Zatz 2004; Kruttschnitt and Gartner 2004.

9. See Belknap and Holsinger 1998; Bloom, Owen, and Covington 2003; Greene, Peters, and Associates 2001; *Juvenile Justice and Delinquency Prevention Act of 1992*. For a history of the evolution of gender-specific programming, see Bloom et al. 2002; Goodkind 2005.

10. Bloom et al. 2002; Bond-Maupin, Maupin, and Leisenring 2002; Britton 2003; Brown, Chesney-Lind, and Stein 2004; Chesney-Lind and Belknap 2004; Gaarder, Rodriguez, and Zata 2004; Giordano, Cernkovich, and Lowery 2004; Hannah-Moffat 2004; McCorkel 2003. See also note 5 (this chapter).

11. Morgan and Peters 2000, Participant Handout 6.

12. Greene, Peters, and Associates 2001; Morgan and Peters 2000.

13. Fullwood 2001, 6.

14. See Orenstein 1994; Brown and Gilligan 1992; Belenky et al. 1986; Leadbeater and Way 1996. See also American Association of University Women 1996, 1998, 2001; Greene, Peters, and Associates 2001. For examples of work in a peer-led, positive, youth leadership-development framework, see Baumgardner and Richards 2000; Carlip 1995; Findlen 1995; Green and Taormino 1997; Jones-Brown and Henriquez 1997; Nam 2001.

15. Greene, Peters, and Associates 2000.

16. Schaffner 2003.

17. Bond-Maupin, Maupin, and Leisenring 2002; Gaarder, Rodriguez, and Zatz 2004; Goodkind 2005; McCorkel 2003.

18. Morgan and Peters 2000, 54.

19. For an ethnography of the gendered organization of a women's prison, see Britton 2003.

20. Lewis 2003; Myers and Williamson 2001.

21. See Gaarder, Rodriguez, and Zatz 2004.

22. The district attorney assumed (correctly) that because I was conducting research with girls, I was a "feminist."

23. Steineger and Peters 2000, 101.

24. Steineger and Peters 2000, 108, 126. See Crick and Grotpeter 1995 and Chapter Four for a fuller discussion of relational aggression.

25. For examples of explorations of debates about sex, culture, and biology, see Butler 1990; Fausto-Sterling 2000; Green and Money 1969. See also Crenshaw 1995; Omi and Winant 1989; Spelman 1990.

26. Black 1991. The interrelated meanings and expressions of sex, gender, culture, and biology are explored in detail in, for example, Lorber 1995; Ferree, Lorber, and Hess 1999; Collins 2004; DeLaurentis 1987; Harris 2000. A sophisticated definition of gender prevails in these texts and elsewhere. See also note 25 (this chapter).

27. Landesman 2004, 32.

28. Finkelhor and Ormrod 2004; training materials such as the CDrom and paper handouts from the Law Enforcement Instructors Alliance October 2005 conference, "Human Trafficking and Sexual Exploitation National Training Seminar," available at http://www.teachcops.com.

29. Finkelhor and Ormrod 2004.

30. Gilman 1985; Collins 2004; hooks 1992. In the Finkelhor and Ormrod National Incidence Based Reporting System report (2004), only 28 percent of juvenile prostitution incidents known to the police involved African Americans.

6 *Conclusion*

1. *Condition* was the term used in this facility to indicate altercations, physical combat, or other incidents requiring all available personnel to rush immediately to a specific unit.
2. Juvenile Court Act (1899), *Ill. Laws*, sec. 132 *et seq.*
3. For alternative representations of young women as complex, competent decision makers, see films such as *Girls Town*, fiction like *Locas* (Yxta Maya Murray 1997), or research such as Way 1998 and Weiss and Fine 2000. See also note 14 in Chapter Five.
4. "Model mugging," where girls are encouraged to hit, kick, jump on, and generally whack at a "mugger" dressed with padded protection, was one of the most popular workshops at girls' conferences in the San Francisco Bay area when I was conducting my research.
5. See Schaffner 2005.
6. Alderden and Perez 2003; Sickmund 2004.
7. See Ayers, Dohrn, and Ayers 2001; Lewis 2003; Ferguson 2000.
8. For more information regarding the Model Standards Project, see note 1 in Chapter Five. See also Currah and Minter 2005.
9. See http://www.chicagogirlscoalition.org.
10. Oral histories of current outreach workers. See also Pfeffer 1997; http://www.cywd.org.
11. See also *Girl Trouble*, http://www.girltrouble.org, a feature-length documentary that follows girls from CYWD through their ordeals in the San Francisco juvenile system.
12. http://www.youarepriceless.org, accessed July 15, 2004.
13. See report titled *Hey Cutie, Can I Get Your Digits?* by the Rogers Park Young Women's Action Team (2003).
14. Health and Medicine Policy Research Group 2003.
15. Missouri data are from interviews and materials disseminated during tours of facilities. See also Mendel 2003.

Bibliography

Books and Articles

Abma, J. C., A. Chandra, W. D. Mosher, L. Peterson, and L. Piccinino. 1997. "Fertility, Family Planning, and Women's Health: New Data from the 1995 National Survey of Family Growth." *Vital and Health Statistics* (National Center for Health Statistics, Hyattsville, MD) 23(19): 1–11.

Acker, Joan.1990. "Hierarchies, Jobs and Bodies: A Theory of Gendered Organizations." *Gender and Society* 4(2): 139–158.

Acoca, Leslie. 1998. "Outside/Inside: The Violation of American Girls at Home, on the Streets, and in the Juvenile Justice System." *Crime and Delinquency* 44(4): 561–589.

———. 1999. "Investing in Girls: A 21st Century Challenge." *Juvenile Justice* 6(1): 3–13.

Acoca, Leslie, and James Austin. 1996. *The Crisis: Women in Prison*. San Francisco: The Women Offender Sentencing Study and Alternative Sentencing Recommendations Project, National Council on Crime and Delinquency.

Acoca, Leslie, and Kelly Dedel. 1998. *No Place to Hide: Understanding and Meeting the Needs of Girls in the California Juvenile Justice System*. San Francisco: National Council on Crime and Delinquency.

Adams, Gerald, Thomas Gulotta, and Mary Anne Clancy. 1985. "Homeless Adolescents: A Descriptive Study of Similarities between Runaways and Throwaways." *Adolescence*, Fall, 715–724.

Adams, Mary Louise. 1997. *The Trouble with Normal*. Toronto: University of Toronto Press.

Addams, Jane. 1909. *The Spirit of Youth and the City Streets*. New York: Macmillan.

Adler, Freda. 1975. *Sisters in Crime: The Rise of the New Female Criminal*. New York: McGraw-Hill.

Agustin, Laura. 2005. "At Home in the Street: Questioning the Desire to Help and Save." In Bernstein and Schaffner, *Regulating Sex*, 67–82.

Alan Guttmacher Institute. 1994. *Sex and America's Teenagers*. Washington, DC: Alan Guttmacher Institute.

Alder, Christine, and Anne Worral. 2004. *Girls' Violence: Myths and Realties*. Albany: State University of New York Press.

Alderden, Megan, and Adrianna Perez. 2003. *Female Delinquents Committed to the Illinois Department of Corrections: A Profile*. Chicago: Illinois Criminal Justice Information Authority.

Alexander, Ruth. 1995. *The "Girl Problem": Female Sexual Delinquency in NY, 1900–1930*. Ithaca, NY: Cornell University Press.

American Association of University Women. 1992. *How Schools Shortchange Girls—The AAUW Report.* New York: Marlowe.

———. 1995. *Getting Smart: What's Working for Girls in School.* Washington, DC: American Association of University Women.

———. 1998. *Separated by Sex: A Critical Look at Single-Sex Education for Girls.* Washington, DC: American Association of University Women.

———. 2001. *Hostile Hallways: The AAUW Survey of Sexual Harassment in America's Schools.* Washington, DC: American Association of University Women.

American Automobile Association. 1997. *Aggressive Driving: Three Studies.* Washington, DC: AAA Foundation for Traffic Safety.

———. 1999. *Controlling Road Rage: A Literature Review and Pilot Study.* Washington, DC: AAA Foundation for Traffic Safety.

American Psychiatric Association. 1994. *Diagnostic and Statistical Manual of Mental Disorders,* 4th ed. Washington, DC: American Psychiatric Association.

Anderson, Elijah. 1997. "Violence and the Inner-City Street Code." In McCord, *Violence and Childhood in the Inner City,* 1–30.

———. 1999. *Code of the Street: Decency, Violence, and the Moral Life of the Inner City.* New York: Norton.

Anzaldua, Gloria. 1987. "La Conciencia de la Mestiza: Towards a New Consciousness." In *Feminisim and "Race,"* edited by Kum-Kum Bhavnani, 93–107. Oxford: Oxford University Press.

Apter, Terri. 1990. *Altered Loves: Mothers and Daughters during Adolescence.* New York: Fawcett Columbine.

Archer, John, ed. *Male Violence.* New York: Routledge.

Artz, Sybelle. 1998. *Sex, Power, and the Violent School Girl.* New York: Teachers College Press.

Austin, Joe, and Michael Nevin Willard. 1998. *Generations of Youth: Youth Cultures in Twentieth-Century America.* New York: New York University Press.

Ayers, William. 1997. *A Kind and Just Parent: The Children of the Juvenile Court.* Boston: Beacon Press.

Ayers, William, Bernardine Dohrn, and Rick Ayers, eds. 2001. *Zero Tolerance: Resisting the Drive for Punishment in Our Schools.* New York: New Press.

Baca Zinn, Maxine, and Bonnie Thornton Dill, eds. 1994. *Women of Color in U.S. Society.* Philadelphia: Temple University Press.

Baker Miller, Jean. 1985. *The Construction of Anger in Women and Men.* Work in Progress 4. Wellesley, MA: Stone Center.

Baskin, Deborah, Ira Sommers, and Jeffrey Fagan. 1993. "The Political Economy of Female Violent Street Crime." *Fordham Urban Law Journal* 20:401–418.

Baumgardner, Jennifer, and Amy Richards. 2000. *Manifesta: Young Women, Feminism, and the Future.* New York: Farrar, Straus & Giroux.

Bay Area Reporter. "It's the Most Violent Time of the Year." 1998. December 10.

Beatty, Cynthia. 1997. *Parents in Prison: Children in Crisis.* Washington, DC: Child Welfare League of America Press.

Beauvoir, Simone, de. 1952. *The Second Sex.* New York: HarperCollins.

Beisel, Nicola. 1997. *Imperiled Innocents: Anthony Comstock and Family Reproduction in Victorian America.* Princeton, NJ: Princeton University Press.

Belenky, Mary Field, Blythe McVicker Clinchy, Nancy Rule Goldberger, and Jill Mattuck Tarule. 1986. *Women's Ways of Knowing: The Development of Self, Voice, and Mind.* New York: BasicBooks.

Belknap, Joanne. 1996. *The Invisible Woman: Gender, Crime, and Justice.* Belmont, CA: Wadsworth.

Belknap, Joanne, and Kristi Holsinger. 1998. "An Overview of Deliquent Girls: How Theory and Practice Have Failed and the Need for Innovative Changes." In Zaplin, *Female Offenders*, 31–64.

Belknap, Joanne, Kristi Holsinger, and Melissa Dunn. 1997. "Understanding Incarcerated Girls: The Results of a Focus Group Study." *Prison Journal* 77(4): 381–404.

Bell, Carl. 1995. "Exposure to Violence Distresses Children and May Lead to Their Becoming Violent." *Psychiatric News* 6(8): 15.

Bernardez, Teresa. 1988. *Women and Anger: Cultural Prohibitions and the Feminine Ideal.* Wellesley, MA: Stone Center.

———. 1991. "Adolescent Resistance and the Maladies of Women: Notes from the Underground." In Gilligan, Rogers, and Tolman, *Women, Girls, and Psychotherapy*, 213–222.

Bernstein, Elizabeth. 2001. "Economies of Desire: Sexual Commerce and Postindustrial Culture." PhD diss., University of California, Berkeley.

Bernstein, Elizabeth, and Laurie Schaffner, eds. 2005. *Regulating Sex: The Politics of Intimacy and Identity.* New York: Routledge.

Bernstein, Mary, and Renate Reimann, eds. 2001. *Queer Families, Queer Politics.* New York: Columbia University Press.

Bhavnani, Kum-Kum, ed. 2001. *Feminism and "Race."* New York: Oxford University Press.

Biglan, Anthony, John Noell, Linda Ochs, Keith Smolkowski, and Carol Metsler. 1995. "Does Sexual Coercion Play a Role in the High-Risk Sexual Behavior of Adolescent and Young Adult Women?" *Journal of Behavioral Medicine* 18(6): 549–568.

Black, Henry. 1991. *Black's Law Dictionary.* Abridged 6th ed. St. Paul, MN: West.

Bloom, Barbara. 2003. *Gendered Justice: Addressing Female Offenders.* Durham, NC: Carolina Academic Press.

Bloom, Barbara, Barbara Owen, and Stephanie Covington. 2003. *Gender-Responsive Strategies: Research, Practice, and Guiding Principles for Women Offenders.* Washington, DC: National Institute of Corrections, U.S. Department of Justice.

Bloom, Barbara, Barbara Owen, Elizabeth Deschenes, and Jill Rosenbaum. 2002. "Moving toward Justice for Female Offenders in the New Millenium: Modeling Gender-Specific Policies and Programs." *Journal of Contemporary Criminal Justice* 18:37–56.

Blumenfeld, Warren, and Diane Raymond. 1988. *Looking at Gay and Lesbian Life.* New York: Philosophical Library.

Bok, Sissela. 1998. *Mayhem: Violence as Public Entertainment.* Reading, MA: Perseus Books.

Bond-Maupin, Lisa, James Maupin, and Amy Leisenring. 2002. "Girls' Delinquency and the Justice Implications of Intake Workers' Perspectives." *Women and Criminal Justice* 13:51–77.

Bourgois, Philippe. 1995. *In Search of Respect: Selling Crack in El Barrio.* New York: Cambridge University Press.

Braithwaite, John, and Kathleen Daly. 1994. "Masculinities, Violence, and Communitarian Control." In Newburn and Stanko, *Just Boys Doing Business?* 189–213.

Braverman, Paula, and Victor Strasburger. 1993. "Adolescent Sexual Activity." *Clinical Pediatrics* 32(11): 658–668.

Breckinridge, Sophonisba P., and Edith Abbott. 1917. *The Delinquent Child and the Home: A Study of the Delinquent Wards of the Juvenile Court of Chicago.* New York: Russell Sage Foundation.

Briere, John N., and Diana M. Elliott. 1994. "Immediate and Long-Term Impacts of Child Sexual Abuse." *The Future of Children: Sexual Abuse of Children* (Center for the Future of Children, David and Lucile Packard Foundation, Los Altos, CA) 4(2): 54–69.

Briggs, Jean. 1979. *Never in Anger: Portrait of an Eskimo Family.* Cambridge, MA: Harvard University Press.

———. 1991. "Mazes of Meanings: The Exploration of Individuality in Culture and of Culture through Individual Constructs." *Psychoanalytic Study of Society* (Analytic Press, Hillsdale, NJ) 16:111–153.

Britton, Dana. 2003. *At Work in the Iron Cage: The Prison as Gendered Organization.* New York: New York University Press.

Brooke, James. 1998. "Homophobia Often Found in Schools, Data Shows." *New York Times,* October 14, sec. A.

Brooks, Kim, Vincent Schiraldi, and Jason Ziedenberg. 2000. *School House Hype: Two Years Later.* Washington, DC: Justice Policy Institute.

Brown, Lyn Mikel. 1998. *Raising Their Voices: The Politics of Girls' Anger.* Cambridge, MA: Harvard University Press.

———. 2003. *Girlfighting: Betrayal and Rejection among Girls.* New York: New York University Press.

Brown, Lyn Mikel, Meda Chesney-Lind, and Nan Stein. 2004. *Patriarchy Matters: Toward a Gendered Theory of Teen Violence and Victimization.* Wellesley Centers for Women Working Paper 417. Wellesley, MA: Center for Research on Women, Wellesley College.

Brown, Lyn Mikel, and Carol Gilligan. 1992. *Meeting at the Crossroads: Women's Psychology and Girls' Development.* Cambridge, MA: Harvard University Press.

Brown, Lyn Mikel, Niobe Way, and Julia Duff. 1999. "The Others in My I: Adolescent Girls' Friendships and Peer Relations." In Johnson, Roberts, and Worell, *Beyond Appearance,* 205–225.

Browne, Angela, and David Finkelhor. 1986. "Impact of Child Sexual Abuse: A Review of the Research." *Psychological Bulletin* 99(1): 66–77.

Brumberg, Joan Jacobs. 1997. *The Body Project: An Intimate History of American Girls.* New York: Random House.

Brydon-Miller, Mary. 2001. "Education, Research, and Action: Theory and Methods of Participatory Action Research." In Tolman and Brydon-Miller, *From Subjects to Subjectivities,* 76–89.

Burke, Kenneth. 1950. *Rhetoric of Motives.* Berkeley: University of California Press.

Busen, N., and Bettina Beech. 1998. "A Collaborative Model for Community-Based Health Care Screening of Homeless Adolescents." *Journal of Professional Nursing* 13:316–324.

Butler, Judith. 1990. *Gender Trouble: Feminism and the Subversion of Identity.* New York: Routledge.

———. 2004. *Undoing Gender.* New York: Routledge.

Campbell, Anne. 1984. *The Girls in the Gang.* New York: Blackwell.

———. 1994. *Men, Women, and Aggression.* New York: Basic Books.

Campbell, Rebecca. 2001. *Emotionally Involved: The Impact of Researching Rape.* New York: Routledge.

Cancian, Francesca, and Steven Gordon. 1988. "Changing Emotion Norms in Marriage: Love and Anger in U.S. Women's Magazines since 1900." *Gender and Society* 2(3): 308–342.

Carlip, Hillary, ed. 1995. *Girl Power: Young Women Speak Out.* New York: TimeWarner.

Carvajal, Doreen. 1999. "Primal Scream: Teaching Tykes to Get a Grip." *New York Times*, November 14, "Week in Review."

Cauffman, Elizabeth. 2004. "A Statewide Screening of Mental Health Symptoms among Juvenile Offenders in Detention." *Journal of the American Academy of Child and Adolescent Psychiatry* 43(4): 430–439.

Cauffman, Elizabeth, S. Shirley Feldman, Jamie Waterman, and Hans Steiner. 1998. "Posttraumatic Stress Disorder among Female Juvenile Offenders." *Journal of the American Academy of Child and Adolescent Psychiatry* 37(11): 1209–1216.

Center for Women Policy Studies. 2001. "'Does It Have to Be Like This?' Teen Women Ask Their Peers about Violence, Hate, and Discrimination." *The Report of the Teen Women Leadership Development Initiative Survey*. Washington, DC: Center for Women Policy Studies.

Centers for Disease Control and Prevention. 2004. *Youth Risk Behavior Surveillance, United States, 2003*. 53 MMWR (SS-2). Washington, DC: U.S. Department of Health and Human Services.

Charles Stewart Mott Foundation. 1994. *A Fine Line: Losing American Youth to Violence*. Flint, MI: Charles Stewart Mott Foundation.

Chase, Nancy, ed. 1999. *Burdened Children: Theory, Research, and Treatment of Parentification*. Thousand Oaks, CA: Sage.

Chesney-Lind, Meda. 1997. *The Female Offender: Girls, Women, and Crime*. Thousand Oaks, CA: Sage.

———. 2004. "Girls and Violence: Is the Gender Gap Closing?" *Applied Research Forum*, Violence against Women Net, a project of the National Resource Center on Domestic Violence. http://www.vawnet.org.

Chesney-Lind, Meda, and Joanne Belknap. 2004. "Trends in Delinquent Girls' Aggression and Violent Behavior: A Review of the Evidence." In Putallaz and Bierman, *Aggression, Antisocial Behavior, and Violence among Girls*, 203–222.

Chesney-Lind, Meda, and Randall Shelden. 1992. *Girls, Delinquency, and Juvenile Justice*. Belmont, CA: Brooks/Cole.

Chodorow, Nancy. 1995. "Gender as a Personal and Cultural Construction." *Signs* 20(3): 516–544.

Cohen, Albert. 1955. *Delinquent Boys: The Culture of the Gang*. Glencoe, IL: Free Press.

Coie, J., and Kenneth Dodge. 1998. "Aggression and Antisocial Behavior." In *Handbook of Child Psychology*, edited by W. Damon, 5th ed., vol. 3, *Social, Emotional, and Personality Development*, edited by N. Eisenberg, 779–862. New York: Wiley.

Collins, Patricia Hill. 1992. *Black Feminist Thought: Knowledge, Consciousness, and the Politics of Empowerment*. New York: Routledge.

———. 2004. *Black Sexual Politics: African Americans, Gender, and the New Racism*. New York: Routledge.

Connell, Robert. 1987. *Gender and Power*. Sydney, Australia: Allen and Unwyn.

Conway, Allan, and Carol Bogdan. 1977. "Sexual Delinquency: The Persistence of a Double Standard." *Crime and Delinquency* 23:131–135.

Conway, Anne. 2005. "Girls, Aggression, and Emotion Regulation." *American Journal of Orthopsychiatry* 75(2): 334–339.

Cooper, Al, David Delmonico, and Ron Burg. 2001. "Cybersex Users, Abusers, and Compulsives." In Davidson and Moore, *Speaking of Sexuality*, 356–367.

Costin, Lela, Howard Jacob Karger, and David Stoesz. 1996. *The Politics of Child Abuse in America*. New York: Oxford University Press.

Covington, Stephanie. 1998. "The Relational Theory of Women's Psychological Development: Implications for the Criminal Justice System." In Zaplin, *Female Offenders*, 113–132.

———. 2003. "A Woman's Journey Home: Challenges for Female Offenders." In *Prisoners Once Removed: The Impact of Incarceration and Reentry on Children, Families, and Communities*, edited by Jeremy Travis and Michelle Waul, 67–104. Washington, DC: Urban Institute Press.

Crenshaw, Kimberle. 1995. "Mapping the Margins: Intersectionality, Identity Politics, and Violence against Women of Color." In *Critical Race Theory: Key Writings That Formed the Movement*, edited by Kimberle Crenshaw, Neil Gotanda, Gary Peller, and Kendall Thomas, 357–383. New York: New Press.

Crick, Nicki. 1997. "Engagement in Gender Normative Versus Nonnormative Forms of Aggression: Links to Social-Psychological Adjustment." *Developmental Psychology* 33(4): 610–617.

Crick, Nicki, and Maureen Bigbee. 1998. "Relational and Overt Forms of Peer Victimization: A Multiinformant Approach." *Journal of Consulting and Clinical Psychology* 66(2): 337–347.

Crick, Nicki, and Jennifer Grotpeter. 1995. "Relational Aggression, Gender, and Social-Psychological Adjustment." *Child Development* 66:710–722.

Crick, Nicki, D. Nelson, J. Morales, C. Cullerton-Sen, J. Casas, and S. Hickman. 2001. "Relational Victimization in Childhood and Adolescence: I Hurt You through the Grapevine." In *Peer Harassment in School: The Plight of the Vulnerable and Victimized*, edited by Jaana Juvonen and Sandra Graham, 196–214. New York: Guilford Press.

Currah, Paisley, and Shannon Minter. 2005. "Unprincipled Exclusions: The Struggle to Achieve Judicial and Legislative Equality for Transgender People." In Bernstein and Schaffner, *Regulating Sex*, 35–50.

Curran, Daniel. 1984. "The Myth of the 'New' Female Delinquent." *Crime and Delinquency* 30(3): 386–399.

Curtin, Mary. 2002. "Lesbian and Bisexual Girls in the Juvenile Justice System." *Child and Adolescent Social Work Journal* 19(4): 285–301.

Dang, Quang H. 1997. *Investigation into the Needs of Lesbian, Gay, Bisexual, Transgender, Queer, and Questioning Youth*. San Francisco: Human Rights Commission of the City and County of San Francisco, July 12.

D'Augelli, Anthony. 1998. "Developmental Implications of Victimization of Lesbian, Gay, and Bisexual Youths." In *Stigma and Sexual Orientation*, edited by Gregory Herek, 193–194. Thousand Oaks, CA: Sage.

D'Augelli, Anthony, and Lawrence Dark. 1995. "Lesbian, Gay, and Bisexual Youths." In *Reason to Hope: A Psychosocial Perspective on Violence and Youth*, edited by Leonard Eron, Jacqueline Gentry, and Peggy Schlegel, 177–196. Washington, DC: American Psychological Association.

Davidson, J. Kenneth, and Nelwyn Moore, eds. 2001. *Speaking of Sexuality: Interdisciplinary Readings*. Los Angeles: Roxbury.

Davis, Katherine. 1929. *Factors in the Sex Life of Twenty-Two Hundred Women*. New York: Harper & Row.

Davis, Nanette. 1999. *Youth Crisis: Growing Up in the High-Risk Society*. Westport, CT: Praeger.

Deisher, Robert, and William Rogers. 1991. "The Medical Care of Street Youth." *Journal of Adolescent Health* 12:500–503.

Delancey Street Foundation. 1997. *San Francisco Juvenile Justice Comprehensive Action Plan*. San Francisco: Delancey Street Foundation.

DeLaurentis, Teresa. 1987. *Technologies of Gender: Essays on Theory, Film, and Fiction.* Bloomington: Indiana University Press.

D'Emilio, John, and Estelle Freedman. 1988. *Intimate Matters: A History of Sexuality in America.* New York: Harper & Row.

Denizet-Lewis, Benoit. 2004. "Friends, Friends with Benefits, and the Benefits of the Local Mall." *New York Times Magazine,* May 30.

DeVault, Marjorie. 1999. *Liberating Method: Feminism and Social Research.* Philadelphia: Temple University Press.

Devine, John. 1996. *Maximum Security: The Culture of Violence in Inner-City Schools.* Chicago: University of Chicago Press.

Devlin, Rachel. 1997. "Female Juvenile Delinquency and the Problem of Sexual Authority in America, 1945–1965." *Yale Journal of Law and the Humanities* 9:147–182.

Devoe, Jill, Katharin Peter, Philip Kaufman, Amanda Miller, Margaret Noonan, Thomas Snyder, and Katrina Baum. 2004. *Indicators of School Crime and Safety,* 2004. NCES 2004–002/NCJ 205290. Washington, DC: U.S. Departments of Education and Justice.

Dietrich, D. 1984. "Psychological Health of Young Adults Who Experienced Early Parental Death: MMPI Trends." *Journal of Clinical Psychology* 40(4): 901–908.

Dohrn, Bernardine. 2004. "All Ellas: Girls Locked Up." *Feminist Studies* 30(2): 302–323.

Donohue, Elizabeth, Vincent Schiraldi, and Jason Ziedenberg. 1998. *School House Hype: School Shootings and the Real Risks Kids Face in America.* Washington, DC: Justice Policy Institute.

Dougherty, Joyce. 1998. "Female Offenders and Childhood Maltreatment: Understanding the Connections." In Zaplin, *Female Offenders,* 227–244.

Duncan, G. J., W. J. Yeung, J. Brooks-Gunn, and J. R. Smith. 1998. "How Much Does Childhood Poverty Affect the Life Chances of Children?" *American Sociological Review* 63:406–423.

Economist. 1998. "The Sex Business." February 14–20, 17–26.

Eder, Donna, with Catherine Evans and Stephen Parker. 1997. *School Talk: Gender and Adolescent Culture.* New Brunswick, NJ: Rutgers University Press.

Eisenstein, Zillah. 1988. *The Female Body and the Law.* Berkeley: University of California Press.

Elkind, David. 1998. *All Grown Up and No Place to Go: Teenagers in Crisis.* New York: Perseus.

Elliott, Delbert, John Hagen, and Joan McCord. 1997. *Youth Violence: Children at Risk.* Congressional Seminar. Washington, DC: American Sociological Association, June 17.

Elliott, Delbert, and Barbara Morse. 1989. "Delinquency and Drug Use as Risk Factors in Teenage Sexual Activity." *Youth and Society* 21(1): 32–60.

Esbensen, Finn-Aage. 2000. "Preventing Adolescent Gang Involvement." *Juvenile Justice Bulletin.* Washington, DC: Office of Juvenile Justice and Delinquency Prevention.

Estes, Richard, and Neil Alan Weiner. 2001. *The Commercial Sexual Exploitation of Children in the U.S., Canada, and Mexico.* Philadelphia: Center for the Study of Youth and Policy, University of Pennsylvania.

Farrington, David. 1996. "The Explanation and Prevention of Youthful Offending." In Hawkins, *Delinquency and Crime,* 68–148.

Fass, Paula, and Mary Ann Mason, eds. 2000. *Childhood in America.* New York: New York University Press.

Fausto-Sterling, Anne. 2000. *Sexing the Body: Gender Politics and the Construction of Sexuality.* New York: Basic Books.

Featherstone, Mike, ed. 1999. *Love and Eroticism.* Thousand Oaks, CA: Sage.

Federal Interagency Forum on Child and Family Statistics. 2005. *America's Children: Key National Indicators of Well-Being, 2005.* Washington, DC: Government Printing Office. Also available at http://www.childstats.gov.

Feinstein, Randi, Andrea Greeblatt, Lauren Hass, Sally Kohn, and Juliana Rana. 2001. *Justice for All? A Report on Lesbian, Gay, Bisexual, and Transgendered Youth in the New York Juvenile Justice System.* New York: Urban Justice Center.

Feldman, S. Shirley, and Glen R. Elliott, eds. 1990. *At the Threshold: The Developing Adolescent.* Cambridge, MA: Harvard University Press.

Ferguson, Ann Arnett. 2000. *Bad Boys: Public Schools and the Making of Black Masculinity.* Ann Arbor: University of Michigan Press.

Fergusson, David, John Horwood, and Annette Beautrais. 1999. "Is Sexual Orientation Related to Mental Health Problems and Suicidality in Young People?" *Archives of General Psychiatry* 56(10): 876–880.

Ferree, Myra Marx, Judith Lorber, and Beth Hess, eds. 1999. *Revisioning Gender.* New York: Sage.

Findlen, Barbara, ed. 1995. *Listen Up: Voices from the Next Feminist Generation.* Seattle: Seal Press.

Fine, Gary Alan, and Kent L. Sandstrom. 1988. *Knowing Children: Participant Observation with Minors.* Newbury Park, CA: Sage.

Fine, Michelle. 1992. *Disruptive Voices: The Possibilities of Feminist Research.* Ann Arbor: University of Michigan Press.

Fineran, Susan. 2001. "Sexual Minority Students and Peer Sexual Harassment in High School." *Journal of School Social Work* 11:50–69.

Finkelhor, David. 1994. "Current Information on the Scope and Nature of Child Sexual Abuse." *The Future of Children: Sexual Abuse of Children* (David and Lucile Packard Foundation, Los Angeles) 4(2): 31–53.

Finkelhor, David, and Larry Baron. 1986. "Risk Factors for Child Sexual Abuse." *Journal of Interpersonal Violence* 1(43): 43–71.

Finkelhor, David, and Lisa Jones. 2004. "Explanations for the Decline in Child Sexual Abuse Cases." *Juvenile Justice Bulletin.* Washington, DC: Office of Juvenile Justice and Delinquency Prevention.

Finkelhor, David, and Richard Ormrod. 2001. "Child Abuse Reported to the Police." *Juvenile Justice Bulletin.* Washington, DC: Office of Juvenile Justice and Delinquency Prevention.

———. 2004. "Prostitution of Juveniles: Patterns from NIBRS." *Juvenile Justice Bulletin.* Washington, DC: Office of Juvenile Justice and Delinquency Prevention.

Fleisher, Joanne, and James Fillman. 1995. "Lesbian and Gay Youth: Treatment Issues." *Counselor*, January/February, 27–28.

Flores-Gonzalez, Nilda. 2002. *School Kids/Street Kids: Identity Development in Latino Students.* New York: Teachers College Press.

Fontaine, Janet, and Nancy Hammond. 1996. "Counseling Issues with Gay and Lesbian Adolescents." *Adolescence* 31(124): 817–830.

Foster Care Youth United (Youth Communications, Inc., New York). 1994. "Interview with 'Sandra,' a Lesbian in the System." January/February, 6.

Freedman, Estelle. 1981. *Their Sisters' Keepers: Women's Prison Reform in America, 1830–1930.* Ann Arbor: University of Michigan Press.

Friedrich-Cofer, L., and A. Huston. 1986. "Television Violence and Aggression: The Debate Continues." *Psychological Bulletin* 100:364–371.

Fullwood, Catlin. 2001. *The New Girls' Movement: Implications for Youth Programs*. New York: Collaborative Fund for Healthy Girls, Healthy Women, Ms. Foundation for Women.

Furstenberg, Jr., Frank, Thomas Cook, Jacquelynne Eccles, Glen Elder Jr., and Arnold Sameroff. 1999. *Managing to Make It: Urban Families and Adolescent Success*. Chicago: University of Chicago Press.

Futterman, Roy, Maria Lorente, and Susan W. Silverman. 2005. "Beyond Harm Reduction: A New Model of Substance Abuse Treatment Further Integrating Psychological Techniques." *Journal of Psychotherapy Integration* 15(1): 3–18.

Gaarder, Emily, Nancy Rodriguez, and Marjarie Zatz. 2004. "Criers, Liars, and Manipulators: Probation Officers' Views of Girls." *Justice Quarterly* 21(3): 547–578.

Galen, B., and Marion Underwood. 1997. "A Developmental Investigation of Social Aggression among Children." *Developmental Psychology* 33:589–600.

Garbarino, James, Nancy Dubrow, Kathleen Kostelny, and Carole Pardo. 1992. *Children in Danger: Coping with Consequences of Community Violence*. San Francisco: Jossey-Bass.

Garbarino, James, and Kathleen Kostelny. 1997. "What Children Can Tell Us about Living in a War Zone." In Osofsky, *Children in a Violent Society*, 32–41.

Gibbs, Nancy. 2001. "The Columbine Effect." *Time*, March 19, 22–38.

Giddens, Anthony. 1992. *The Transformation of Intimacy: Sexuality, Love, and Eroticism in Modern Societies*. Stanford, CA: Stanford University Press.

Gilgun, Jane. 1986. "Sexually Abused Girls' Knowledge about Sexual Abuse and Sexuality." *Journal of Interpersonal Violence* 1(3): 309–325.

Gilligan, Carol. 1982. *In a Different Voice: Psychological Theory and Women's Development*. Cambridge, MA: Harvard University Press.

Gilligan, Carol, Nona Lyons, and Trudy Hanmer, eds. 1989. *Making Connections: The Relational Worlds of Adolescent Girls at Emma Willard School*. Cambridge, MA: Harvard University Press.

Gilligan, Carol, Annie Rogers, and Deborah Tolman, eds. 1991. *Women, Girls, and Psychotherapy: Reframing Resistance*. New York: Haworth Press.

Gilligan, James. 1996. *Violence: Reflections on a National Epidemic*. New York: Vintage Books.

Gilman, Sander. 1985. "Black Bodies, White Bodies: Toward an Iconography of Female Sexuality in Late Nineteenth-Century Art, Medicine, and Literature." *Critical Inquiry* 12 (Autumn): 204–242.

Giordano, Peggy. 1999. "Girls, Guys, and Gangs: The Changing Social Context of Female Delinquency." In *Female Gangs in America*, edited by Meda Chesney-Lind and John Hagedorn, 90–99. Chicago: Lakeview Press.

Giordano, Peggy, Stephen Cernkovich, and Allen Lowery. 2004. "A Long-Term Follow-Up of Serious Adolescent Female Offenders." In Putallaz and Bierman, *Aggression, Antisocial Behavior, and Violence among Girls*, 186–202.

Girls Inc. and the Office of Juvenile Justice and Delinquency Prevention. 1996. *Prevention and Parity: Girls in Juvenile Justice*. Washington, DC: U.S. Department of Justice.

Glueck, Sheldon, and Eleanor Glueck. 1934. *Five Hundred Delinquent Women*. New York: Knopf.

Golding, J. 1999. "Child Sexual Abuse." In *Support for Survivors,* edited by the California Coalition against Sexual Assault, 77–113. Oakland, CA: California Coalition against Sexual Assault.

Goldman, Marion. 1987. "Prostitution, Economic Exchange, and the Unconscious." In *Advances in Psychoanalytic Sociology,* edited by Jerome Rabow, Gerald Platt, and Marion Goldman, 187–209. Malabar, FL: Krieger.

Gonzales, Patrick, C. Calsyn, L. Jocelyn, K. Mak, D. Kastberg, S. Arafeh, T. Williams, and W. Tsen. 2000. *Pursuing Excellence: Comparisons of Eighth-Grade Science and Mathematics Achievement from a U.S. Perspective, 1995–1999.* Washington, DC: National Center for Education Statistics.

Goodkind, Sara. 2005. "Gender-Specific Services in the Juvenile Justice System: A Critical Examination." *Affilia* 20(1): 52–70.

Goodwin, Marjorie. 2002. "Building Power Asymmetries in Girls' Interaction." *Discourse and Society* 13(6): 715–730.

Gordon, Linda. 1988. *Heroes of Their Own Lives.* New York: Penguin Books.

Green, Karen, and Trista Taormino, eds. 1997. *A Girl's Guide to Taking Over the World.* New York: St. Martin's Press.

Green, Richard, and John Money. 1969. *Transsexualism and Sex Reassignment.* Baltimore: Johns Hopkins Press.

Greene, Peters, and Associates. 2000. *Beyond Gender Barriers: Programming Specifically for Girls.* Nashville: Office of Juvenile Justice and Delinquency Prevention.

———. 2001 [1998]. *Guiding Principles for Promising Female Programming: An Inventory of Best Practices.* Washington, DC: Office of Juvenile Justice and Delinquency Prevention.

Greenfield, Lawrence. 1997. *Sex Offenses and Offenders: An Analysis of Data on Rape and Sexual Assault.* Washington, DC: Bureau of Justice Statistics, U.S. Department of Justice.

Greenfield, Lawrence, and Tracy Snell. 1999. "Women Offenders." *Bureau of Justice Statistics, Special Report.* Washington, DC: U.S. Department of Justice.

Griffin, Christine. 1993. *Representations of Youth: The Study of Youth and Adolescence in Britain and America.* Cambridge, MA: Polity Press.

Griffiths, Vivienne. 1995. *Adolescent Girls and Their Friends: A Feminist Ethnography.* New York: Avebury Press.

Grover, Sonja. 2004. "Why Won't They Listen to Us? On Giving Power and Voice to Children Participating in Social Research." *Childhood: A Global Journal of Child Research* 11(1): 81–93.

Gutierrez, P. 1999. "Suicidality in Parentally Bereaved Adolescents." *Death Studies* 23(4): 359–370.

Hagedorn, John. 1994. "Homeboys, Dope Fiends, Legits, and New Jacks." *Criminology* 32:197–219.

———. 1997. *People and Folks: Gangs, Crime, and the Underclass in a Rustbelt City.* Chicago: Lake View Press.

Hahn-Rafter, Nicole. 1995. *Partial Justice: Women, Prisons, and Social Control.* New Brunswick, NJ: Transaction.

Hall, G. Stanley 1904. *Adolescence—Its Psychology and Its Relations to Physiology, Anthropology, Sociology, Sex, Crime, Religion and Education.* New York: Appleton.

Haney, Lynne. 1996. "Homeboys, Babies, Men in Suits: The State and the Reproduction of Male Dominance." *American Sociological Review* 61(October): 759–778.

Hannah-Moffat, Kelly. 2004. "Losing Ground: Gendered Knowledges, Parole Risk, and Responsibility." *Social Politics* 11(3): 363–385.

Harris, Angela. 2000 [1990]. "Race and Essentialism and Critical Legal Theory." In *Critical Race Theory*, edited by Richard Delgado and Jean Stefancic, 261–274. Philadelphia: Temple University Press.

Harris, Linda, Robert W. Blum, and Michael Resnick. 1991. "Teen Females in Minnesota: A Portrait of Quiet Disturbance." In Gilligan, Rogers, and Tolman, *Women, Girls, and Psychotherapy*, 119–136.

Harvey, Penelope, and Peter Gow, eds. 1994. *Sex and Violence: Issues in Representation and Experience*. New York: Routledge.

Harway, Michele, and Marsha Liss. 1999. "Dating Violence and Teen Prostitution: Adolescent Girls in the Justice System." In Johnson, Roberts, and Worell, *Beyond Appearance*, 277–300.

Havel, Vaclav. [1978] 1991. "The Power of the Powerless." In *Open Letters*, 125–214. New York: Knopf.

Hawkins, J. David, ed. 1996. *Delinquency and Crime: Current Theories*. New York: Cambridge University Press.

Haynie, Dana. 2003. "Contexts of Risk? Explaining the Link between Girls' Pubertal Development and Their Delinquency Involvement." *Social Forces* 82:355–397.

Hayward, Mark D., Toni P. Miles, Eileen M. Crimmins, and Yu Yang. 2000. "The Significance of Socioeconomic Status in Explaining the Racial Gap in Chronic Health Conditions." *American Sociological Review* 65(6): 910–930.

Health and Medicine Policy Research Group. 2003. *Healing Girls in the Juvenile Justice System: The Challenge to Our Community, Proceedings of the July 2003 Conference*. Chicago: Health and Medicine Policy Research Group. http://www.hmprg.org.

Hennessey, Marianne, Julian Ford, Karen Mahoney, Susan Ko, and Christine Siegfried. 2004. *Trauma among Girls in the Juvenile Justice System*. Los Angeles: National Child Traumatic Stress Network.

Henry J. Kaiser Family Foundation. 2003. *National Survey of Adolescents and Young Adults: Sexual Health Knowledge, Attitudes and Experiences*. Menlo Park, CA: Henry J. Kaiser Family Foundation.

Herdt, Gilbert, ed. 1989. *Gay and Lesbian Youth*. New York: Harrington Park Press.

Herman, Judith. 1981. *Father-Daughter Incest*. Cambridge, MA: Harvard University Press.

———. 1992. *Trauma and Recovery*. New York: Basic Books.

Herrera, Veronica, and Laura Ann McCloskey. 2001. "Gender Differences in the Risk for Delinquency among Youth Exposed to Family Violence." *Child Abuse and Neglect* 25:1037–1051.

———. 2003. "Sexual Abuse, Family Violence, and Girls' Antisocial Behavior: Findings from a Longitudinal Study." *Violence and Victims* 18(3): 319–334.

Hey, Valerie. 1997. *The Company She Keeps: An Ethnography of Girls' Friendship*. Bristol, PA: Open University Press.

Hirschi, Travis. 1969. *Causes of Delinquency*. Berkeley: University of California Press.

Hochschild, Arlie. 1975. "The Sociology of Feeling and Emotion: Selected Possibilities." In *Another Voice: Feminist Perspectives on Social Life and Social Science*, edited by Marcia Millman and Rosabeth Moss Canter, 280–307. New York: Anchor Books.

———. 1989. *The Second Shift: Working Parents and the Revolution at Home*. New York: Viking Press.

Holden, George, Robert Geffner, and Ernest Jouriles, eds. 1998. *Children Exposed to Marital Violence: Theory, Research, and Applied Issues.* Washington, DC: American Psychological Association.

Holsinger, Kristi. 2000. "Feminist Perspectives on Female Offending: Examining Real Girls' Lives." *Women and Criminal Justice* 12:23–51.

Holsinger, Kristi, and Alexander Holsinger. 2005. "Differential Pathways to Violence and Self-Injurious Behavior: African American and White Girls in the Juvenile Justice System." *Journal of Research in Crime and Delinquency* 42(2): 211–242.

hooks, bell. 1992. *Black Looks: Race and Representation.* Boston: South End Press.

Hsia, Heidi, George Bridges, and Rosalie McHale. 2004. "Disproportionate Minority Confinement: Year 2002 Update." NCJ Report 201240. Washington, DC: Office of Juvenile Justice and Delinquency Prevention.

Huesmann, Rowell, Jessica Moise-Titus, Cheryl-Lynn Podolski, and Leonard Eron. 2003. "Longitudinal Relations between Children's Exposure to TV Violence and Their Aggressive and Violent Behavior in Young Adulthood." *Developmental Psychology* 39(2): 201–221.

Human Rights Watch. 2001. *Hatred in the Hallways: Violence and Discrimination against Lesbian, Gay, and Bisexual and Transgender Youth in U.S. Schools.* New York: Human Rights Watch.

Humes, Edward. 1996. *No Matter How Loud I Shout: A Year in the Life of Juvenile Court.* New York: Simon & Schuster.

Hunter, J. 1990. "Violence against Lesbian and Gay Male Youths." *Journal of Interpersonal Violence* 5(3): 295–300.

Hurtado, Aida. 2003. *Voicing Chicana Feminisms: Young Women Speak Out on Sexuality and Identity.* New York: New York University Press.

Hymowitz, Carolyn, and Michaele Weissman. 1978. *A History of Women in America.* New York: Bantam Books.

Irvine, Janice, ed. 1994. *Sexual Cultures and the Construction of Adolescent Identities.* Philadelphia: Temple University Press.

Irwin, John. 1970. *The Felon.* Englewood Cliffs, NJ: Prentice Hall.

Jacobs, Janet L. 1993. "Victimized Daughters: Sexual Violence and the Empathic Female Self." *Signs* 19(1): 126–145.

Jakobsen, Janet, and Ann Pellegrini. 2004. *Love the Sin: Sexual Regulation and the Limits of Religious Tolerance.* New York: Beacon Press.

James, Allison, and Alan Prout, eds. 1997. *Constructing and Reconstructing Childhood: Contemporary Issues in the Sociological Study of Childhood.* London: Falmer Press.

James, Jennifer, and William Thornton. 1980. "Women's Liberation and the Female Delinquent." *Journal of Research in Crime and Delinquency* 20:230–244.

Janus, Mark-David, Arlene McCormack, Ann Wolbert Burgess, and Carol Hartman. 1987. *Adolescent Runaways: Causes and Consequences.* Lexington, MA: Lexington Books.

Jencks, Christopher, and Susan Mayer. 1990. "The Social Consequences of Growing Up in a Poor Neighborhood." In *Inner-City Poverty in the United States,* edited by Laurence Lynn and Michael McGreary, 111–186. Washington, DC: National Academy Press.

Jenkins, Esther, and Carl Bell. 1997. "Exposure and Response to Community Violence among Children and Adolescents." In Osofsky, *Children in a Violent Society,* 9–31.

Johnson, Norine, Michael Roberts, and Judith Worell, eds. 1999. *Beyond Appearance: A New Look at Adolescent Girls.* Washington DC: American Psychological Association.

Jones-Brown, Delores, and Zelma Henriquez. 1997. "Mentoring as a Juvenile Justice Strategy." *Social Justice* 24(4): 212–233.

Jonson-Reid, Melissa, and Richard P. Barth. 2000. "From Maltreatment Report to Juvenile Incarceration: The Role of Child Welfare Services." *Child Abuse and Neglect* 24(4): 505–520.

Jordan, Karen. 2000. "Substance Abuse among Gay, Lesbian, Bisexual, Transgender, and Questioning Adolescents." *School Psychology Review* 29(2): 201–206.

Kantrowitz, Barbara, and Pat Wingert. 1999. "Beyond Littleton: How Well Do You Know Your Kid?" *Newsweek*, May 10, 36–60.

Kaplan, Elaine Bell. 1997. *Not Our Kind of Girl: Unraveling the Myths of Black Teenage Motherhood.* Berkeley: University of California Press.

Kataoka, Sheryl, Bonnie Zima, Dierdre Dupre, Kathleen Moreno, Xiaowei Yang, and James McCracken. 2001. "Mental Health Problems and Service Use among Female Juvenile Offenders: Their Relationship to Criminal History." *Journal of the American Academy of Child and Adolescent Psychiatry* 40(5): 549–555.

Katz, Jack. 1988. *Seductions of Crime: Moral and Sensual Attractions in Doing Evil.* New York: Basic Books.

Kaufman, K. 2005. "Childhood Mourning: Prospective Case Analysis of Multiple Losses." *Death Studies* 29(3): 237–249.

Keller, Kenneth. 2002. "Juvenile Female Offenders in Cook County: Trends and Outcomes." Paper presented at the American Society of Criminology annual meetings, Chicago.

Kelley, Robin D. G. 1996. "Kickin' Reality, Kickin' Ballistics: Gansta Rap and Postindustrial Los Angeles." In *Droppin' Science: Critical Essays on Rap Music and Hip Hop Culture,* edited by William Eric Perkins, 117–158. Philadelphia: Temple University Press.

Kelly, Barbara Tatem, Terence Thornberry, and Carolyn Smith. 1997. "In the Wake of Childhood Maltreatment." *Juvenile Justice Bulletin.* Washington, DC: Office of Juvenile Justice and Delinquency Prevention.

Kennedy, Michael. 1991. "Homeless and Runaway Youth Mental Health Issues: No Access to the System." *Journal of Adolescent Health* 12:576–579.

Ketterlinus, Robert, Michael Lamb, Katherine Nitz, and Arthur Elster. 1992. "Adolescent Nonsexual and Sex-Related Behaviors." *Journal of Adolescent Research* 7(4): 431–456.

Kilpatrick, D., K. Ruggiero, R. Acierno, B. Saunders, H. Resnick, and C. Best. 2003. "Violence and Risk of PTSD, Major Depression, Substance Abuse/Dependence, and Comorbidity: Results from the *National Survey of Adolescents.*" *Journal of Consulting and Clinical Psychology* 1(4): 692–700.

Klein, Malcolm, Cheryl Maxson, and Jody Miller. 1995. *The Modern Gang Reader.* Los Angeles: Roxbury.

Kleinman, Arthur, Veena Das, and Margaret Lock. 1997. *Social Suffering.* Berkeley: University of California Press.

Konopka, Gisela. 1966. *The Adolescent Girl in Conflict.* Englewood, NJ: Prentice Hall.

Kooy, Elizabeth. 2002. *The Status of Automatic Transfers to Adult Court in Cook County, Illinois, October 1999 to September 2000.* Chicago: Cook County Office of the Public Defender.

Kruks, Gabe. 1991. "Gay and Lesbian Homeless/Street Youth: Special Issues and Concerns." *Journal of Adolescent Health* 12(7): 515–518.

Kruttschnitt, Candace, and Rosemary Gartner. 2004. *Marking Time in the Golden State: Women's Imprisonment in California.* Cambridge: Cambridge University Press.

Kumpfer, Karol. 1993. *Strengthening America's Families: Promising Parenting Strategies for Delinquency Prevention.* Washington, DC: Office of Juvenile Justice and Delinquency Prevention.

———. 1994. *Family Strengthening in Preventing Delinquency: A Literature Review.* Washington, DC: Office of Juvenile Justice and Delinquency Prevention.

Kumpfer, Karol, and Connie Tait. 2000. *Family Skills Training for Parents and Children.* Washington, DC: Office of Juvenile Justice and Delinquency Prevention.

Kunzel, Regina. 1993. *Fallen Women, Problem Girls: Unmarried Mothers and the Professionalization of Social Work, 1890–1945.* New Haven, CT: Yale University Press.

Kurwa, Nishat. 1998. "Do Schools Condone Harassment of Gay Students?" *San Francisco Examiner,* May 19, sec. D.

La Ferla, Ruth. 2003. "Underdressed and Hot: Dolls Moms Don't Love." *New York Times,* October 26, sec. 9.

Lamb, Sharon. 2001. *The Secret Lives of Girls: What Good Girls Really Do—Sex Play, Aggression, and Their Guilt.* New York: Free Press.

Lancaster, Roger, and Micaela di Leonardo, eds. 1997. *The Gender/Sexuality Reader.* New York: Routledge.

Landesman, Peter. 2004. "Sex Slaves on Main Street: The Girls Next Door." *New York Times Magazine,* January 25.

Lareau, Annette. 2003. *Unequal Childhoods: Class, Race, and Family Life.* Berkeley: University of California Press.

Lauer, Marc, and Meda Chesney-Lind, eds. 2002. *Invisible Punishment: The Collateral Consequences of Mass Imprisonment.* New York: Free Press.

Leadbeater, Bonnie Ross, and Niobe Way, eds. 1996. *Urban Girls: Resisting Stereotypes, Creating Identities.* New York: New York University Press.

Leiberman, Jethro. 1981. *The Litigious Society.* New York: Basic Books.

Lerner, Harriet. 1985. *The Dance of Anger.* New York: HarperCollins.

Lerner, R., and N. Galambos. 1998. "Adolescent Development: Challenges and Opportunities for Research, Programs, and Policies." *Annual Review of Psychology* 49:413–446.

Lesage, Julia. 1985. "Women's Rage." In *Marxism and the Interpretation of Culture,* edited by Cary Nelson and Larry Grossberg, 419–428. Champagne: University of Illinois Press.

Leschied, Alan, Anne Cummings, Michelle Van Brunschot, Alison Cunningham, and Angela Saunders. 2001. "Agression in Adolescent Girls: Implications for Policy, Prevention, and Treatment." *Canadian Psychology* 42(3): 200–215.

Levesque, Roger. 2000. *Adolescents, Sex, and the Law: Preparing Adolescents for Responsible Citizenship.* Washington, DC: American Psychological Association.

Levine, Felice, and Katherine Rosich. 1996. *Social Causes of Violence: Crafting a Science Agenda.* Washington, DC: American Sociological Association.

Levine, Judith. 2002. *Harmful to Minors: The Perils of Protecting Children from Sex.* Minneapolis: University of Minnesota Press.

Levine, Kay. 2003. "Prosecution, Politics and Pregnancy: Enforcing Statutory Rape in California." PhD diss., School of Jurisprudence and Social Policy, University of California at Berkeley.

Lewis, Amanda. 2003. *Race in the Schoolyard: Negotiating the Color Line in Classrooms and Communities.* New Brunswick, NJ: Rutgers University Press.

Lobel, Kerry, ed. 1986. *Naming the Violence: Speaking Out about Lesbian Battering.* Emeryville, CA: Seal Press.

Lockwood, Daniel. 1997. "Violence among Middle School and High School Students: Analysis and Implications for Prevention." *Research in Brief.* Washington, DC: National Institute of Justice, Office of Justice Programs, U.S. Department of Justice.

Loeber, Rolf. 1996. "Developmental Continuity, Change, and Pathways in Male Juvenile Problem Behaviors and Delinquency." In Hawkins, *Delinquency and Crime,* 1–27.

Lorber, Judith. 1995. *Paradoxes of Gender.* New Haven, CT: Yale University Press.

Luker, Kristin. 1984. *Abortion and the Politics of Motherhood.* Berkeley: University of California Press.

———. 1996. *Dubious Conceptions: The Politics of Teenage Pregnancy.* Cambridge, MA: Harvard University Press.

Luster, Tom, and Stephen A. Small. 1997. "Sexual Abuse History and Number of Sex Partners among Female Adolescents." *Family Planning Perspectives* 29(5): 204–211.

MacKinnon, Catherine. 1989. *Toward a Feminist Theory of the State.* Cambridge, MA: Harvard University Press.

Madriz, Esther. 1997. *Nothing Bad Happens to Good Girls: Fear of Crime in Women's Lives.* Berkeley: University of California Press.

Males, Mike. 1999. *Framing Youth: Ten Myths about the Next Generation.* Monroe, ME: Common Courage Press.

Mann, Coramae Richey. 1984. *Female Crime and Delinquency.* University: University of Alabama Press.

Martin, Karin. 1996. *Puberty, Sexuality, and the Self: Girls and Boys at Adolescence.* New York: Routledge.

Maxfield, Michael, and Earl Babbie. 2005. *Research Methods for Criminal Justice and Criminology,* 4th ed. Belmont, CA: Thomson Wadsworth.

McCord, Joan, ed. 1997. *Violence and Childhood in the Inner City.* Cambridge: Cambridge University Press.

McCorkel, Jill. 2003. "Embodied Surveillance and the Gendering of Punishment." *Journal of Contemporary Ethnography* 32(1): 41–76.

McKay, Matthew, Peter Rogers, and Judith McKay. 1989. *When Anger Hurts: Quieting the Storm Within.* Oakland, CA: New Harbinger.

Mendel, Dick. 2003. "Small Is Beautiful: Missouri Shows the Way on Juvenile Corrections." In *Juvenile Justice at a Crossroads,* 28–36. Baltimore: Annie E. Casey Foundation.

Mennel, Robert. 1973. *Thorns and Thistles: Juvenile Delinquents in the United States, 1825–1940.* Hanover: University of New Hampshire Press.

Meredith, Robyn. 1999. "Truants' Parents Face Crackdown across the U.S." *New York Times,* December 6, sec. A.

Messerschmidt, James. 1997. *Crime as Structured Action: Gender, Race, Class, and Crime in the Making.* Thousand Oaks, CA: Sage.

Michael, Robert, John Gagnon, Edward Laumann, and Gina Kolata. 1994. *Sex in America: A Definitive Survey.* Boston: Little, Brown.

Miller, Jody. 2001. *One of the Guys: Girls, Gangs, and Gender.* New York: Oxford University Press.

Miranda, Marie. 2003. *Homegirls in the Public Sphere.* Austin: University of Texas Press.

Mohanty, Chandra Talpade. 2003. *Feminism without Borders: Decolonizing Theory, Practicing Solidarity.* Durham, NC: Duke University Press.

Mohr, Wanda. 1997. "Making the Invisible Victims of Domestic Violence Visible." *Domestic Violence Report* 2(6): 81–82.

Moore, Henrietta. 1994. "The Problem of Explaining Violence in Social Sciences." In Harvey and Gow, *Sex and Violence,* 138–155.

Moore, Kristen Anderson, Christine Winquist Nord, and James L. Perterson. 1989. "Nonvoluntary Sexual Activity among Adolescents." *Family Planning Perspectives* 21(3): 110–114.

Moretti, Marlene, Candice Odgers, and Margaret Jackson, eds. 2004. *Girls and Aggression: Contributing Factors and Intervention Principles.* New York: Kluwer Academic.

Morgan, Joan. 2000. *When Chickenheads Come Home to Roost: A Hip Hop Feminist Breaks It Down.* New York: Simon & Schuster.

Morgan, Marcia, and Sheila Peters. 2000. "Training Curriculum for Policymakers, Administrators, and Managers." In Greene, Peters, and Associates, *Beyond Gender Barriers: Programming Specifically for Girls,* n.p.

Moskowitz, Harry, John Griffith, Carla DiScala, and Robert Sege. 2001. "Serious Injuries and Deaths of Adolescent Girls Resulting from Interpersonal Violence." *Archives of Pediatric Adolescent Medicine* 155:903–908.

Murray, John. 1997. "Media Violence and Youth." In Osofsky, *Children in a Violent Society,* 72–96.

Murray, Yxta Maya. 1997. *Locas.* New York: Grove Press.

Myers, Kristen, and Passion Williamson. 2001. "Race Talk: The Perpetuation of Racism through Private Discourse." *Race & Society* 4:3–26.

Naffine, Ngaire. 1987. *Female Crime: The Construction of Women in Criminology.* Sydney, Australia: Allen and Unwyn.

Nam, Vickie, ed. 2001. *Yell-oh Girls!* New York: HarperCollins.

Naples, Nancy. 2003. *Feminism and Method: Ethnography, Discourse, and Activist Research.* New York: Routledge.

Nathanson, Constance. 1991. *Dangerous Passage: The Social Control of Sexuality in Women's Adolescence.* Philadelphia: Temple University Press.

National Center for Education Statistics. 2004. *Societal Support for Learning: Public Effort to Fund Education.* Washington, DC: U.S. Department of Education. http://www.nces.ed.gov.

National Foster Parent Association. 2004. *Fact Sheet.* http://www.nfpainc.org.

Ness, Carol. 1998. "Gay Bias Rising among Top Students." *San Francisco Examiner,* November 12, sec. A.

Newburn, Tim, and Elizabeth Stanko, eds. 1994. *Just Boys Doing Business? Men, Masculinities, and Crime.* New York: Routledge.

Newport, Frank. 2001. *Americans See Women as Emotional and Affectionate and Men as More Aggressive: Gender Specific Stereotypes Persist in Recent Gallup Poll.* Gallup Organization Poll Analyses. February 21. http://www.gallup.com.

Obeidallah, Dawn, and Felton Earls. 1999. *Adolescent Girls: The Role of Depression in the Development of Delinquency.* Research Preview. Washington, DC: National Institute of Justice.

O'Brien, Patricia. 2001. *Making It in the "Free World": Women in Transition from Prison.* Albany: State University of New York Press.

O'Connell Davidson, Julia. 2005. *Children and the Global Sex Trade.* Cambridge, MA: Polity Press.

O'Connell Davidson, Julia, and Derek Layder. 1998. *Methods, Sex, and Madness.* New York: Routledge.

Odem, Mary. 1995. *Delinquent Daughters: Protecting and Policing Adolescent Female Sexuality in the United States, 1885–1920.* Chapel Hill: North Carolina University Press.

Odem, Mary, and Steven Schlossman. 1991. "Guardians of Virtue: The Juvenile Court and Female Delinquency in Early 20th Century Los Angeles." *Crime and Delinquency* 37(2): 186–203.

Office of Juvenile Justice and Delinquency Prevention. 1999. "Minorities in the Juvenile Justice System." *Juvenile Justice Bulletin.* 1999 National Report Series. Washington, DC: Office of Juvenile Justice and Delinquency Prevention.

O'Hare, William, and Mark Mather. 2003. *The Growing Number of Kids in Severely Distressed Neighborhoods: Evidence from the 2000 Census.* A Kids Count/Population Reference Bureau Report on Census 2000. Baltimore: Annie E. Casey Foundation; Washington, DC: Population Reference Bureau.

Olders, H. 1989. "Mourning and Grief as Healing Processes in Psychotherapy." *Canadian Journal of Psychiatry [Revue Canadienne de Psychiatrie]* 34(4): 271–278.

O'Leary, Claudine, and Olivia Howard. 2001. *The Prostitution of Women and Girls in Metropolitan Chicago: A Preliminary Prevalence Report.* Chicago: Center for Impact Research.

Olmedo, Irma. 2004. "Language Mediation among Emergent Bilingual Children." *Linguistics and Education* 14(2): 143–162.

Omi, Michael, and Howard Winant. 1989. *Racial Formation in the United States: From the 1960s to the 1980s.* New York: Routledge.

Orenstein, Peggy. 1994. *Schoolgirls: Young Women, Self-Esteem, and the Confidence Gap.* New York: Doubleday.

Osofsky, Joy, ed. 1997. *Children in a Violent Society.* New York: Guilford Press.

———. 1998. "Children as Invisible Victims of Domestic and Community Violence." In Holden, Geffner, and Jouriles, *Children Exposed to Marital Violence,* 95–120.

O'Toole, Laura, and Jessica Schiffman, eds. 1997. *Gender Violence: Interdisciplinary Perspectives.* New York: New York University Press.

Owen, Barbara, and Barbara Bloom. 1997. *Profiling the Needs of Young Female Offenders: Final Report to the Executive Staff of the California Youth Authority.* Washington, DC: National Institute of Justice.

———. 1998. *Modeling Gender-Specific Services in Juvenile Justice: Policy and Program Recommendations.* Sacramento, CA: Office of Criminal Justice Planning.

Owens, Robert. 1998. *Queer Kids: The Challenges and Promise for Lesbian, Gay, and Bisexual Youth.* New York: Haworth Press.

Pajer, Kathleen, William Gardner, Robert Rubin, James Perel, and Stephen Neal. 2001. "Decreased Cortisol Levels in Adolescent Girls with Conduct Disorder." *Archives of General Psychiatry* 58:297–302.

Parsons, Talcott. 1942. "Age and Sex in Social Structure of the United States." *American Sociological Review* 7(5): 604–616.

Pastor, Jennifer, Jennifer McCormick, and Michelle Fine. 1996. "Makin' Homes: An Urban Girl Thing." In Leadbeater and Way, *Urban Girls*, 15–34.

Patillo, Mary, David Weiman, and Bruce Western, eds. 2004. *Imprisoning America: The Social Effects of Mass Incarceration.* New York: Russell Sage Foundation.

Perez McCluskey, Cynthia. 2002. *Understanding Latino Delinquency.* New York: LFB Scholarly Publishing.

Pfeffer, Rachel. 1997. *Surviving the Streets: Girls Living on Their Own.* New York: Garland.

Phelps, Linda. 1979. "Female Sexual Alienation." In *Women: A Feminist Perspective,* edited by Joann Freeman, 18–26. Palo Alto, CA: Mayfield.

Phillips, Lynn. 1999. "Recasting Consent: Agency and Victimization in Adult-Teen Relationships." In *New Versions of Victims: Feminists Struggle with the Concept,* edited by Sharon Lamb, 82–107. New York: New York University Press.

———. 2000. *Flirting with Danger: Young Women's Reflections on Sexuality and Domination.* New York: New York University Press.

Pinderhughes, Howard. 1997. *Race in the Hood: Conflict and Violence among Urban Youth.* Minneapolis: Minnesota University Press.

Pipher, Mary. 1994. *Reviving Ophelia: Saving the Lives of Adolescent Girls.* New York: Ballantine Books.

Pisciotta, Alexander. 1982. "Saving the Children: The Promise and Practice of *Parens Patriae,* 1838–1898." *Crime and Delinquency* 28(3): 410–425.

Pollak, Otto, and Alfred Friedman, eds. 1969. *Family Dynamics and Female Sexual Delinquency.* Palo Alto, CA: Science and Behavior Books.

Pollock, Joycelyn. 1999. *Criminal Women.* Cincinnati: Anderson.

Ponton, Lynn. 2000. *The Sex Lives of Teenagers: Revealing the Secret World of Adolescent Boys and Girls.* New York: Penguin Books.

Pope, Carl, Rick Lovell, and Steven Brandl. 2001. *Voices from the Field: Readings in Criminal Justice Research.* Belmont, CA: Wadsworth Thomson.

Pough, Gwendolyn. 2004. *Check It While I Wreck It: Black Womanhood, Hip Hop Culture, and the Public Sphere.* Boston: Northeastern University Press.

Poulin, Anne Bowen. 1996. "Female Delinquents: Defining Their Place in the Justice System." *Wisconsin Law Review* 1996(3): 549–551.

Powers, Jane, and Barbara Jaklitsch. 1989. *Understanding Survivors of Abuse: Stories of Homeless and Runaway Adolescents.* Lexington, MA: Lexington Books.

Proweller, Amira. 1998. *Constructing Female Identities: Meaning Making in an Upper Middle Class Youth Culture.* Albany: State University of New York Press.

Putallaz, Martha, and Karen Bierman, eds. 2004. *Aggression, Antisocial Behavior, and Violence among Girls.* New York: Guilford Press.

Puzzanchera, C., W. Kang, R. Poole, and Y. Wan. 2002. *Easy Access to Juvenile Populations.* http://www.ojjdp.ncjrs.org.

Pynoos, R., and S. Eth. 1985. "Developmental Perspective on Psychic Trauma in Childhood." In *Trauma and Its Wake,* edited by Charles Figley, 193–216. New York: Brunner/Mazel.

Reinharz, Shulamit. 1992. *Feminist Methods in Social Research.* Oxford: Oxford University Press.

Remafedi, Gary, and Robert Blum. 1986. "Working with Gay and Lesbian Adolescents." *Pediatric Annals* 15(11): 773–783.

Resources for Youth. 2000. *Information Exchange.* San Rafael, CA: Resources for Youth.

Rich, Adrienne. [1978] 1986. "Compulsory Heterosexuality and the Continuum of Lesbian Existence." In *Feminist Frontiers II: Rethinking Sex, Gender, and Society,* edited by Laurel Richardson and Verta Taylor, 120–141. New York: McGraw-Hill.

Richardson, Laurel, Verta Taylor, and Nancy Whittier. 2003. *Feminist Frontiers,* 5th ed. New York: McGraw-Hill.

Richie, Beth E. 1996. *Compelled to Crime: The Gender Entrapment of Battered Black Women.* New York: Routledge.

———. 2002. "The Social Impact of Mass Incarceration of Women." In *Invisible Punishment: The Collateral Consequences of Mass Imprisonment,* edited by Marc Lauer and Meda Chesney-Lind, 136–149. New York: Free Press.

Roberts, Dorothy. 2002. *Shattered Bonds: The Color of Child Welfare.* New York: Basic Civitas Books.

Rogers, Betty. 1999. "Bitter Harvest: How the Sexual Exploitation of Girls Has Become Big Business in Thailand." *Ms.,* October/November, 45–55.

Rogers Park Young Women's Action Team. 2003. *"Hey Cutie, Can I Get Your Digits?" A Report about the Street Harassment of Girls in Rogers Park.* Chicago: Friends of Battered Women and Their Children, August.

Rose, Tricia. 1994. *Black Noise: Rap Music and Black Culture in Contemporary America.* Middletown, CT: Wesleyan University Press.

———. 2003. *Longing to Tell: Black Women's Stories of Sexuality and Intimacy.* New York: Farrar, Straus & Giroux.

Rosen, Ruth. 1982. *The Lost Sisterhood: Prostitution in America, 1900–1918.* Baltimore: Johns Hopkins University Press.

Rosenberg, Harold, and Kristina Phillips. 2003. "Acceptability and Availability of Harm-Reduction Interventions for Drug Abuse in American Substance Abuse Treatment Agencies." *Psychology of Addictive Behaviors* 17(3): 202–210.

Rosenthal, Susan L., Lisa M. Lewis, and Sheila S. Cohen. 1996. "Issues Related to the Decision-Making of Inner City Adolescent Girls." *Adolescence* 31(12): 731.

Ross, Catherine E., and John Mirowsky. 2001. "Neighborhood Disadvantage, Disorder, and Health." *Journal of Health and Social Behavior* 42(3): 258–276.

Rowe, David. 1996. "An Adaptive Strategy Theory in Crime and Delinquency." In Hawkins, *Delinquency and Crime,* 268–324.

Rubin, Gayle. 1975. "The Traffic in Women: Notes on the 'Political Economy' of Sex." In *Toward an Anthropology of Women,* edited by Rayna Reiter, 157–210. New York: Monthly Review Press.

Rubin, Lillian. 1990. *Erotic Wars: What Happened to the Sexual Revolution?* New York: HarperPerennial.

Runtz, Marsha, and John Briere. 1986. "Adolescent 'Acting Out' and Childhood History of Sexual Abuse." *Journal of Interpersonal Violence* 1(3): 326–334.

Ryan, Kevin. 2004. *Juvenile Detention Center Investigation: An Examination of Conditions of Care for Youth with Mental Health Needs.* Trenton, NJ: Office of the Child Advocate.

Ryan, Suzanne, Jennifer Manlove, and Kerry Franzetta. 2003. *The First Time: Characteristics of Teens' First Sexual Relationships.* Child Trends Research Brief. Washington, DC: Child Trends.

"San Francisco Foster Care Fact Sheet." 1996. Unpublished document prepared by Rebecca Carabez, San Francisco General Hospital Child Protection Center, on file with author.

San Francisco Task Force on Prostitution. *Final Report.* 1996. San Francisco: Mayor's Office.

Sanchez-Jankowski, Martin. 1991. *Islands in the Street: Gangs and American Urban Society.* Berkeley: University of California Press.

Savin-Williams, Ruth. 2001. "Dating and Romantic Relationships among Gay, Lesbian, and Bisexual Youths." In Davidson and Moore, *Speaking of Sexuality,* 306–316.

Savin-Williams, Ruth, and Thomas Berndt. 1990. "Friendship and Peer Relations." In Feldman and Elliott, *At the Threshold,* 277–307.

Schaffner, Laurie. 1997. "Families on Probation: Court-Ordered Parenting Skills Classes for Parents of Juvenile Offenders." *Crime and Delinquency* 43(4): 412–437.

———. 1999a. *Teenage Runaways: Broken Hearts and "Bad Attitudes."* New York: Haworth Press.

———. 1999b. "Violence and Female Delinquency: Gender Transgressions and Gender Invisibility." *Berkeley Women's Law Journal* 14:40–65.

———. 2003. *The Study of the Girls Link Collaborative: The Evaluation of Girls Link.* Technical Report. Chicago: Cook County Bureau of Public Safety and Judicial Coordination, Juvenile Justice Commission of Cook County, October. http://www.ajfo.org.

———. 2005. "Capacity, Consent, and the Construction of Adulthood." In Bernstein and Schaffner, *Regulating Sex,* 189–205.

Scheler, Max. 1994. *Ressentiment.* Milwaukee: Marquette University Press.

Scherzer, Teresa. 1998. "Domestic Violence in Lesbian Relationships: Findings of the Lesbian Relationships Research Project." In *Journal of Lesbian Studies "Gateways to Improving Lesbian Health and Health Care,"* edited by Christy Ponticelli, 29–47. New York: Haworth Press.

Schlosser, Eric. 1997. "The Business of Pornography." *U.S. News and World Report,* February.

Schlossman, Steven L. 1977. *Love and the American Delinquent: The Theory and Practice of "Progressive" Juvenile Justice, 1825–1920.* Chicago: University of Chicago Press.

Scholinski, Daphne. 1997. *The Last Time I Wore a Dress.* New York: Riverhead Books.

Schur, Edwin. 1984. *Labeling Women Deviant: Gender, Stigma, and Social Control.* Philadelphia: Temple University Press.

———. 1997. "Sexual Coercion in American Life." In *Gender Violence: Interdisciplinary Perspectives,* edited by Laura O'Toole and Jessica Schiffman, 80–91. New York: New York University Press.

Scott, James C. 1985. *Weapons of the Weak: Everyday Forms of Peasant Resistance.* New Haven, CT: Yale University Press.

Scott, Joseph W., and Albert Black. 1999. "Deep Structures of African American Family Life: Female and Male Kin Networks." In *The Black Family: Essays and Studies,* 6th ed., edited by Robert Staples, 232–240. Belmont, CA: Wadsworth.

Scripps Howard. 1996. "Teen-Girl Crime Wave Swamps Sweet 16 Image." *Arizona Republic,* December 4, sec. A.

Sedgwick, Eve Kosofsky. 1993. "How to Bring Your Kids Up Gay." In *Fear of a Queer Planet,* edited by Michael Warner, 69–81. Minneapolis: University of Minnesota Press.

Sharpe, Sue. 1976. *"Just Like a Girl": How Girls Learn to Be Women.* New York: Penguin Books.

Shelden, Randall, Sharon Tracy, and William Brown. *Youth Gangs in American Society,* 2nd ed. Belmont, CA: Wadsworth.

Shoemaker, Donald. 1996. *Theories of Delinquency: An Examination of Explanations of Delinquent Behavior,* 3rd ed. New York: Oxford University Press.

Sickmund, Melissa. 2004. *Juveniles in Corrections.* National Report Series. Washington, DC: Office of Juvenile Justice and Delinquency Prevention.

Sickmund, Melissa, T. J. Sladky, and Wei Kang. 2004. *Census of Juveniles in Residential Placement Databook, 2001.* http://www.ojjdp.ncjrs.org/ojstatbb/cjrp/.

Sickmund, Melissa, Howard Snyder, and Eileen Poe-Yamagata. 1997. *Juvenile Offenders and Victims: 1997 Update on Violence.* Washington, DC: Office of Juvenile Justice and Delinquency Prevention.

Siegel, Larry. 2005. *Criminology, the Core,* 2nd ed. Belmont, CA: Thomson Wadsworth.

Siegfried, Christine, Susan Ko, and Ann Kelley. 2004. *Victimization and Juvenile Offending.* Los Angeles: Juvenile Justice Working Group, National Child Traumatic Stress Network.

Silverman, A. B., H. Reinharz, and R. Giaconia. 1996. "The Long-Term Sequelae of Child and Adolescent Abuse: A Longitudinal Community Study." *Child Abuse and Neglect* 20:708–723.

Silverman, Jay, Anita Raj, Lorelei Mucci, and Jeanne Hathaway. 2001. "Dating Violence against Adolescent Girls and Associated Substance Abuse, Unhealthy Weight Control, Sexual Risk Behavior, Pregnancy, and Suicidality." *Journal of the American Medical Association* 280(5): 572–579.

Simkins, Sandra, and Sarah Katz. 2002. "Criminalizing Abused Girls." *Violence against Women* 8(12): 1474–1499.

Simmons, Rachel. 2002. *Odd Girl Out: The Hidden Culture of Aggression in Girls.* New York: Harcourt.

Simon, Rita. 1975. *The Contemporary Woman and Crime.* Washington, DC: Government Printing Office.

Singer, M., T. Anglin, L. Song, and L. Lunghofer. 1995. "Adolescents' Exposure to Violence and Associated Symptoms of Psychological Trauma." *Journal of the American Medical Association* 273(6): 477–482.

Sisters Empowering Sisters. 2003. *Respect Me, Don't Media Me.* A Participatory Research Report. Chicago: Girls Best Friend Foundation.

Smart, Carol, and Barry Smart, eds. 1978. *Women, Sexuality, and Social Control.* Boston: Routledge.

Smith, Carolyn. 1997. "Factors Associated with Early Sexual Activity among Urban Adolescents." *Social Work* 42:334–346.

Smith, Carolyn, Terrence Thornberry, and Timothy Ireland. 2004. "Adolescent Maltreatment and Its Impact: Timing Matters." *Prevention Researcher* 11(1): 7–11.

Smith, Dorothy. 1987. *The Everyday World as Problematic: A Feminist Sociology.* Boston: Northeastern University Press.

Smith-Rosenberg, Carroll. 1985. *Disorderly Conduct: Visions of Gender in Victorian America.* New York: Oxford University Press.

Snitow, Ann, Christine Stansell, and Sharon Thompson. 1983. *Powers of Desire: The Politics of Sexuality.* New York: Monthly Review Press.

Snyder, Howard. 1998. *Serious, Violent, and Chronic Juvenile Offenders: An Assessment of the Extent of and Trends in Officially-Recognized Serious*

Criminal Behavior in a Delinquent Population. Washington, DC: Office of Juvenile Justice and Delinquency Prevention.

———. 2000. *Sexual Assault of Young Children as Reported to Law Enforcement: Victim, Incident, and Offender Characteristics.* Washington, DC: National Center for Juvenile Justice, U.S. Department of Justice.

———. 2005. "Juvenile Arrests 2003." *Juvenile Justice Bulletin.* Washington, DC: U.S. Department of Justice.

Snyder, Howard, C. Puzzanchera, and W. Kang. 2005. *Easy Access to FBI Statistics 1994–2002.* http://ojjdp.ncjrs.org/ojstatbb/ezaucr/.

Snyder, Howard and Melissa Sickmund. 2006. *Juvenile Offenders and Victims: 2006 National Report.* Washington DC: Office of Juvenile Justice and Delinquency Prevention.

Snyder, Howard, and Melissa Sickmund. 1999. *Juvenile Offenders and Victims: 1999 National Report.* Washington, DC: Office of Juvenile Justice and Delinquency Prevention.

Soderlund, Gretchen. 2005. "Running from the Rescuers: New US Crusades against Sex Trafficking and the Rhetoric of Abolition." *National Women's Studies Journal* 17 (Fall): 3, 64–87.

Spelman, Elizabeth V. 1990. *Inessential Woman: Problems of Exclusion in Feminist Thought.* Boston: Beacon Press.

Stack, Carol. 1997. *All Our Kin.* New York: BasicBooks.

Stahl, Anne L. 2003. *Delinquency Cases in Juvenile Courts, 1999.* OJJDP Fact Sheet. Washington, DC: Office of Juvenile Justice and Delinquency Prevention, September.

Stahl, Anne L., T. Finnegan, and W. Kang. 2003. *Easy Access to Juvenile Court Statistics: 1985–2000.* http://ojjdp.ncjrs.org.

Stannard, Una. 1971. "The Mask of Beauty." In *Woman in Sexist Society: Studies in Power and Powerlessness,* edited by Vivian Gornick and Barbara Moran, 187–203. New York: Signet.

Steffensmeier, Darrell, and Emilie Allan. 1996. "Gender and Crime: Toward a Gendered Theory of Female Offending." *Annual Review of Sociology* 22:459–487.

———. 1998. "The Nature of Female Offending: Patterns and Explanation." In Zaplin, *Female Offenders,* 5–30.

Stein, Nan. 2001. "Sexual Harassment Meets Zero Tolerance: Life in K–12 Schools." In Ayers, Dohrn, and Ayers, *Zero Tolerance,* 143–154.

Stein, Nancy, Susan Roberta Katz, Esther Madriz, and Shelley Shick, special eds. 1997. "Losing a Generation: Probing the Myths and Realities of Youth and Violence." *Social Justice* 24(4).

Steineger, Melissa, and Sheila Peters. 2000. *Beyond Gender Barriers: Programming Specifically for Girls: "Training of Trainers Curriculum."* Nashville: Greene, Peters, and Associates; Washington, DC: Office of Juvenile Justice and Delinquency Prevention.

Steiner, Claude. 1997. *Achieving Emotional Literacy.* New York: Avon.

Steiner, H., I. Garcia, and Z. Matthews. 1997. "Posttraumatic Stress Disorder in Incarcerated Juvenile Delinquents." *Journal of the American Academy of Child and Adolescent Psychiatry* 36(3): 357–365.

Stephens, Sharon, ed. 1995. *Children and the Politics of Culture.* Princeton, NJ: Princeton University Press.

Stewart, Anna, Susan Dennison and Elissa Waterson. 2002. "Pathways from Child Maltreatment to Juvenile Offending." *Australian Institute of Criminology:*

Trends and Issues in Crime and Criminal Justice, no. 241. Canberra, Australia: Australian Institute of Criminology.

Stock, Jacqueline, Michelle Bell, Debra Boyer, and Frederick Connell. 1997. "Adolescent Pregnancy and Sexual Risk-Taking among Sexually Abused Girls." *Family Planning Perspectives* 29(5): 200–203.

Sudbury, Julia. 2005. *Global Lockdown: Race, Gender, and the Prison-Industrial Complex.* New York: Routledge.

Sullivan, Kathleen. 1998. "Gay Youths Struggle in Personal Hell." *San Francisco Examiner and Chronicle,* July 26, sec. D.

Sutherland, Donald. 1939. *Principles of Criminology.* Philadelphia: Lippincott.

Sykes, Gresham, and David Matza. 1957. "Techniques of Neutralization: A Theory of Delinquency." In *Theories of Deviance,* 4th ed., edited by Stuart Traub and Craig Little, 203–213. Itasca, IL: Peacock, 1994.

Tannen, Deborah. 1998. *The Argument Culture: Stopping America's War of Words.* New York: Ballantine Books.

Tappan, Paul. 1947. *Delinquent Girls in Court: A Study of the Wayward Minor Court of NY.* New York: Columbia University Press.

Teplin, Linda, Karen Abram, Gary McClelland, Mina Dulcan, and Amy Mericle. 2002. "Psychiatric Disorders in Youth in Juvenile Detention." *Archives of General Psychiatry* 59(12): 1133–1143.

Thomas, William Isaac. 1923. *The Unadjusted Girl.* New York: Harper & Row.

Thompson, Sharon. 1994. "What Friends Are For: On Girls' Misogyny and Romantic Fusion." In Irvine, *Sexual Cultures and the Construction of Adolescent Identities,* 228–249.

———. 1995. *Going All the Way: Teenage Girls' Tales of Sex, Romance, and Pregnancy.* New York: Hill & Wang.

Thorne, Barrie. 1993. *Gender Play: Girls and Boys in School.* New Brunswick, NJ: Rutgers University Press.

Tice, Karen. 1998. *Tales of Wayward Girls and Immoral Women: Case Records and the Professionalization of Social Work.* Chicago: University of Illinois Press.

Tolman, Deborah. 2002. *Dilemmas of Desire: Teenage Girls Talk about Sexuality.* Cambridge, MA: Harvard University Press.

Tolman, Deborah, and Mary Brydon-Miller, eds. 2001. *From Subjects to Subjectivities: A Handbook of Interpretive and Participatory Methods.* New York: New York University Press.

Tolman, Deborah, and Tracy Higgins. 1996. "How Being a Good Girl Can Be Bad for Girls." In *"Bad Girls/Good Girls": Women, Sex, and Power in the Nineties,* edited by Nan Bauer Maglin and Donna Perry, 205–225. New Brunswick, NJ: Rutgers University Press.

Tonry, Michael, and Mark Moore, eds. 1998. *Youth Violence.* Chicago: University of Chicago Press.

Tucker, Jennifer, and Leslie Wolfe. 1997. *Victims No More: Girls Fight Back against Male Violence.* Washington, DC: Center for Women Policy Studies.

Umberson, Debra, and Meichu Chen. 1994. "Effects of a Parent's Death on Adult Children: Relationship Salience and Reaction to Loss." *American Sociological Review* 59(1): 152–168.

Underwood, Marion. 2003. *Social Aggression among Girls.* New York: Guilford Press.

U.S. Census Bureau. 2003. "Table 5: Percent of People in Poverty." *Poverty 2002.* http://www.census.gov.

U.S. Department of Health and Human Services. 2003. *Overview of Findings from the 2003 National Survey on Drug Use and Health*. Washington, DC: Office of Applied Studies, Substance Abuse and Mental Health Services Administration. http://www.samhsa.gov.

U.S. Department of Labor. 2005. "Census of Fatal Occupational Injuries: All U.S. Fatalities in All Sectors, Homicides, All Workers." *Bureau of Labor Statistics Data*. http://www.bls.gov.

Vance, Carol, ed. 1984. *Pleasure and Danger: Exploring Female Sexuality*. Boston: Routlege.

van der Kolk, Bessel, ed. 1987. *Psychological Trauma*. Washington, DC: American Psychiatric Press.

van der Kolk, Bessel, and Mark Greenberg. 1987. "The Psychobiology of the Trauma Response: Hyperarousal, Constriction, and Addiction to Traumatic Re-exposure." In van der Kolk, *Psychological Trauma*, 63–88.

Veysey, Bonita. 2003. *Adolescent Girls with Mental Health Disorders Involved with the Juvenile Justice System*. Washington, DC: National Center for Mental Health and Juvenile Justice. http://www.ncmhjj.com.

VIBE. 2001. *Hip Hop Divas*. New York: Three Rivers Press.

Walkerdine, Valerie. 1998. "Popular Culture and the Eroticization of Little Girls." In *The Children's Culture Reader*, edited by Henry Jenkins, 254–264. New York: New York University Press.

Walkerdine, Valerie, Helen Lucey, and June Melody. 2001. *Growing Up Girl: Psychosocial Explorations of Gender and Class*. New York: New York University Press.

Way, Niobe. 1996. "Between Experiences of Betrayal and Desire: Close Friendships among Urban Adolescents." In Leadbeater and Way, *Urban Girls*, 173–192.

———. 1998. *Everyday Courage: The Lives and Stories of Urban Teenagers*. New York: New York University Press.

Weiss, Lois, and Michele Fine, eds. 2000. *Construction Sites: Excavating Race, Class, and Gender among Urban Youth*. New York: Teachers College Press.

Wellesley Centers for Women. 1998. "An Interview with Nan Stein." *Research Report*, Spring.

Wells, L. Edward, and Joseph Rankin. 1995. "Juvenile Victimization: Convergent Validation of Alternative Measurements." *Journal of Research in Crime and Delinquency* 32(3): 287–307.

West, Candace, and Don Zimmerman. 1987. "Doing Gender." *Gender and Society* 1(2): 125–151.

West, Elliot, and Paula Petrik, eds. 1992. *Small Worlds: Children and Adolescence in America, 1850 to 1950*. Kansas City: Missouri University Press.

West Group. 2003. *California Juvenile Laws and Rules*. St. Paul, MN: Thomson West.

Widom, Cathy Spatz. 1989. "Child Abuse, Neglect, and Violent Criminal Behavior." *Criminology* 27(2): 251–271.

Widom, Cathy Spatz, and J. Kuhns. 1996. "Childhood Victimization and Subsequent Risk for Promiscuity, Prostitution, and Teenage Pregnancy: A Prospective Study." *American Journal of Public Health* 86(11): 1607–1612.

Wilcox, Brian. 1999. "Sexual Obsessions: Public Policy and Adolescent Girls." In Johnson, Roberts, and Worell, *Beyond Appearance*, 333–354.

Wing, Adrienne, and Christine A. Willis. 1997. "Critical Race Feminism: Black Women and Gangs." *Journal of Gender, Race, and Justice* 1(1): 141–176.

Wolf, Diane, ed. 1997. *Feminist Dilemmas in Fieldwork*. Boulder, CO: Westview Press.

Wolfe, Leslie, and Jennifer Tucker. 1998. *Report of the Summit on Girls and Violence*. Washington, DC: Center for Women Policy Studies.

Wood, Jennifer, David Foy, Carole Goguen, Robert Pynoos, and C. Boyd James. 2002. "Violence Exposure and PTSD among Delinquent Girls." In *Trauma and Juvenile Delinquency: Theory, Research, and Interventions*, edited by Ricky Greenwald, 109–126. New York: Haworth Press.

Woodhead, Martin. 1997. "Psychology and the Construction of Children's Needs." In James and Prout, *Constructing and Reconstructing Childhood*, 63–84.

Wordes, Madeline, and Michell Nunez. 2002. *Our Vulnerable Teenagers: Their Victimization, Its Consequences, and Directions for Prevention and Intervention*. Oakland, CA: National Council on Crime and Delinquency.

Wyatt, Edward. 2001. "Sexual Attacks in New York City's Schools Are Up Sharply." *New York Times*, June 3.

Yates, Gary, Richard Mackenzie, Julia Pennbridge, and E. Cohen. 1988. "A Risk Profile Comparison of Runaway Youth and Non-runaway Youth." *American Journal of Public Health* 78:820.

Yates, Gary, Richard Mackenzie, Julia Pennbridge, and Avon Swofford. 1991. "A Risk Profile Comparison of Homeless Youth Involved in Prostitution and Homeless Youth Not Involved." *Journal of Adolescent Health* 12:545–548.

Zaplin, Ruth, ed. 1998. *Female Offenders: Critical Perspectives and Effective Interventions*. Gaithersburg, MD: Aspen.

Zemsky, Beth. 1991. "Coming Out against All Odds: Resistance in the Life of a Young Lesbian." *Women and Therapy: A Feminist Quarterly* 11(3/4): 185–200.

Zimring, Franklin. 1998. *American Youth Violence*. New York: Oxford University Press.

Selected Legal and Public Documents

California Government Code, sec. 13965 (2000).

Civil Rights Act of 1964, Title VII, Public Law 88-352.

Davis v. Monroe County Board of Education, 526 U.S. 629 (1999).

Juvenile Court Act (1899), *Ill. Laws*, sec. 132 *et seq.*

Juvenile Justice and Delinquency Prevention Act of 1974, revised 1992, codified at *U.S. Code* 42, sec. 5601.

Juvenile Justice Crime Prevention Act (2000), *California Government Code*, sec. 30061 *et seq.*

Roper v. Simmons 125 U.S. 1183 (2005).

Runaway and Homeless Youth Act of 1974, Title III of the *Juvenile Justice and Delinquency Prevention Act of 1974*.

United Nations. *United Nations Convention on the Rights of the Child*. 1989. New York: United Nations.

Victims of Trafficking and Violence Protection Act of 2000. Public Law 106-386, 106th Cong. (October 28, 2000).

Films and Videos

Anger Management. 2002. Color, 106 minutes. Feature comedy. Rated PG-13. Director, Peter Segal. Starring Jack Nicholson, Adam Sandler. Columbia TriStar.

Girlfight. 2000. Color, 110 minutes. Feature drama. Rated R. Director, Karyn Kusama. Starring Michele Rodriguez. Columbia TriStar.

Girls Town. 1996. Feature drama. Rated R. Director, Jim McKay. Starring Lili Taylor, Bruklyn Harris, Anna Grace, Aunjanue Ellis. October Films.
Girl Trouble. 2004. Color, 74 minutes, Documentary. Not Rated. Producers, directors, and cinematographers: Lexi Leban, Lidia Szajko. http://www.girltrouble.org.
Million Dollar Baby. 2004. Color, 132 minutes. Rated PG-13. Director, Clint Eastwood. Warner Bros. Entertainment.
Orphan Trains, 1854–1929. 2000. Color, 60 minutes. Documentary. Directors and producers, Janet Graham, Edward Gray. PBS.
Set It Off. 1996. Color, 123 minutes. Rated R. Director, F. Gary Gray. Featuring Jada Pinkett Smith, Queen Latifah. New Line Cinema.
Thirteen. 2003. Color, 100 minutes. Feature drama. Rated R. Director, Catherine Hardwicke. Starring Holly Hunter. Twentieth Century Fox Productions.

Selected Research Resources

Air America: http://www.airamericaradio.com
Alan Guttmacher Institute: http://www.agi-usa.org
American Youth Policy Forum: http://www.aypf.org
Building Blocks for Youth: http://www.buildingblocksforyouth.org
Center for Young Women's Development: http://www.cywd.org
Center on Juvenile and Criminal Justice: http://www.cjcj.org
Centers for Disease Control and Prevention, Youth Risk Behavior Survey: http://www.cdc.gov/HealthyYouth/yrbs/index.hem
Child Trends DataBank: http://www.childtrends.org
Child Welfare League of America: http://www.cwla.org
Children's Defense Fund: http://www.childrensdefense.org
Critical Resistance: http://www.criticalresistance.org
Democracy Now: http://www.democracynow.org
Federal Bureau of Investigation, *Uniform Crime Reports*: http://www.fbi.gov/ucr/ucr.htm
FindLaw: http://www.findlaw.com
Girls Inc.: http://www.girlsinc.org
Girls Study Group: http://www.girlsstudygroup.rti.org
LexisNexis: http://www.lexis.com
National Criminal Justice Reference Service: http://www.ncjrs.org
National Institute of Justice: http://www.nijpcs.org
Office of Juvenile Justice and Delinquency Prevention: http://www.ojjdp.ncjrs.org
Sentencing Project: http://www.sentencingproject.org
Soros Foundation: http://www.soros.org/about/foundations
UNICEF: http://www.unicef.org
Vera Institute for Justice: http://www.vera.org
Youth Law Center: http://www.ylc.org
Youth Today: http://www.youthtoday.org/youthtoday

Index

abuse: in girls' narratives, 142; incidence of, 60; and later troubling behaviors, 208n. 34; reconfiguring meaning of, 58–59; responses to, 63; use of term, 4; verbal, 65. *See also* childhood sexual abuse

acquiescence, expected from women, 123

acting in, defined, 130

activism, feminist, 151

actresses, as beauty ideal, 108

Addams, Jane, 38, 39

adjudicated, use of term, 36

adjudication: in juvenile court, 118; of juveniles as adults, 49, 117; and power, 180; for violent offenses, 133

Adler, Freda, 151

adolescence: contemporary, 137; defined, 35; and early sexual contact, 108–109; and gender, 156; psychosexual tasks in, 100; psychosocial framing of, 131–132

adolescents: emotional responses of, 43; in research design, 44; use of term, 34. *See also* teenagers

adult court: compared with juvenile court, 117; transfer to, 18, 180

adulthood: defining, 82; gendered construction of, 180; protecting young women from, 178–179; social constructions of, 35

adults: and best interests of child, 177; demographics of sample of, 52–53, 53 *illus.*; distrust of, 55; trial as, 49

advertising: directed at girl children, 123, 124 *illus.*; sexual images promoted by, 103; violence in, 131

African American girls, 50 *table,* 55 *table,* 82; in detention, 79–80; and dominant media, 84–85, 135; in intake process, 20–33; prostitution label for, 164; and shifting norms, 123, 124 *illus.*

African Americans: and family integrity, 92; media's stereotypical refrains about, 135; substance dependence among, 89

after-school programs, 17

age: of adult participants, 52; in detention, 24; of girls in court system, 49; of juvenile offenders, 36–37

aggression: and abuse, 58, 63, 71, 74–75; context for, 176; and gender, 121, 126–130; girls', 128, 171–172; masculine, 127; and media exposure to violence, 72; normalization of, 130–131; relational, 7, 129, 161; and sexual trauma, 58; social, 128–129; as survival strategy, 120; use of term, 210n. 6; victim-to-offender theory of, 208; and witnessing violence, 71, 74–75

Ala-Teen meetings, 57

About the Author

Laurie Schaffner is the author of *Teenage Runaways: Broken Hearts and "Bad Attitudes"* (Haworth Press 1999) and is co-editor with Elizabeth Bernstein of *Regulating Sex: The Politics of Intimacy and Identity* (Routledge 2005). She teaches at the University of Illinois at Chicago and is a community partner with Girl Talk—a project for young women involved in the Cook County (Illinois) juvenile court system.